An
introduction
to population
geography

An introduction to population geography

WILLIAM F. HORNBY
Principal Lecturer in Geography
Sheffield City Polytechnic

MELVYN JONES
Senior Lecturer in Geography
Sheffield City Polytechnic

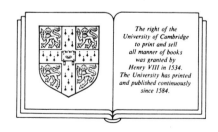

The right of the
University of Cambridge
to print and sell
all manner of books
was granted by
Henry VIII in 1534.
The University has printed
and published continuously
since 1584.

CAMBRIDGE UNIVERSITY PRESS
CAMBRIDGE

NEW YORK   NEW ROCHELLE
MELBOURNE   SYDNEY

Published by the Press Syndicate of the University of Cambridge
The Pitt Building, Trumpington Street, Cambridge CB2 1RP
32 East 57th Street, New York, NY 10022, USA
10 Stamford Road, Oakleigh, Melbourne 3166, Australia

First published 1980
Sixth printing 1987

Printed in Great Britain at the University Press, Cambridge

Library of Congress Cataloguing in Publication Data

Hornby, William Fredric.
An introduction to population geography.
Bibliography: p.
Includes index.
1. Population geography. 2. Population geography
– Case studies. I. Jones, Melvyn, joint author.
II. Title
HB1951.H67   301.32   78-74536
ISBN 0 521 21395 9

Contents

Acknowledgements

The authors and publisher would like to thank the following for permission to reproduce illustrations:

Food and Agricultural Organization of the United Nations for the title photograph for Part I and for Fig. 4.9.

Oxfam for Figs. 2.4, 4.1 and 9.2 and for the title photographs for Parts II and III

David and Charles (Holdings) Ltd and Professor G. M. Howe for Figs. 2.9 and 2.11, from *Man, Environment and Disease in Britain*

Thomas Nelson and Sons Ltd and Professor G. M. Howe for Fig. 2.12, from *National Atlas of Disease Mortality*

Longman Group Ltd and W. T. W. Morgan for Figs. 3.2, 3.3 and 3.4, from *East Africa*

Macmillan, London and Basingstoke and C. Clark for Fig. 3.9, from *Population Growth and Land Use*

The American Geographical Society for Fig. 3.10, from an article 'Changes in urban density gradients through time for "Western" and "Non-Western" cities' by B. J. L. Berry *et al.* in *Geographical Review* (1963), vol. 53, and Fig. 14.3, from an article by W. Zelinsky in *Geographical Review* (1971), vol. 61

The University of Chicago Press and P. M. Hauser and O. D. Duncan for Fig. 4.6, from *The Study of Population*

Weidenfeld and Nicolson and E. A. Wrigley for Fig. 4.7, from *Population and History*

The Camera Press for Figs. 4.11, 6.4, 10.2, 11.1, 11.2, 14.1, 14.2, 16.4, 17.3, 17.4 and 19.1

The High Commissioner for the Republic of Singapore for Fig. 8.1.

Faim et Developpement for Fig. 9.4.

Popperfoto for Fig. 13.1

The Ministry of Overseas Development and The British Council for the two advertisements in Fig. 13.3

The Automobile Association for Fig. 13.4

British Railways Board for Fig. 13.7

Pergamon Press and H. D. Clout for Fig. 13.8, from *Rural Geography: An Introductory Survey*

J. Allan Cash for Fig. 13.5 and the title photograph to Part IV

Kenneth Jury and Laurence Woodley for Fig. 16.2

Pergamon Press and R. Lawton for Figs. 15.1 and 15.2 from *The Journey to Work in Britain – Some Trends and Problems*, Regional Studies vol. 2

Thanks are also due to the following for permission to reproduce extracts:

Hutchinson Publishing Group Ltd and Terry Coleman for an extract from *Passage to America*

Times Newspapers Ltd for an extract '120,000 Somali nomads settled on the land' from *The Times* of 23 August 1975. Reproduced from *The Times* (London) by permission

Preface

This book deals with particular themes within the field of human geography, and is designed primarily to meet the needs of students embarking on geographical studies at an advanced level. It is appropriate for the radically revised A-level syllabuses now set by, for example, the Joint Matriculation Board, London University and the Oxford and Cambridge Board. There is clearly a need for students at this level to understand certain concepts and models basic to the appreciation of spatial patterns and processes. This conceptual understanding must be allied to a considerable background knowledge and a wide range of statistical and cartographic skills. This raises a number of fundamental issues concerning the selection and organisation of teaching approaches and resources to provide an interesting and effective teaching programme. The selection and presentation of themes in this book reflect the changing emphasis in geography and represent an attempt to meet the students' needs. At the same time the book provides a useful introduction to population geography for students in higher education.

The book considers two major themes: population growth and distribution, and population mobility. In each case a general examination of the theme is followed by a series of detailed case studies selected from developed and less developed regions of the world. This reflects the need for students to have both a general knowledge of a broad field of study and a detailed knowledge of specific cases. Each case study is concerned with the elucidation and exemplification of selected concepts, models or themes in the setting of a particular area. The decision to separate the detailed case studies from the general chapters was a difficult one but, on balance, is considered likely to be the most helpful approach at this level.

To help students to develop a fuller understanding of many of the concepts introduced in the text a considerable number of exercises has been included. These are mainly of the data-response type increasingly being used by examination boards and require students to analyse and comment upon data from a wide range of sources. For the convenience of teachers and students these exercises are grouped together at the end of the book, but they form an integral part of the book and have been arranged in a sequence which closely relates to the order in which particular themes are introduced in the text.

The extensive bibliography includes both sources which are specifically referred to in the text and some suggestions for further reading within the general field of study.

We wish to acknowledge help and advice provided by colleagues, especially Miss E. M. Fyfe for assistance with Case Study 10.

W. F. H.
M. J.

Part One

Population growth and distribution: some general considerations

1 Introduction: components of population change and problems of measurement

In the mid-1970s the population of the world increased by approximately 70 million every year, an increment roughly equivalent to the addition of the total occupants of ten cities the size of Liverpool or Sheffield to the world's population every month or of one such city every three days. The rate at which population is increasing varies considerably from place to place. Many countries in Africa, Latin America and Southern Asia record growth rates four times as high as those in some parts of Western Europe. Geographers are concerned with these and other spatial variations in the world's population as well as with changes in the total world population. In this part of the book we shall briefly examine the basic components of population change and the problems of measuring change. We shall then go on to consider various aspects of world population growth, population distribution and the relationships between population growth and resource utilisation. There will also be some mention of population movements, but an examination in depth of these is the primary concern of the second part of the book.

First, it is important to be clear about what we mean by 'population' and to appreciate some of the difficulties involved in population measurement. The word 'population' can be used in several different ways. A biologist, for example, might refer to a collection of animals or plants as a population, whereas a geographer would be more likely to confine his use of the word to collections of human beings. Thus a geographer might refer to, say, 'the population of Sydney', but on consideration it can be seen that such an expression has no very precise meaning unless further details are given. Does it, for example, refer to the people who are normally resident in Sydney? If so, what does 'normally' mean in this context? Does it refer to the people who were resident in Sydney on a particular day in a particular year? If it does, should not a particular time also be specified, as the number of residents would obviously change during the course of a day as a result of births and deaths and of people moving into Sydney to live or leaving the city to live elsewhere? And does the 'population of Sydney' include any other people whose homes are outside the city boundary but who travel daily to work in Sydney?

Consideration of such questions as these makes it clear that the term 'population' is often used by geographers in a way which it is difficult to relate to a precise numerical value. Indeed, the term is frequently applied to collections of people of which the exact numbers and composition are changing almost all the time. In such circumstances it may be virtually impossible to provide for a population a numerical value which is both up-to-date and accurate. In short, a study of population is essentially a study of a dynamic and not of a static situation.

There are two basic ways in which population change takes place. First, a population may increase or decline as a result of natural change, i.e. as a result of the number of people being born or dying within the community. Secondly, it may alter as a result of migration, with people moving into or away from the place where the community lives. Thus the total population of any particular community represents the balance between two components – the natural change component and the migration change component. This can be shown diagrammatically as in Fig. 1.1. This diagram emphasises the dynamic nature of population and can be applied at different scales; to a city or to a country, for example.

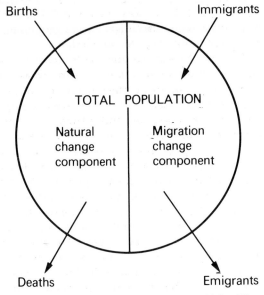

Births Immigrants

TOTAL POPULATION

Natural change component Migration change component

Deaths Emigrants

1.1 Components of population change. (After Haggett, 1975.)

The relative significance of the two components varies greatly from place to place and through time. The migration change component is likely to be of greater relative importance in, for example, part of a town where new houses are being built than in the same area when building programmes have been completed. After the initial occupation of such an area, migration would be likely to become less important than natural increase because there is a high probability that the area would be largely populated by young, in many cases newly married, people with a resultant high birth rate. Migration would not cease entirely as some people would move away to be replaced by new migrants, but it would be considerably less significant than earlier. In time, further changes would occur as the population aged, the birth rate declined, the death rate increased and new migrants moved in. Similar dynamic patterns can be traced on a larger scale in, for example, some parts of the United States which were settled by European migrants in the nineteenth century. In general, however, the natural change component is far more significant at the national level than is the migration change component and, of course, the latter can be ignored when dealing with changes in the total population of the world (though this may not always be so if other planets suitable for human settlement are discovered and developed).

Most national population censuses attempt to overcome the difficulties arising from the continuing changes in population totals by basing calculations on a rigid series of instructions concerning the date and time to which census data refer and the categories of people who should be included or excluded from the totals. It is easy to see that problems can arise in carrying out a census. Though it is common to base the collection of data on the places where people reside and so exclude problems of daily travel to work and so on, many other difficulties exist. For example, should people working temporarily overseas be included in the total population? Should sailors be excluded if they are at sea when the census is taken? Should someone who lives and works in London from Monday to Friday but returns to spend the weekend with his family in Manchester be recorded as a resident of London or Manchester? No doubt you can think of other problems involved in taking a census in a country like Great Britain, but these almost pale into insignificance when compared with the problems of some other countries. In some tropical areas, for example, quite large numbers of people are nomadic and it is easy for such people to be omitted altogether from the census count. Others, perhaps suspicious of the motives of government officials asking them questions, may deliberately give false information.

The problems involved in carrying out a census in a less developed country have been epitomised in recent years by the example of Nigeria. The first official Nigerian census was in 1911, but this and later censuses in 1921 and 1931 were little more than estimates and did not involve an organised enumeration of the total population. There was no census in 1941 because of World War 2 and the first attempt at a full enumeration was in the early 1950s. A shortage of trained staff and other organisational problems caused this census to be taken over a period of approximately nine months from July 1952 to April 1953, with each of the three main regions being enumerated in turn rather than simultaneously. The total population of the country according to this census was approximately 30 million. Before the next census, in 1962, Nigeria achieved political independence and the census took place in a period of political tension. There was considerable controversy about the census results and the national government decided that the results were so unreliable as to be unacceptable; a new census was taken in the following year. This, which recorded a total population of 55.6 million, was accepted by the government though there was still some doubt about its accuracy.

Even allowing for a considerable margin of error, the census made it clear that Nigeria had a notably larger population than any other African state. It also implied that there had been a population growth rate in excess of 6% per annum since the previous census – almost an impossibility unless natural increase had been accompanied by massive immigration, of which there was no evidence on the scale necessary. With no means of directly checking the accuracy of either of the censuses concerned, most demographers concluded that the 1952/3 total probably represented an under-assessment and the 1963 total an over-assessment, with a total of 50 million being suggested by some as a reasonably accurate estimate of the 1963 population.

Before 1973, various political changes and a re-organisation of state boundaries occurred but, despite these and other steps taken by the government in power at the time to ensure an accurate enumeration, the preliminary results of the 1973 census showed an astonishing total of 79 million people. Even on the basis of the original 1963 total of 55.6 million this represented an annual increase of over 3.5% a year throughout the period between the censuses, a rate considerably in excess of most estimates though just within the bounds of possibility. Census data for individual states were even more confusing however, with three of the twelve states having almost doubled their population, two others having apparently decreased in numbers and some having increased at rates roughly in accordance with expectations. These results again gave rise to considerable controversy and have been rejected by the government which replaced the one in power at the time of the 1973 census. Obviously, Nigeria's population total is still a matter of dispute.

Though Nigeria's census problems have possibly received more publicity than those of many other countries, they are by no means unique. Some countries have not even attempted a full enumeration and estimates can be extremely inaccurate. They may also be used for political purposes as was evident in 1975 when the population of Spanish Sahara (now West Sahara) was variously quoted as being from 75,000 up to ten times that number in different press reports put out before Spain handed over political control to Morocco and Mauritania. Clearly, any study of population must take into account the possibility that population estimates and even official population statistics based on census enumerations may well be inaccurate. It is important to remember this in relation to the comments made in the remainder of this book and the statistics on which such comments are based.

2 World population growth

Though population data for many countries in the modern world are of doubtful validity, information concerning earlier periods is generally even less reliable. Despite this, several attempts have been made to chart the patterns of population growth and distribution in the past (see, for example, Trewartha, 1969), based on such evidence as archaeological remains, population structures and densities of modern communities with economies similar to those of some earlier groups and, for more recent periods, a variety of written evidence and estimates based on surveys of different kinds.

The origins of man are still the subject of considerable dispute, speculation concerning this being based on a limited number of fragments of skeletons, some of the earliest of which have been discovered in recent years in East and North-east Africa. Modern man (*Homo sapiens*) can be traced back for over a million years but, during most of that period, the number of people on earth was very small in comparison with the present population. Rates of population growth were very slow, and the economic basis of existence was hunting and food-gathering. Primitive communities with this type of economy gradually spread, possibly from early bases in tropical Africa and Asia, to occupy much of the world. As recently as 10,000 years ago, when man first began to cultivate crops and domesticate animals, estimates suggest that the entire world population probably totalled only 5 million, a figure roughly equivalent to the present populations of small countries such as Denmark or Scotland.

This period of economic change when man first became a farmer rather than a hunter (often described as the Neolithic Revolution) drastically altered the relationship between man and his environment, and further changes followed. These included the development of permanent rather than the earlier shifting cultivation, the introduction of new technological aids such as the plough, increases in production and exchange of agricultural and other commodities (which in turn helped to make possible the growth of cities) and the discovery of how to smelt and make use of metals. During the long period between the Neolithic Revolution and the beginning of early modern times (in about 1650) population is thought to have increased at a considerably faster rate on average than in the pre-Neolithic era, though no doubt the rate fluctuated through time and between different groups.

The total world population probably reached 500 million by about 1650 and has since grown at an ever-increasing rate (see Fig. 2.1). Between 1650 and 1830, a period of 180 years, the total population approximately doubled to reach 1,000 million. In the following hundred years it doubled again and since 1930 it has

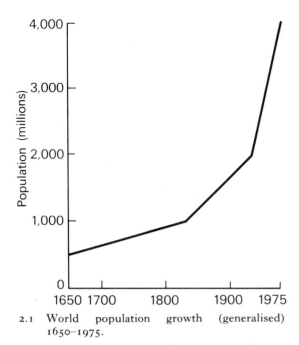

2.1 World population growth (generalised) 1650–1975.

clear that the relationship between births and deaths is fundamental to this. Measurements of births and deaths can be expressed in several different ways, but they are most commonly indicated in the form of crude birth rates and crude death rates. These can be simply calculated, as shown below, on the basis of data which are fairly easily available:

Crude birth rate (expressed as number of live births per 1,000 persons)

$$= \frac{\text{Total number of live births in 1 year} \times 1,000}{\text{Total mid-year population}}$$

Crude death rate (expressed as number of deaths per 1,000 persons)

$$= \frac{\text{Total number of deaths in 1 year} \times 1,000}{\text{Total mid-year population}}$$

doubled yet again, exceeding 4,000 million in the mid-1970s according to many estimates. If some forecasts prove correct the next doubling will take only thirty-five years, so that by the year 2010 the world population could total approximately 8,000 million, though the most recent evidence suggests that the rate of increase is at last beginning to slow down slightly. An increase on anything approaching this scale in such a short space of time is extremely difficult to comprehend, however, amounting to an average annual increase of about twice the present population of the United Kingdom, or more than a thousand times the number of people that fill Wembley Stadium on FA Cup Final day. The possibility of population growth on such a scale is seen by many people as a serious threat to man's survival. The use of terms like 'population explosion' tends to encourage such concern and it is easy to view the future of the world with considerable gloom. If the situation is to be understood, however, it is important to examine what has happened in the recent past so that likely future developments can be more fully appreciated and assessed.

Look again at Fig. 1.1. From what has already been said, it is clear that only the natural growth component of total population need be considered when dealing with population growth for the world as a whole. The diagram makes it

The difference between the two rates is known as the rate of natural increase, though this is usually expressed as a percentage. Thus in 1971 the United Kingdom had a crude birth rate of 16.6 per thousand, a crude death rate of 11.9 per thousand and a rate of natural increase of 0.47% per year. Whereas the rate of natural increase is related solely to birth and death rates, the rate of population growth is also concerned with changes brought about by migration. Thus Jamaica, with an estimated crude birth rate of 31 per thousand and a crude death rate of 7 per thousand in 1976 had a rate of natural increase of 2.4% but a population growth rate of only 1.9% because of the effects of emigration.

The terms 'crude' birth rate and 'crude' death rate are used because it is possible to use more precise, less crude ways of measuring fertility and mortality. For example, fertility might be calculated by relating the number of births to the number of women of child-bearing age in the community rather than to the whole population. We shall look at some of these alternative measurements later. In the meantime, it is important to remember that crude rates may conceal quite marked variations within a community – between different age groups for example – as well as suffering from inaccuracy, in some cases, because of a shortage of accurate basic data. Where the terms 'birth

5

rate' and 'death rate' are used elsewhere in this book they should be taken to mean crude birth or crude death rate.

An examination of the information available concerning birth and death rates, and of population changes resulting from the difference between these, led to the suggestion that many European countries have passed through four main stages of population change in modern times. This pattern of population development is often described as the *demographic* or *vital transition*, and Fig. 2.2 is an attempt to represent it in the form of a model. Further research has indicated that particular countries do not, in many cases, conform in detail to all aspects of the pattern suggested by the model, but it nevertheless provides a useful indication of general patterns of change and a yardstick against which the experience of individual countries can be measured.

Until at least the middle of the eighteenth century, the limited evidence available suggests that both birth and death rates had fluctuated between 30 and 40 per thousand in most countries for several centuries. It seems likely that fluctuations were greatest in death rates as populations were affected by periodic wars, famines and diseases, but the long-term effect of these was, with a few major exceptions, usually slight. One such exception was the fourteenth-century plague, later known as the Black Death, which resulted in the death of between 10% and 50% of the population of England. The general situation was therefore one in which the population remained at a low, though fluctuating, level with high birth and death rates maintaining a rough balance so that changes in population totals were slow and slight in comparison with those of later periods. This situation is represented by stage 1 in Fig. 2.2.

During the eighteenth or early nineteenth century the death rate began to decline in many European countries. This declining death rate was initially associated with improvements in nutrition and increased political stability but, by the second half of the nineteenth century, better sanitation, improved personal hygiene and increased medical knowledge became important contributory factors (although the decline in certain infectious diseases is not fully understood) and the death rate fell more rapidly. There was no immediate corresponding fall in birth rates (see stage 2 in Fig. 2.2) and the difference between birth and death rates resulted in rapid population growth. Indeed, in some areas fertility actually increased, largely because people married earlier as a result of changing socio-economic conditions in this period. The United Kingdom provides one example of such an area and here, as death rates fell and fertility increased, population growth reached a maximum of 1.6% per annum in the 1820s. It is worth noting that this figure, though high for the period in which it occurred, is considerably lower than the rate of growth experienced in many countries in Asia, Africa and Latin America since 1950. In most European countries the nineteenth century was a period of population growth on a scale not previously experienced, though there were variations in the pattern of growth between different

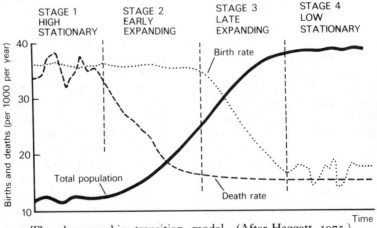

2.2 The demographic transition model. (After Haggett, 1975.)

countries both in degree and in the time at which changes occurred.

As many of the major diseases of temperate areas were controlled and improved standards of health and sanitation had their effect, the death rate in most European countries gradually levelled off at a much lower level than that of stage 1. By the 1920s and 1930s countries such as Sweden, the Netherlands and the United Kingdom had death rates well below 20 per thousand and though these continued to decline, largely as a result of the greater control over infant mortality, the rate of this decline was much slower than previously. In this same period (stage 3 in Fig. 2.2) birth rates began to decline dramatically. This fall in the birth rate is less simply explained than the earlier fall in death rates. In most European countries it seems to have been associated with the development of a predominantly urban-industrial society in which the desire for, and possibly the economic value of, large families decreased. In addition better methods of birth control made it possible for parents to restrict the size of their families if they so wished.

More recently both birth and death rates have reached a stage where they are relatively stable and where population change is in the form of a slow natural rate of increase with the birth rate slightly higher than the death rate on average (see stage 4 in Fig. 2.2). It is interesting to note that in contrast with the stage 1 situation the tendency in stage 4 is for the birth rate to fluctuate more than the death rate. This phenomenon will be discussed in some of the detailed case studies. By the middle of the twentieth century many European countries had reached stage 4 of the demographic transition and natural increase rates in Europe today are generally below 1 %, while in some countries, including the German Democratic Republic (East Germany) and the German Federal Republic (West Germany), Belgium, Austria, Hungary and Sweden, they have fallen to below 0.5 %.

A pattern of demographic change similar to that outlined above has also occurred, or appears to be occurring, in several countries outside Europe. Most of these countries, e.g. Canada, Australia and the USA (see Case Study 2), have a population which has strong links with Europe in terms of its origins, but a demographic transition of the 'European' type has also occurred in some areas which have no clear ethnic links with Europe. Japan provides a good illustration of this and, as it developed into an industrial state similar to some European countries, it also appeared to develop along similar demographic lines. As in the case of the United Kingdom, birth rates probably increased in stage 2 and the limited data available suggest that population increases in the period 1880 to 1910 were the result not only of a declining death rate but also of an increasing birth rate (probably from about 25 per thousand to 34 per thousand), giving a slightly unusual stage 2 in the demographic cycle. Since about 1920, however, birth and death rates have first declined and then stabilised, with minor fluctuations, so that by 1974 the birth rate was 18.6 per thousand, the death rate 6.5 per thousand and the natural increase rate 1.2 %, giving a pattern of demographic development similar to that of many European countries (see Exercise 1, p. 145). Singapore is another Asian country which appears to be following a rather similar pattern though at a later date than Japan (see Case Study 4).

Much interest and attention is now focused on the demographic situation in a large number of countries, mainly in Africa, Latin America and Asia, which are at a lower level of economic development than those mentioned so far and are sometimes grouped together as 'less developed' countries (LDCs), a term which will be examined in more detail later. In most LDCs a situation similar to that of stage 1 in Fig. 2.2 has been succeeded since about 1950 by one in which the death rate has declined dramatically but, as yet, no substantial change has occurred in the birth rate, though recent evidence suggests this may have begun in some countries. At present natural increase rates in excess of 2.5 % per annum are common and rates exceeding 3 % occur in some countries, including Algeria, Kenya, Mexico, Pakistan, Thailand, Tunisia and Venezuela. This situation (see Fig. 2.3) is, in some ways, comparable with stage 2 in the European demographic transition model, though fertility in Europe was generally lower in this period of change than is the case in any LDCs today and population growth rates in LDCs are generally higher than was the case in nineteenth-century Europe (in part because of their lower marriage age for women). It cannot

7

be assumed that the demographic development of LDCs will necessarily follow a pattern similar to that of most European countries. Even if this did happen, however, time is a crucial factor, for massive annual increases in population are now occurring in Asia, Africa and Latin America in countries which are already facing grave problems in feeding their existing populations. The basic problem is that whereas death rates have fallen markedly, in response to the provision of better medical facilities and disease eradication programmes in particular, there has so far been only limited evidence of a desire on the part of parents in these countries to reduce the size of their families. In these circumstances, it is not surprising that many governments have introduced family planning and other forms of population control programmes.

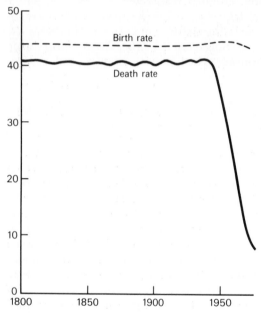

2.3 The demographic transition in LDCs.

The attitudes of both governments and individuals towards family planning in LDCs vary considerably. During the 1950s and 1960s many governments accepted the need for family planning programmes and have since endeavoured to introduce them, with differing degrees of success. In India, for example, the birth rate was still in excess of 40 per thousand in the early 1970s despite an extensive family planning programme (see Case Study 5). In Jamaica, by contrast, the birth rate fell from 43.1 per

thousand to 34.8 per thousand between 1960 and 1971, and in similar periods it dropped from 40.9 to 34.5 per thousand in Peninsular Malaysia and from 35.1 to 19.7 per thousand in Hong Kong.

Other countries have remained strongly opposed to family planning programmes. There are several reasons for this opposition. Some governments believe that population increase is an essential element in the economic development of their countries. Many Brazilians, for example, would argue that the resources of the Amazon Basin can only be developed effectively if Brazil has a much larger population than at present. (An argument of this kind clearly raises the issue of what is the optimum population for a particular area, a theme which is examined in more detail in Chapter 4.) There is also a belief in many LDCs that the efforts of people living in areas like North America and Western Europe to encourage family planning programmes in less affluent areas than their own are not without self-interest. It is argued that people living in the more economically developed areas are concerned to preserve present world economic patterns and so ensure that rapid population growth in LDCs does not result in a shortage of the products at present consumed by those living in North America, Western Europe and similar areas. In short, programmes of family planning are seen as a means of preserving high standards of living in some areas at the expense of others which already have much lower living standards.

Hostile attitudes of this kind are fostered by the way in which some family planning programmes have emphasised the necessity of birth control with little reference to the circumstances or needs of individuals. There has been a tendency to group together all LDCs and imply that they have identical problems – notably that of having too many people and not enough food. It has also been implied that the provision of contraceptive devices and advice on a massive scale – especially if accompanied by large-scale propaganda – will resolve most of these problems. In many cases such an approach is doomed to failure, or at best will have only limited success. Birth control is unlikely to be an attractive idea to a peasant farmer who relies on his children to help him farm his land and to act as an insurance for his old age in a

2.4 Two brothers in Bihar, India, in 1967 during a severe drought which caused many farmers to leave their farms. The father of these boys had gone to Calcutta in search of work and, though their mother worked from dawn to dusk digging wells, she could not earn enough to feed her family adequately. In such circumstances it is easy to see why few children may survive to maturity.

country, where, as in most LDCs, there is no such thing as an old age pension. One recent estimate suggested that an average Indian couple would need to have at least six children to be reasonably sure that one son would reach maturity (see Fig. 2.4). In these circumstances, family planning might rightly be viewed as having more rather than fewer children. This sort of individual attitude provides one reason why family planning programmes in some countries, such as India are not fully effective despite strong governmental backing. There are many other factors which also militate against birth control. For example, in much of Latin America, and in some other parts of the world, the influence of the Roman Catholic church has restricted the spread and effectiveness of family planning as has the widespread attitude that a man's social status is to some extent determined by the number of children he has sired.

Attitudes in some Communist countries, including China, have fluctuated through time, one rather confusing element in this being that while Marxist theorists tend to oppose birth control as a means of restricting the number of children, they are prepared to acknowledge its importance as a means of female emancipation.

Education seems to be a significant influence on the size of families. More-educated parents tend to have fewer children, as illustrated in Fig. 2.5 for Hong Kong. This is no doubt related to other factors such as the different social and economic opportunities available to more-educated people in most societies. It also emphasises the fact that the most successful family planning programmes have generally been conducted in areas where economic changes have also been occurring, such as Hong Kong and Singapore (see Case Study 4). Indeed it would seem reasonable to conclude from the available evidence that relatively few individuals in LDCs are likely to adopt birth control measures unless radical changes occur in their traditional way of life, so that they have greater economic security, better social security in their old age, improved educational opportunities and a higher degree of female emancipation. In short, people must be in a situation

9

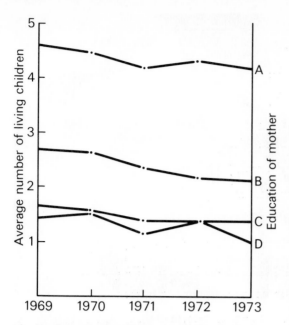

A No formal education

B Primary education

C Secondary education

D University education

2.5   Number of living children in relation to education of mothers in Hong Kong. (Data based on
survey of new patients at Hong Kong Family
Planning Association clinics in years indicated.)
Note the negative relationship between educational attainment of mothers and the number of
children born, and the decline in average
number of births irrespective of educational
attainment of mothers. (Source: *The Family
Planning Association of Hong Kong: 23rd
Annual Report 1973–4.*)

where they perceive some real advantage in
restricting the size of their families before they
are likely to practise birth control. Thus so-
called family planning programmes which are
dominated by attempts to encourage birth control without consideration of other aspects of
social and economic change will probably fail.
While the birth rate remains high in many
LDCs, exceeding 50 per thousand in some,
such as Kenya, Niger and Saudi Arabia, death
rates have reached very low levels in many
countries. Some, such as Jamaica, Peninsular
Malaysia and Venezuela have a death rate below
10 per thousand. This is a result of greatly improved public health facilities and, in particular,
the control of the major tropical diseases and

the great reduction in infant mortality. Many
countries have reduced infant mortality to only
one-third of the 1950 level.

The potential for further increases in population of LDCs is very great. There is scope for
further decline in the death rates of many
countries. It also seems unlikely that there will
be a rapid fall in birth rates, because a large
proportion of the population of most LDCs has
still to pass through the fertile age range (usually
regarded for statistical purposes as being
between the ages of 15 and 44). This leads us
to an investigation of the age structures of
particular populations and the effect these have
on population growth.

Age structure and population growth

The population structure or age composition of
a particular population has a strong influence on
the rate of population increase. Fig. 2.6 shows
the percentage of the population aged less than
15 years for selected countries in 1975. The
difference between the LDCs and the more
economically advanced countries is striking and
shows how young the populations of the LDCs
are. It also emphasises the fact that in the course
of the next few years, as these youngsters pass
through the fertile age group (15–44 years), the
crude birth rate in most LDCs is likely to
remain high unless there are striking reductions
in the number of children born to each woman.
Additionally, the low death rates in LDCs are
partly a function of the age structure in these
countries where the majority of the population
is relatively young.

A more detailed examination of the age structure of a particular population can be made
through the use of population pyramids. These
are diagrams which consist of a series of hori-
zontal bars representing successive age ranges
(normally at 5-year intervals), with the total
males in each group recorded to the left and
females to the right of a vertical axis, each 5-year
total normally being expressed as a percentage
of the total population. Fig. 2.7 (pp. 11–12)
contains a series of such population pyramids
(also known as age–sex pyramids).

The pyramid for Kenya is fairly representa-
tive of many LDCs. The broad base and narrow
tip of the pyramid represent a situation in which
there is a large percentage of young people and

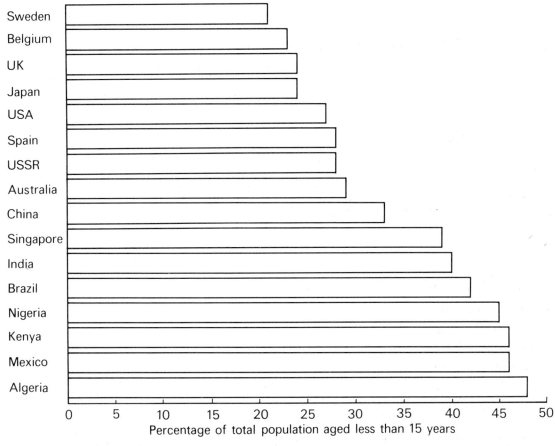

2.6 Percentage of total population aged less than 15 years in selected countries in 1975. (Source: 1976 World Population Data sheet of the Population Reference Bureau, Inc.)

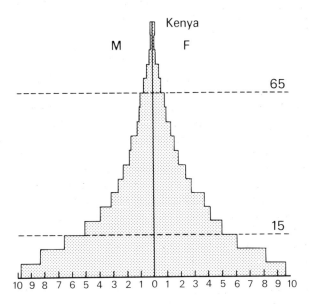

2.7 (For explanation and continuation of figure, see over.)

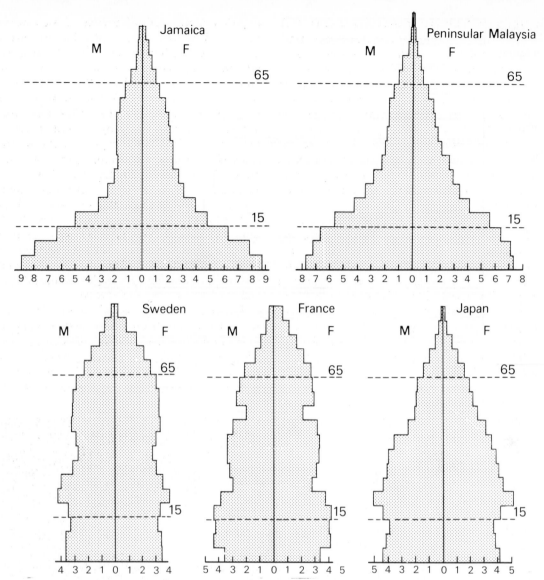

2.7 Population pyramids for Kenya (1969), Jamaica (1965), Peninsular Malaysia (1970), Sweden (1970), France (1968) and Japan (1970). (Note: In these and all subsequent population pyramids the data are arranged in 5-year age groups represented as a percentage of the total population.)

relatively few old people. The pyramid for Peninsular Malaysia is slightly different, with a smaller percentage of the total in the lowest age groups (42.8 % under 15 years old compared to 48.4 % in Kenya) but also a smaller difference between the totals in various age groups in the lower part of the age range. These differences reflect the greater effect of family planning schemes and the greater control over death rates, in particular a reduced rate of infant mortality, in Peninsular Malaysia. It is significant that living standards in Peninsular Malaysia have risen noticeably in recent years (see Fig. 2.8). As regards older people the difference between the two pyramids is less marked, though a slightly greater proportion of the total population survived to reach the age of 65 in Peninsular Malaysia than in Kenya.

It is important to remember that a population pyramid does not only reflect births and deaths but usually also migration patterns. This is noticeable in the case of Jamaica where large-scale unemployment (estimated at over 30 % by some experts in the mid-1970s) has led to migration on a considerable scale. One effect of this has been to lower the rate of growth of the Jamaican population as a result of the 'loss' of people in the fertile age groups. The narrowing of the population pyramid for the 20- to 50-year-old groups clearly shows the impact of migration, especially of men, on the population structure, though in other respects the pyramid is fairly typical of LDCs.

The population pyramids for more economically developed countries contrast strongly with those for LDC's tending to show much less variation between different age groups and thus being more rectangular than triangular in shape. The pyramids for Sweden, France and Japan all show the effects of much lower birth rates and generally lower death rates over a considerable period of time. Some individual differences between the countries are apparent, however. These include the effects of the later decline of the birth rate in Japan compared with Sweden and France, the impact on the population structure of France of high death rates and a substantial reduction in births during the two world wars, and the marked effect on the Japanese age structure of the 'baby boom' which followed World War 2. The birth rate also rose in France after World War 2 and the marked decline in the 1960s has been succeeded more recently by a slight increase, these fluctuations being typical of the fourth stage of the 'European' demographic transition model. It can be seen that Sweden, France and Japan all have less than 25 % of their population aged less than 15 years. It therefore seems likely that they will have considerably lower birth rates than Kenya, Peninsular Malaysia, Jamaica and other LDCs as a result. This would only *not* be the case if the size of families in developed countries were much greater than in the LDCs, and this seems very improbable.

The effect which the age structure of a population has on crude birth and death rates obviously limits the value of these rates as a means of showing fertility and mortality levels. Alternative methods have therefore been devised which try to overcome this limitation. These include:

2.8 Mineworkers in Malaysia. The clothing and vehicles of these mineworkers reflect a higher standard of living than is usual in most tropical areas. The living standards of agricultural workers have also begun to improve recently in much of Peninsular Malaysia and government attempts to bring about further improvements in social and economic conditions are likely to have significant effects on family planning programmes.

(a) *General fertility rate.* This relates the number of births in any year to the number of women in the fertile age group (15–44 years). It is usually expressed as so many births per thousand women in the fertile age group per year.

(b) *Age-specific fertility rate.* This relates the number of births in any year to the number of women in a specific age group (e.g. 20–24 years) and is again usually expressed as so many births per thousand women in the specific age group per year.

(c) *Age-specific mortality rate.* This is similar to (b), being calculated on the basis of the number of deaths per thousand persons in a specific age group in a selected year.

(d) *Gross reproduction rate.* This is defined as the average number of female children that a woman will produce during the whole of her reproductive period, if current fertility rates prevail.

(e) *Net reproduction rate.* This is similar to (d) but amended to take account of females who die before passing through the fertile age group. A net reproduction rate of 1 implies that a population is exactly replacing itself, of less than 1 that it is failing to do so and of more than 1 that the population is likely to increase because the number of potential mothers in the next generation is being increased.

Whatever means are used to measure rates of population change, it is difficult to forecast the future pattern of growth with any certainty. Developments in the years ahead will inevitably be affected by influences which change through time, such as social attitudes to family planning. It is useful, however, to examine the experiences of particular countries as these may indicate likely patterns of development elsewhere. In addition they illustrate in more detail some of the developments which have already occurred. The case studies in Part II demonstrate something of the nature of, and the problems involved in, population change and may have relevance on a wider scale.

Disease and population growth

That disease is an important variable in population change has already been alluded to. Disease is likely either to have severe socio-economic effects (e.g. an above-average number of days' absence from work through sickness, which may lead to worsening housing conditions and nutritional standards, which in turn may lead to susceptibility to other diseases, etc.) or to lead to death. Widespread disease-induced deaths obviously unbalance age structures and may have crippling demographic consequences, sometimes for generations. For instance, early deaths on a large scale as a result of disease will obviously affect fertility rates in the immediate future if they occur among adults in the fertile age range and in the longer term if they occur among infants. It is important to distinguish between the two major groups of diseases – infectious (communicable) and degenerative – for they are of varying significance in different parts of the world.

Infectious diseases are caused by pathogenic (disease-carrying) bacteria and viruses. Bacteria are among the smallest of living organisms and they penetrate or are engulfed by body cells. Viruses are even smaller. They are parasitic and cannot survive outside living cells. The rate of reproduction of bacteria and viruses is extremely high. Howe (1972) cites the example of a cut infected by a thousand of the streptococcal bacteria, which will within twelve hours produce approximately 10–100 million streptococci if left to grow unchecked. This number is sufficient to kill a human being.

Bacteria or viruses may be introduced into the body directly, by swallowing (as in the case of cholera, dysentery and typhoid), by breathing in (e.g. diphtheria, scarlet fever and smallpox) or through wounds (e.g. tetanus). Alternatively they may be introduced indirectly by a carrier (vector), as in the case of malaria via the *Anopheles* mosquito, the plague via the rat flea (*Xenopsylla cheopsis*) and typhus via the body louse (*Pediculus humanis corporis*).

One of the most important distinguishing characteristics of infectious diseases is their ability to spread rapidly as epidemics. This characteristic is well illustrated by selected British examples, perhaps the best known of which is the bubonic plague (the Black Death) which reached Britain in 1348. Bubonic plague is an infectious disease of certain rodents and is passed on to human beings through the bite of infected fleas which live on the rodents. The host in medieval times was the black or house

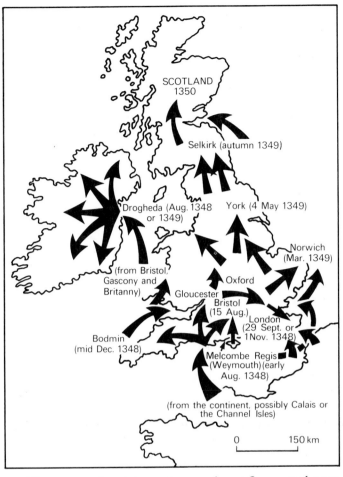

SCOTLAND
1350

Selkirk (autumn 1349)

Drogheda (Aug. 1348
or 1349)

York (4 May 1349)

Norwich
(Mar. 1349)

(from Bristol,
Gascony and
Britanny)

Oxford

Gloucester

Bristol
(15 Aug.)

London
(29 Sept. or
1 Nov. 1348)

Bodmin
(mid Dec. 1348)

Melcombe Regis
(Weymouth) (early
Aug. 1348)

(from the continent, possibly Calais or
the Channel Isles)

0   150 km

2.9   The progress of the Black Death in
the British Isles in the fourteenth
century. (After Howe, 1972.)

rat (*Rattus rattus*) and the vector was the rat flea. The house rat infested the wattle and daub, thatched dwellings of the poor and was particularly widespread in towns. The disease is thought to have started in the Indian sub-continent between 1340 and 1342. It expanded into Europe via the Crimea in 1346, having been brought there by an invading Tartar army which probably contracted it in Asia Minor. The plague entered Britain at what is now Weymouth in Dorset early in August in 1348, from Calais or the Channel Islands. The disease spread through Dorset, Devon and Somerset and reached Bristol by 15 August (Fig. 2.9). It had struck in Gloucester, Oxford and London by the autumn. East Anglia and Lincolnshire succumbed in the spring of 1349, by May it had reached York and by mid-summer was in North Wales. By the spring of 1350 it had affected most of Scotland. Some scholars claim that the population of Britain was halved between 1348

and 1350, others that it was reduced by 30%; one scholar believes that the plague reduced the population by no more than 10%. What is clear is that the effect of the plague was uneven; pastoral and hilly districts suffered least, while river and sea ports were worst hit.

Since the Black Death a large number of other rapidly spreading, but fortunately less potent, infectious diseases have been recorded in these islands. In the sixteenth century, for instance, a disease of uncertain origin called sweating sickness or English sweat diffused over the country with varying degrees of severity on a number of occasions.

In the seventeenth century there were several outbreaks of plague, in which the inhabitants of London were the principal sufferers: in the epidemic of 1603 over 33,000 in the capital died; in 1625 the London death toll was over 41,000 and in the Great Plague of 1665 there were over 65,000 deaths in London.

In the nineteenth century cholera epidemics occurred in 1817–23 and 1827–33. The second of these began in the Ganga Valley in 1826 and quickly spread through the Punjab and Afghanistan into South-east Europe. The disease had reached Berlin by August 1831 and Hamburg in October. It was in Sunderland on 19 October 1831 that the disease first occurred in Britain. By the beginning of 1834 almost 22,000 had died in England and Wales, over 25,000 in Ireland and 9,500 in Scotland.

A relatively small cholera epidemic which occurred in the Soho district of London in 1854 is renowned because of the map showing deaths from the epidemic which appeared in the second edition of John Snow's essay 'On the Mode of Communication of Cholera' (Fig. 2.10). The 'cholera field', as Snow called it, was centred on a pump in Broad Street and extended for about 200 metres around it. Within this area more than 500 people died from cholera between 1 and 10 September 1854.

2.10 The 'cholera field' around Broad Street pump, Soho, London, 1854.

Snow pointed out that most of the dead had been users of the Broad Street pump, whereas those living in the area and obtaining water elsewhere were unaffected. This was the first time a relationship between cholera and contaminated water had been proven.

By the beginning of the twentieth century the significance of infectious diseases in Britain had been greatly reduced and continued improvements in public water supplies, sewage systems and public and private hygiene had virtually eliminated them as major killers by the 1970s. However, occasionally outbreaks have occurred, some of which have been severe. Between 1947 and 1958, for instance, over 50,000 people contracted poliomyelitis, but vaccination programmes which began in 1956 have since made the disease extremely rare.

National and international programmes to eradicate infectious diseases have been significant features of the development of health systems in the last forty years. Malaria, which before World War 2 was the world's most powerful single cause of sickness and death, has undergone the most comprehensive eradication campaigns.

In Sri Lanka, for instance, the estimated expectation of life at birth rose from 43 years in 1946 to 52 in 1947 and the population subsequently grew very rapidly. This type of change, which had taken fifty years in the countries of Western Europe, was put down at the time to the spraying of malarial areas with DDT, an insecticide which had been developed during World War 2. Scholars now disagree about whether there was a single cause–effect relationship between spraying with DDT and population change in Sri Lanka. Because of the ambiguous way in which deaths were reported in Sri Lanka in the 1940s it is not possible to make a statistical comparison of deaths from malaria before and after 1947. Supporters of DDT spraying argue that the use of insecticides not only reduced the number of deaths from malaria but also indirectly affected population growth by reducing the number of malaria-induced miscarriages and by increasing the amount of sexual intercourse among adults no longer weakened by the disease. More cautious observers point out that during the critical period of initial post-war population growth, war-time food shortages ended, milk and milk products became more widely available and maternity services were substantially increased.

In spite of programmes of control and eradication infectious diseases are still potent disablers and killers in LDCs. In developed urbanised countries such diseases have been largely brought under control or eliminated by a combination of environmental improvements, health education, legislation and the widespread use of vaccines and antibiotics. But in such countries deaths from infectious diseases have been replaced by deaths from degenerative diseases in middle and later life. Although called degenerative their aetiology (cause) is still imperfectly understood and for some at least there is evidence that environmental factors contribute to their development. The most important degenerative diseases are heart disease, cerebro-vascular disease (stroke), cancer, and respiratory diseases such as bronchitis and asthma. In the United Kingdom, for instance, in the period 1959–63 the major causes of death for men were heart disease and cerebro-vascular disease (Fig. 2.11). For females, strokes were the major cause followed by coronary heart disease. Death from pneumonia and stomach cancer were about the same for both sexes, but those from lung cancer and bronchitis were much more severe for men than for women. Female deaths from cancer of the breast and the uterus were also of some significance.

It is useful to explore the geographical distribution of mortality from degenerative diseases in an advanced country. Howe's *A National Atlas of Disease Mortality in the United Kingdom* (1970) provides a detailed analysis at this level. Figs. 2.12 (*a*) and (*b*) are simplified versions of maps in that atlas. Instead of using conventional geographical base maps Howe used what he called demographic base maps in which he employed squares and diamonds of various sizes to represent urban and rural populations respectively. In each of the maps he used the standardised mortality ratio (SMR), which is the national expectation of mortality from that particular disease. An SMR in excess of 100 indicates a mortality rate above the national average and an SMR below 100 indicates a mortality rate below the national average. Fig. 2.12(*a*) shows those areas in which the number of deaths among males from ischaemic heart disease during the period 1959–63 was moder-

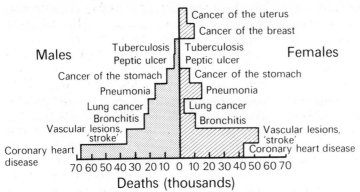

Cancer of the uterus
Cancer of the breast

Males   Females

Tuberculosis | Tuberculosis
Peptic ulcer | Peptic ulcer
Cancer of the stomach | Cancer of the stomach
Pneumonia | Pneumonia
Lung cancer | Lung cancer
Bronchitis | Bronchitis
Vascular lesions, 'stroke' | Vascular lesions, 'stroke'
Coronary heart disease | Coronary heart disease

70 60 50 40 30 20 10 0 10 20 30 40 50 60 70

Deaths (thousands)

2.11 Average annual deaths by cause in the United Kingdom, 1959–63. (After Howe, 1972.)

ately or extremely high. (Ischaemic heart disease results from a decreased blood supply to the heart. This may be due to the narrowing or blocking of the coronary arteries.) The map shows that those parts of the country to the north of a line from the Humber to the Bristol Channel generally had high SMRs and those to the south had low SMRs on the whole. Areas with particularly high SMRs occurred in Scotland, Northern Ireland, Lancashire, West Yorkshire and South Wales. Rural–urban differences in mortality rates are not revealed.

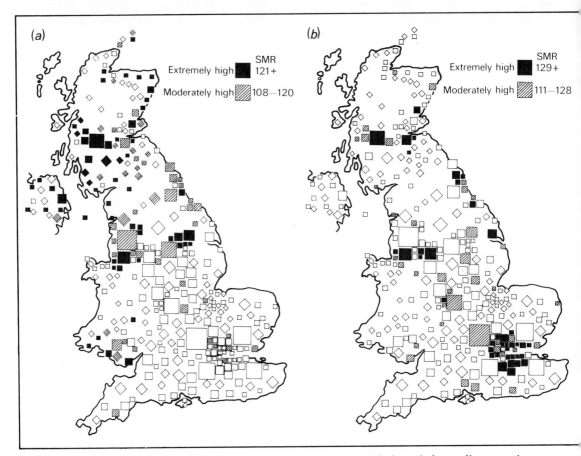

2.12 Mortality among males in the United Kingdom, 1959–63, from (a) ischaemic heart disease and (b) lung-bronchus cancer. (After Howe, 1970.)

In the world as a whole deaths from this disease are a feature of nations which are economically advanced, and populations which are well nourished and predominantly employed in non-manual occupations. In the United Kingdom the reverse seems to be true, with the affluent south-east experiencing relatively low mortality rates in the period under discussion. Heart disease, like a number of other degenerative diseases, appears to be caused by a number of inter-related factors including high fat levels, tension and stress, cigarette smoking, physical inactivity, obesity and diabetes. Another suspected contributory factor is soft water, which is characteristic of large areas of western and northern Britain.

Deaths among males from cancer of the trachea, lung and bronchus (Fig. 2.12b) in the same period reveal a rather different pattern. Although Lancashire and parts of Scotland have high mortality rates, as they do in the case of heart disease, there are two additional major concentrations of high mortality rates – north-east England and Greater London – and two smaller concentrations – West Bromwich and Kingston-upon-Hull. By contrast, Kent and Sussex, the South-west, Wales, East Anglia, the East Midlands, Cumbria and the Borders, Southern Scotland, the Scottish Highlands and Northern Ireland all have relatively low mortality ratios. The map also suggests a heavy concentration of deaths in urban areas. Again, as in the case of heart disease, no single cause of lung–bronchus cancer can be identified. In the main, people living in areas of heavy industry are the greatest sufferers. Suspected contributory factors are smoking habits and air pollutants, including smoke, dust, exhaust gases from motor vehicles and effluents of particular industries.

3 Some aspects of population distribution

World patterns

The present irregular spatial distribution of population throughout the world represents the current stage of a continually changing pattern of adjustment by millions of individuals to the variety of physical and cultural factors which affect them. Although modern technology enables man to live on almost any part of the earth's surface if he so chooses, certain areas have tended to discourage settlement, partly because of the physical discomfort and difficulties of living there but also because they offer comparatively few opportunities for providing man with a means of livelihood. Such areas include zones of extreme aridity, the highest mountain areas and zones with very low temperatures but, although these zones are usually very sparsely populated, limited areas of more dense settlement occur within them as, for example, in the oil-mining regions of the Sahara and the urban centres of the Soviet northlands. Other parts of the world, such as the agriculturally productive alluvial lowlands of southern Asia, offer particular physical attractions to man and may therefore be more densely populated than adjacent areas. It would be misleading, however, to suggest that patterns of population distribution are determined by physical factors alone, for within the broad framework of physical attractions and constraints cultural factors strongly influence the detailed pattern of distribution.

These cultural factors are of many different kinds. Levels of economic development and technology, for example, affect the number of people which can be supported in a particular area. The largely industrialised society of the United Kingdom can support far more people than could a society based on shifting cultivation in the same area and the irrigation farming of the Nile Valley or parts of the lower Ganga Basin supports more people than was possible in such areas before irrigation techniques were developed. Perhaps less obviously, such factors as political organisation, religious beliefs, levels of education and social attitudes can influence, directly or indirectly, birth and death rates, population mobility and types and patterns of settlement, which all contribute to the pattern of population distribution in a particular area.

Population distribution at a continental scale is marked by some striking contrasts, as is apparent from Table 3.1. Over half the world's people live in Asia (excluding USSR) on a little over 20% of the world's land area, more than four times as many as in any other continent. Europe (excluding USSR) ranks second in terms of total numbers and has a higher population density than Asia, more than three times the average density for the world as a whole. Africa, the third continent in terms of popula-

Table 3.1. *World population data (by regions)*

	Pop. estimate mid-1976 (millions)	Total pop. as % world total	Rate of pop. growth, annual %[a]	Crude birth rate[b]	Crude death rate[b]	Infant mortality rate[c]	Surface area (km² × 10⁻³)	Area as % world area	Pop. density per km²	Pop. projection to A.D. 2000 (millions)[d]	Total pop. as % world total A.D. 2000
World	4,019	—	1.8	30	12	105	135,830	—	29.6	6,214	—
Africa	413	(10.3)	2.6	46	20	152	30,391	(22.4)	13.6	815	(13.1)
North America	239	(5.9)	0.8	15	9	16	21,515	(15.8)	11.1	294	(4.7)
Latin America (incl. Central America)	326	(8.1)	2.8	37	9	75	20,566	(15.1)	15.9	606	(9.8)
Asia (excl. USSR)	2,287	(56.9)	2.0	33	13	121	27,580	(20.3)	82.9	3,612	(58.1)
Europe (excl. USSR)	476	(11.8)	0.6	15	10	22	4,937	(3.6)	96.4	540	(8.7)
Oceania	22	(0.5)	1.8	22	10	53	8.510	(6.3)	2.6	33	(0.5)
USSR	257	(6.4)	0.9	18	9	28	22,402	(16.5)	11.5	314	(5.1)

General sources: 1976 World Population Data sheet of the Population Reference Bureau, Inc. and *UN Demographic Yearbook 1975*.
[a] Based on population changes during period since 1970.
[b] Per thousand. For more developed areas based on registration of births for most recent year available (usually 1973 or 1974). For less developed areas based on UN estimates for 1970–75 period.
[c] Annual deaths to infants under 1 year of age per 1,000 live births. Sources as for note a.
[d] Based on UN medium variant projections to population totals as estimated for mid-1975.

tion size, has a much lower population density than either Europe or Asia but its population is growing at a much faster rate than that of Europe so that it is currently 'gaining' on Europe by nearly 8 million people each year. Rates of growth in much of Asia are comparable with those in many African countries but the lower rates in China (estimated at 1.7% per annum) and Japan (2.3%) reduce the continental average considerably. Latin America has the highest average rate of all, in marked contrast to the more economically advanced area of North America, which has a growth rate comparable with those of Europe and the USSR. These variations in population growth rates between different continents, which will be considered in a different context later, emphasise the dynamic nature of population distribution patterns.

There are, of course, also major variations in distribution within particular continents. Fielding (1974) suggests that three major generalisations can be made:

1 The highest densities are in areas of favourable physical environment, irrigation being an important 'cultural' improvement of some areas which have seasonal or unreliable rainfall but are otherwise physically attractive.

2 People are attracted to live in areas of low elevation, with more than half the world's population occupying areas below 200 metres above sea level.

3 Population clusters along the borders of continents and countries, leaving interiors empty by comparison. Approximately two-thirds of the world's population lives within about 500 kilometres of the coast.

These generalisations are clearly exemplified in Asia, where there is a particular concentration in the marginal lowland areas of India, southeast Asia, China and Japan, in contrast to the sparsely populated upland interior of the continent. The other major concentrations of dense population on a world scale are associated with the industrialised societies of Europe and North America, which have developed high levels of urbanisation during recent centuries. Between them, the lowland areas of south and east Asia and the major mid-latitude zones of Europe and eastern North America contain approximately half the world's people on about 5% of the world's land area.

There is also a striking concentration of the world's population into comparatively few countries. Table 3.2 shows the fifteen countries which had estimated populations of over 50 million each in 1976. Very dominant even in this group are China and India which, assuming the estimates given in the table are reasonably accurate, contain over one-third of the world's population between them. (It is particularly important to emphasise the considerable doubts concerning the accuracy of Chinese population data, though few demographers would argue for a total substantially lower than that suggested.) The first five countries named in the table contain over half the world's population, and perhaps just as striking is the fact that, although there are more than 160 nation-states with populations in excess of 200,000, only slightly over 30% of the world's people live outside the fifteen countries named in Table 3.2.

The variations in rates of population growth between different countries will inevitably lead to changes in the rank order of these countries in terms of their population totals as time passes. If the population projections for A.D. 2000 listed in Table 3.2 are reasonably accurate the five countries which had the highest population totals in 1976 seem likely to retain their relative positions in A.D. 2000. Japan, however, is likely to fall from sixth to eleventh in rank order as a result of the faster growth rates anticipated in the five countries ranked immediately below it in 1976. Various other minor changes are suggested by the information in Table 3.2. What is not apparent from the table is that if all the world's countries are considered, instead of merely the leading fifteen of 1976, the same series of projections suggests that the four European countries in the table will have been 'relegated' from the top fifteen altogether by A.D. 2000. Their anticipated replacements would be the Philippines (with a projected population increase from 44.0 million in 1976 to 86.3 million in A.D. 2000), Thailand (43.3 to 86.0 million), Turkey (40.2 to 71.3 million) and Iran (34.1 to 67.0 million). This again emphasises the possible effects of the high growth rates expected in many of the less economically advanced countries in the next few decades.

Population projections

We have already explained how difficult it is to obtain accurate data about population. Obviously any attempts to calculate the likely

Table 3.2. *Population data for selected countries*

	Pop. estimate mid-1976 (millions)	Rank order: total pop. 1976	Total pop. as % world total 1976	Rate of pop. growth, annual %[a]	Pop. projection to A.D. 2000 (millions)[b]	Rank order: projected pop. A.D. 2000
China	836.8	(1)	20.8	1.7	1,126.0	(1)
India	620.7	(2)	15.4	2.0	1,051.4	(2)
USSR	257.0	(3)	6.4	0.9	314.0	(3)
USA	215.3	(4)	5.4	0.8	262.5	(4)
Indonesia	134.7	(5)	3.4	2.1	230.3	(5)
Japan	112.3	(6)	2.8	1.2	132.7	(11)
Brazil	110.2	(7)	2.7	2.8	207.5	(6)
Bangladesh	76.1	(8)	1.9	2.7	144.8	(8)
Pakistan	72.5	(9)	1.8	2.9	146.4	(7)
Nigeria	64.7	(10)	1.6	2.7	135.1	(9)
Mexico	62.3	(11)	1.6	3.5	134.4	(10)
German Federal Republic	62.1	(12)	1.5	0.2	66.5	(12)
Italy	56.3	(13)	1.4	0.8	61.7	(15)
United Kingdom	56.1	(14)	1.4	0.1	62.3	(13)
France	53.1	(15)	1.3	0.8	61.9	(14)

General source: 1976 World Population Data sheet of the Population Reference Bureau, Inc.
[a] Based on population changes during period since 1970.
[b] Based on UN medium variant projections to population totals as estimated for mid-1975.

population for the year 2000, or any other date in the foreseeable future, are even more open to question. Even the estimates of population totals in the ten-year interval between censuses in economically advanced countries tend to be quite inaccurate at times. Inter-censal estimates of this kind are produced by amending the census population totals to take account of (*a*) changes resulting from natural increase or decrease and (*b*) changes occasioned by migration. Past experience in countries with sophisticated methods of recording population change has shown that population estimates tend to become less reliable with each year that passes after a census, however carefully records are kept. In countries where methods of recording population data are much less effective, the problem of making accurate estimates is clearly much greater. Many countries still lack efficient means of registering births and deaths and, even in developed countries, information relating to migration is often unreliable and incomplete. Thus even short-term estimates of population change may be inaccurate.

Long-term forecasts are obviously much less likely to be accurate. Estimates of population change over long periods of time are usually known as population projections and, although a detailed explanation of the methods used in making such projections is not appropriate here, it is useful to be aware of the bases on which they have been calculated. Most projec-

tions are now based on refinements of the component method, which was devised in the late nineteenth century. This involves subdividing a population into groups of either males or females within a relatively narrow age range (often either one or five years) and assessing likely changes in each of these groups (or cohorts) on the basis of certain assumptions concerning fertility, mortality and migration over a period of time. It is not usually considered satisfactory to use this method in stages of more than five years at a time. A projection of, say, twenty-five years would involve carrying out a series of calculations each reflecting likely changes during periods of five years or less to particular cohorts.

The assumptions made concerning particular variables are clearly of fundamental importance, yet many possibilities exist and it is not surprising that population projections have become notorious for their inaccuracy. Recent changes in birth rates in Great Britain have led to drastic revisions in the forecasts of population that were made in the mid-1960s. Some such forecasts anticipated a total population of 80 million in Great Britain by A.D. 2000, whereas most forecasts made in the mid-1970s were below 65 million (see Fig. 3.1*a* and *b*). In terms of national planning, inaccurate projections can cause major problems. This became apparent in the mid-1970s when teacher unemployment in the United Kingdom developed on a large scale. Far more teachers were trained than was necessary to teach the number of children in schools, largely because the scale of the decline in birth rates was not accurately anticipated by educational planners. Similar problems can occur in, for example, the fields of housing provision, health services and labour supply.

Because of the many problems inherent in population projections it is becoming more usual for demographers to calculate a series of projections based on different assumptions rather than producing only a single projection. This series of projections, called variants, is not usually averaged out but is seen as indicating a range of possibilities. Recent population projections for Great Britain provide a good illustration of this approach.

Projections of the population of Great Britain and of its constituent countries by sex and age were first produced in the 1920s. Since 1955,

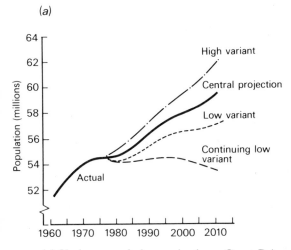

(*a*)

3.1 (*a*) Variant population projections, Great Britain 1974–2011. (Based on Fig. 2, *Variant Population Projections 1974–2011*, HMSO, 1975).

(b)

		High variant	Central projection	Low variant	Continuing low variant
1974 (base population)					
0–14	12,800				
15–64/59[a]	32,522				
65/60 and over[b]	9,200				
All ages	54,522				
1991					
0–14		13,305	12,319	11,428	10,275
15–64/59[a]		34,633	34,573	34,543	34,542
65/60 and over[b]		9,680	9,680	9,680	9,680
All ages		57,618	56,572	55,651	54,497
2011					
0–14		13,721	12,400	11,181	9,143
15–64/59[a]		38,725	37,481	36,339	34,591
65/60 and over[b]		9,804	9,804	9,804	9,804
All ages		62,250	59,685	57,324	53,538

[a] 15–64 for males; 15–59 for females.
[b] 65 and over for males; 60 and over for females.

3.1 (b) Variant population structure projections 1991 and 2011.

new projections, using the component method, have been made every year. Until the mid-1970s these projections were based on a single set of assumptions concerning the three components of population change: births, deaths and net migration. The strategy of drawing up a single projection was favoured up to that time on the grounds that it provided a common framework or a consistent starting point for all population-related planning. But despite warnings, false implications were read into the single projection, in particular that future population could be determined with a high degree of accuracy.

Because of this problem there was pressure to publish a range of population projections based on different assumptions concerning fertility, mortality and migration. The United Nations, for example, requested countries to undertake 1970-based projections incorporating fertility at 'high' and 'low' as well as 'medium' levels as a contribution to new world projections. In 1974 the Office of Population Censuses and Surveys published for Great Britain variant population projections for the period 1974–2011. It was thought that the publication of the variants as well as the central projection would help users in two ways:

1 by giving some idea of the magnitude of the uncertainty in the population projection and

hence enabling users to test the sensitivity of their plans to possible future population variations; and

2 by enabling users to assess the costs and implications if the birth trend, population growth, etc., were either above or below the central projection.

The main features of the variant projections for Great Britain are summarised in Fig. 3.1 (a) and (b). The high and low variants have been relatively narrowly spaced in order to give a useful measure of the uncertainty to be attached to the central projection. Very broadly spaced variants would, while covering more future possibilities, be relatively worthless for educational planners, for those users concerned with man-power questions, and for those concerned with the provision of services for old people, all of whom need to devise a limited number of alternative plans.

The projections show that it is the fertility component that is surrounded by most uncertainty. The projected population aged 0–14 in 1991 varies by more than 3 million and by 2011 by more than 4.5 million. Further uncertainty is caused by the fact that by the latter date the various projected child populations of 1991 will have entered the adult group. Thus by 2011, according to these projections, the population

24

of Great Britain may be as low as 53.5 million (about 1 million less than the base population in 1974) or as high as 62.25 million.

Mapping population distribution and density

So far we have confined discussion of population distribution and density to a consideration of differences on a world scale and have made no attempt to map these, largely because maps on such a scale are so generalised as to be almost meaningless. The cartographic representation of population data presents particular problems even when dealing with considerably smaller areas, largely because of the near impossibility of precisely locating populations on a map, even where detailed information is available from censuses or similar sources.

The most common type of population distribution map in which an attempt is made to pinpoint the location of population as precisely as possible is the dot map. Fig. 3.2 is a fairly typical example of this kind of map and shows the main problems of attempting to construct a dot distribution map, i.e. how many people should be represented by a single dot, where should each dot be placed and what should be the physical size of the dots themselves? Clearly the resultant map is a compromise. The dot size has been kept small to allow for as much flexibility as possible – a larger dot size would have meant either that dots would overlap, which is clearly undesirable, or that their value would have to be reduced. Despite this, with a dot value of 10,000 people the location of particular dots can be a major problem, for in East Africa there are very few agglomerations of 10,000 people – only fourteen in the whole of mainland Tanzania, for example. Thus the location of dots is inevitably symbolic to some extent. Even if dots with a value of only 100 people had been used it would have been difficult to locate them accurately in some of the most sparsely populated zones of northern Kenya, where the few permanent settlements are small in size and some groups are semi-nomadic and therefore have no permanent 'location'. Moreover, if dots of a lower value than 10,000 people had been used cartographic problems would have arisen in representing some of the more densely populated areas such as the

Kenya Highlands and the areas fringing Lake Victoria unless the basic map-scale had been enlarged. Even on the present basis it has been found impossible to use dots effectively to show the four largest towns (Nairobi and Mombasa in Kenya, Kampala in Uganda and Dar-es-Salaam in Tanzania). This is a common problem and cartographers frequently use symbols such as proportional circles, squares or even spheres to show larger settlements on maps of this kind.

An alternative to the population distribution map is a population density map (see Fig. 3.3). Though some such maps attempt to indicate a relationship between population totals and cultivated land, inhabited area or other similar measures, the vast majority of population density maps simply indicate the relationship between total population and total land area. Fig. 3.3 is of this type and indicates clearly some of the variations in population density which exist within East Africa. The map suffers from the fundamental weakness of all density maps in that population totals are related to units of area within which there is not a uniform distribution of population. The densities mapped thus represent averages for the particular units of area. Even where these units are comparatively small, as in Fig. 3.3, there are considerable variations in density. For example, in Kigezi in south-west Uganda (A in Fig. 3.3) although the average density is over 100 per square kilometre there are quite extensive areas of forest and game reserve which have very low population densities. In the Bwindi forest area within Kigezi, approximately 300 square kilometres in extent, the population consists of only about 100 pygmies, though adjacent parishes have population densities of more than 600 per square kilometre (Kagambirwe, 1972).

Obviously, the smaller the units of area used the more likely it is that density maps will give an accurate representation of reality. But there are more likely to be problems in obtaining data for small units of area, especially in LDCs. In addition, however small the units it is difficult to avoid the artificial visual impression created by the boundaries of the units. In Fig. 3.3, though there are quite marked changes in density between, for example, the Kenya Highlands and the areas to the south of these as a result of distinct changes in physical character, the

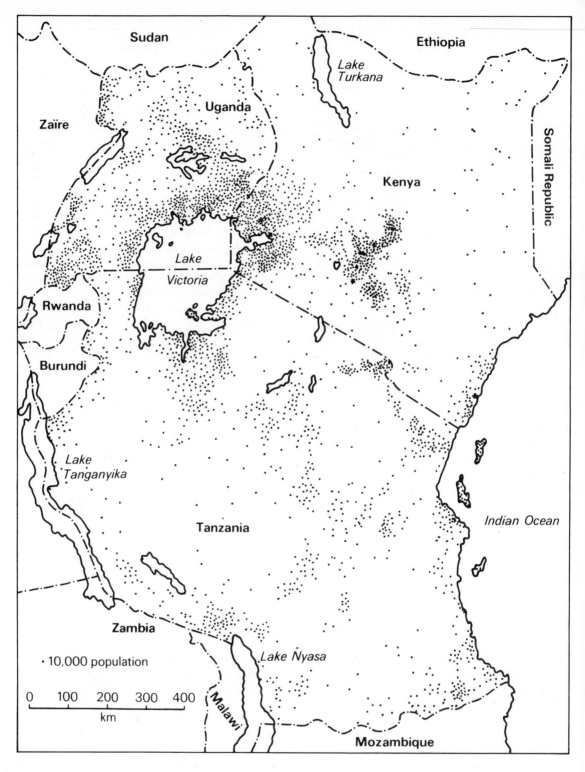

3.2 Distribution of population in East Africa excluding the four largest towns. (After Morgan, 1973): based on data published in national censuses 1967–9.)

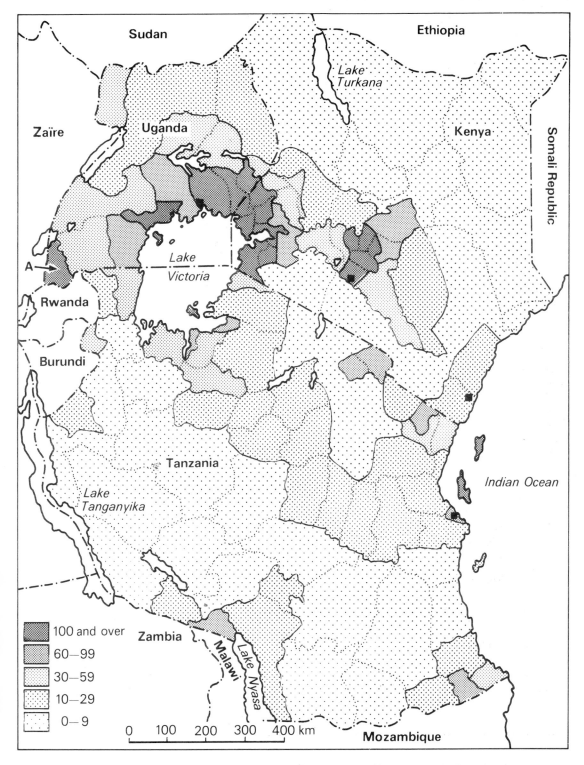

3.3 Density of population per square kilometre in East Africa. (After Morgan, 1973: data sources as for Fig. 3.2.)

'break line' between different areas is not quite as clear-cut as the map implies. In cases where suitable data are available, some cartographers have mapped densities on the basis of grid squares of a particular size but, though this sometimes gives a better impression than using administrative units as a unit of area, it introduces a different kind of artificiality, for densities obviously do not alter in a formal pattern of squares. One other aspect of density maps is perhaps worth mentioning at this stage and that is the crucial importance of the class boundaries chosen. For example, it is easy to assume that any of the areas in central Tanzania shown in Fig. 3.3 as being within the density class 10–29 people per square kilometre has a density which is more similar to that of any other area within the same class than it is to the density of any area in another class. But this is not necessarily true. Two units of area with densities of 9 and 11 people per square kilometre would fall into different density classes, even though their densities are much more similar than those of two units with, say, 11 and 28 people per square kilometre which would fall into the same density class. With this problem in mind, it is clear that careful thought needs to be given to the division of density values into suitable classes if these are not to be very misleading.

Despite the problems involved in constructing population distribution and density maps both can provide a useful indication of spatial variations in the pattern of population distribution to users who are aware of the limitations of such maps. A useful graphic method of showing variations in population concentration in a very different way is through the construction of Lorenz curves (see Fig. 3.4). This technique, which was initially devised to indicate concentrations of income or wealth, can be used when information about an area is available in equivalent units (e.g. parishes or counties), and so can frequently be employed in dealing with population data. Units of area are ranked in order of density of population and then populations and areas of these units are totalled for each density class. Cumulative percentages of area can then be plotted against cumulative percentages of population on a graph and the points joined together to form a 'curve'. If all the units of area had similar densities this curve would follow the diagonal,

indicating an even distribution of population throughout the total area concerned. Normally, of course, there is considerable deviation from this and the more 'bowed' the Lorenz curve, the greater is the unevenness of distribution of population.

Thus, in Fig. 3.4, Uganda is shown to have the most evenly distributed population of the three East African countries, though even there 30 % of the population occupies approximately 60 % of the total area, largely a reflection of the low densities in the more arid parts of the country. In Kenya distribution is markedly more uneven, with the densely populated areas of the Kenya Highlands and Lake Victoria Lowlands accounting for the bulk of the total population and 80 % of the total area containing well under 20 % of the total population. This more sparsely populated area is mainly in the regions of low rainfall in north and north-east Kenya.

Urbanisation

The most striking examples of population concentration occur in urban areas. Several large Indian cities have population densities within their inner areas of well over 1,000 per hectare, with Bombay, in places, reaching densities in excess of 3,000 per hectare. Other cities in LDCs have similar densities: e.g. Ibadan with

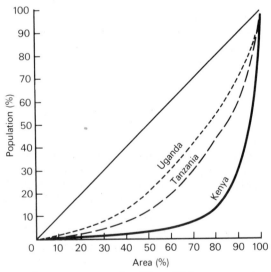

3.4 Lorenz curves for East African countries. (After Morgan, 1973: data sources as for Fig. 3.2.)

28

3.5 A typical street in central Singapore, built in the mid-nineteenth century and consisting of three-storey shophouses. Part of the ground floor of each building is occupied by a shop or small industrial concern but the remainder of the shophouse is divided into numerous small cubicles in which families of as many as eight or ten people may occupy an area only 3 metres square. Districts like this are being replaced by high-rise flats, in which approximately half of Singapore's population now lives.

over 2,000 per hectare in parts of the old walled town, and Singapore with over 2,500 per hectare in parts of the 'shophouse' core (see Fig. 3.5). In the past, similar densities have been recorded in industrialised countries, with New York's lower East side having densities of approximately 2,500 per hectare in 1900, for example, but today densities of even 1,000 per hectare are rare in more developed countries as a result of urban renewal programmes, improved living standards, and better communications that allow people to live further from their place of work.

Although cities were already in existence more than 5,000 years ago, it is only in the relatively recent past that urban dwellers have comprised a substantial proportion of the total world population. As recently as 1800 probably only 3 % of the world's people lived in settlements with a population of more than 5,000. By 1900 this proportion was between four and five times as great as a hundred years earlier and by the mid-1970s it was approximately 40 % of the total world population. In terms of actual numbers this represents an increase from about 80 million in 1800 to nearly twenty times as many in the mid-1970s.

Comparison of the level of urbanisation (i.e. the proportion of the total population living in urban areas, usually expressed as a percentage) between different countries is difficult because the definition of 'urban areas' varies greatly and has also changed through time. In some cases urban areas are defined solely in terms of numbers, as in Ghana where they are described as 'localities of 5,000 or more inhabitants' and Venezuela where they consist of 'centres with a population of 1,000 or more inhabitants'. In other areas they are defined in administrative terms, as in Tanzania where the urban population comprises the residents of sixteen 'gazetted townships' and in Ecuador where the urban areas are defined as 'capitals of provinces and cantons'. Some definitions are far more complex, however, and take into account a wide range of factors. An interesting example of this type is provided by the Philippines where urban areas are defined as:

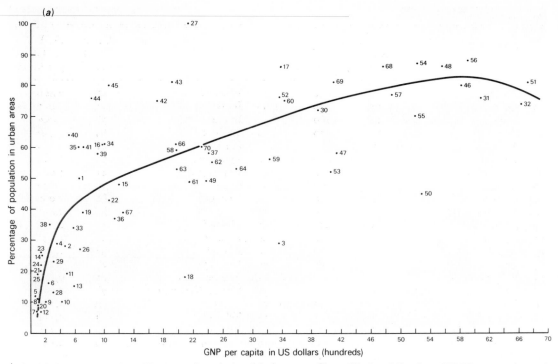

3.6 (a) A scattergraph to illustrate the relationship between Gross National Product (GNP) per capita and the percentage of total population living in urban areas in the mid-1970s.

Cities and municipalities having a population density of 1,000 or more persons per square kilometre. Central districts of municipalities and cities having a population density of 500 or more persons per square kilometre. Central districts regardless of population density having the following: networks of streets; six or more commercial or recreational establishments and some amenities of a city, e.g. town hall, church, public plaza, market place, school, hospital. *Barrios* conforming to the conditions listed above and having 1,000 or more inhabitants whose occupation is neither farming nor fishing.

Despite the difficulty of making accurate comparisons between countries with different definitions of urban areas, it is clear that there is, in general, a marked contrast between developed and less developed countries. In the former, urbanisation levels in excess of 70 % are not uncommon though there is by no means a uniform pattern. In the mid-1970s in Northwest Europe alone urbanisation levels ranged from over 80 % in such countries as Belgium, German Federal Republic and Sweden to just over 50 % in Ireland and even less in Norway. There also appears to be some statistical evi-

dence to show that the more urbanised the country is, the higher its wealth as measured by Gross National Product (see Fig. 3.6 and Exercise 10).

Urbanisation in developed areas has been closely associated with industrial expansion, agricultural changes and the development of efficient transport networks. The evolution of the factory system encouraged the growth of larger settlements than had the earlier domestic industries, while improvements in agriculture and the development of new forms of transport enabled the concentrations of population in urban areas to be provided with the food, raw materials and other items they needed. These economic changes occurred first in Western Europe and were accompanied by the transfer of workers from agricultural to industrial and service occupations, which resulted in a movement of people from rural to urban areas. Similar changes occurred in North America (where the number of people employed in agriculture in the United States decreased from over 70 % of the total employed population in 1820 to less than 40 % by 1900 and less than 5 % in 1970), and in other now economically

		Urban popula- tion (%)	GNP (US $ per capita)			Urban popula- tion (%)	GNP (US $ per capita
1	Algeria	50	650	37	Puerto Rico	58	2,400
2	Egypt	43	280	38	Bolivia	35	250
3	Libya	29	3,360	39	Brazil	58	900
4	Ghana	29	350	40	Colombia	64	510
5	Mali	12	70	41	Peru	60	710
6	Nigeria	16	240	42	Venezuela	75	1,710
7	Upper Volta	7	80	43	Argentina	81	1,900
8	Ethiopia	11	90	44	Chile	76	820
9	Kenya	10	200	45	Uruguay	80	1,060
10	Mozambique	10	420	46	Denmark	80	5,820
11	Rhodesia	19	480	47	Finland	58	4,130
12	Tanzania	7	140	48	Iceland	86	5,550
13	Angola	15	580	49	Ireland	52	2,370
14	Zaïre	25	150	50	Norway	45	5,280
15	Rep. of South Africa	48	1,200	51	Sweden	81	6,720
				52	United Kingdom	76	3,360
16	Iraq	61	970	53	Austria	52	4,050
17	Israel	86	3,380	54	Belgium	87	5,210
18	Saudi Arabia	18	2,080	55	France	70	5,190
19	Turkey	39	690	56	German Federal Rep.	88	5,890
20	Bangladesh	9	100				
21	India	20	130	57	Netherlands	77	4,880
22	Iran	43	1,060	58	Bulgaria	59	1,770
23	Pakistan	26	130	59	Czechoslovakia	56	3,220
24	Sri Lanka	22	130	60	German Democratic Rep.	75	3,430
25	Burma	19	90				
26	Malaysia	27	660	61	Hungary	49	2,140
27	Singapore	100	2,120	62	Poland	55	2,450
28	Thailand	13	300	63	Greece	53	1,970
29	China	23	300	64	Italy	53	2,770
30	Japan	72	3,880	65	Portugal	26	1,540
31	Canada	76	6,080	66	Spain	61	1,960
32	United States	74	6,640	67	Yugoslavia	39	1,250
33	Guatemala	34	570	68	Australia	86	4,760
34	Mexico	61	1,000	69	New Zealand	81	4,100
35	Cuba	60	640	70	USSR	60	2,300
36	Jamaica	37	1,140				

3.6 (b) The data from which the graph was compiled.
(Source: 1976 World Population Data sheet of the Population Reference Bureau, Inc.)

advanced countries such as Australia and Japan. The extreme of urban development is to be seen in the great metropolitan areas such as London, New York and Tokyo, all of which have populations in excess of 10 million according to recent estimates.

Although urban population increases in the period between 1750 and 1950 occurred principally in what are now economically advanced countries, more recently such growth has been of increasing importance in LDCs. Some countries within this group, notably in Latin America, already have urbanisation levels comparable with those of more developed countries (see Fig. 3.6). The urban population of all LDCs more than doubled in total between 1950 and 1970 with a rate of increase more than twice that of developed countries during the same period. Moreover, with urbanisation levels in much of Africa and Asia still below 30 % in the mid-1970s, there is ample possibility of further growth. As rates of urban growth in the more economically advanced areas are now in decline, it seems certain that future urban population

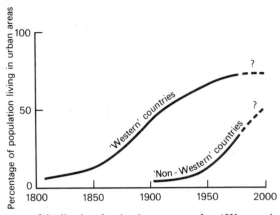

3.7 Idealised urbanisation curves for 'Western' and 'non-Western' countries. (After Haggett, 1975.)

increases will be concentrated mainly in less developed areas.

It would be wrong to assume that the LDCs are merely following a pattern set at an earlier stage by the present industrialised countries. Since 1950 the *average* population increase of urban areas in southern Asia, Africa and Latin America has been in excess of 4% per annum and many individual cities are today increasing at rates of more than 6% per annum. By contrast, most European countries during their period of most rapid urbanisation registered increases in urban population of little more than 2% per annum, though rates of growth in some North American and Australian cities, boosted by immigration from Europe, were closer to those of cities in LDCs at the present time. Fig. 3.7 illustrates the different patterns of growth in what Haggett (1975) called 'Western' and 'non-Western' countries, typically representing the experiences of European nations and the LDCs. The former group has typically had a period of slow growth followed by a sharp increase in growth rate in the second half of the nineteenth century and a gradual levelling out thereafter. The typical curve for a LDC indicates a later but much more rapid period of growth which in most cases shows little sign of slowing down at present, though this could take place in the future. Clearly such curves are generalised and individual countries are likely to follow slightly different patterns.

The differences in rates of growth reflect other economic, social and demographic differences. The growth of cities in nineteenth-century Europe was very heavily dependent on migration from the countryside into the cities, as natural increase within the cities was limited by the high mortality rates which prevailed when sanitation was often poor, water supplies frequently polluted, malnutrition common and medical provision limited. In 1861, for example, Liverpool still had a crude death rate of 29.0 per thousand and a natural increase rate of only 0.5%. Substantial decreases in urban death rates in many cases did not long precede the falling birth rates which have been a feature of most European cities in the twentieth century.

By contrast, natural increase rates in the cities of LDCs at the present time are often high. Health standards and medical provision are usually better than in surrounding rural areas and death rates have, in many cases, decreased by as much in the period between 1950 and 1975 as was the case in a period three times as long in the nineteenth and early twentieth centuries in many European cities. Meanwhile birth rates remain high, often approaching and sometimes exceeding 30 per thousand per annum. The limited amount of research into desired family size in the urban areas of LDCs suggests that in many cases five or six children still represent a desirable aim for many parents, especially amongst the poorer and less educated groups. Social attitudes to family size appear to be beginning to change, but it is not yet clear whether the pattern of decreasing family size followed by more developed countries will be repeated exactly, or, if it is, how long this will take. Thus, with high birth rates and low death rates, sometimes described as a combination of pre-industrial fertility and post-industrial mortality, natural increase rates often exceed 2% and even reach 3% per annum in some cases (e.g. in Manila).

To this rapid rate of natural increase is added the massive influx of migrants from rural areas. The migrants, despite the limited industrial development in many cities, perceive the possibility of greater opportunities being available in the urban areas than exist in the often poverty-stricken rural areas, where rapid rates of natural increase again exacerbate existing problems. The proportion of the urban population increase which results from natural increase compared with that which results from migration varies, but migration is often responsible for more than half the total increase. Thus migration to Nairobi in the 1960s is estimated to have accounted for approximately 50% of the city's population growth in that period and about 70% of Sao Paulo's increase between 1950 and 1970 is thought to be attributable to migration.

In the mid-1970s the balance of world urban population between developed and less developed countries was approximately even, but this is rapidly changing as can be seen from Fig. 3.8. By A.D. 2000 it is estimated that more than 60% of the world's population living in agglomerations of over 20,000 people will be in the countries that are at present less developed. This forecast assumes an increase of nearly 750 million people in the urban population of those countries between 1980 and 2000 and would obviously give rise to enormous problems in housing and provision of other amenities. These serious problems will arise in areas where similar difficulties have already resulted in the extensive development of squatter settlements and a wide range of other urban problems.

Since 1800 a major shift in the world's population distribution has taken place, with the rapid growth of urban populations, first in the present industrialised countries and more recently in LDCs, where growth continues at a rapid rate. On a different scale, population distributions *within* individual cities have also tended to change through time. This indicates again some of the contrasts between developed and less developed countries.

Within urban areas it is usually possible to differentiate contrasting functional zones that characteristically have different residential population densities. Examination of the pattern of residential populations has recently involved the use of a method known as gradient analysis. Investigations by Clark (1967) of residential population density gradients for thirty-six cities in different parts of the world showed that, in general, densities decline with increasing distance from the city centre, normally decreasing most sharply near the centre and less markedly as distance from the centre increases. Since the data used in plotting density gradients are based on the averaging of information available for administrative or census units which are approximately equidistant from the city centre, it is clear that the gradients as plotted may obscure

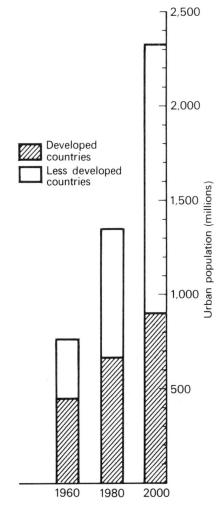

3.8 Estimated world urban population growth A.D. 1960–2000. The totals relate to settlements of population over 20,000. (Source: UN Dept of Economic and Social Affairs, 1970.)

differences which exist within particular concentric zones around the city centre. This is especially true of large urban agglomerations which incorporate subsidiary centres within the urban area. Factors like this should be borne in mind when drawing conclusions based on density gradients.

Fig. 3.9 indicates how the density gradient for London has changed through time, largely as a result of changing transport facilities. The steep gradient for 1801 indicates a stage when transport provision was limited and people had to live close to where they worked. Later stages indicate first an increase and later a decrease in

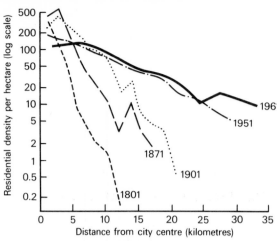

3.9 Residential density profiles for London in selected years. (After Clark, 1967.)

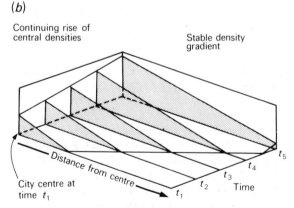

Central densities first increase, later decline

Outward migration of zone of maximum density

Distance from centre

Decreasing density gradients

City centre at time t_1

t_1 t_2 t_3 t_4 t_5 Time

(b)

Continuing rise of central densities

Stable density gradient

Distance from centre

City centre at time t_1

t_1 t_2 t_3 t_4 t_5 Time

3.10 Changes in urban density gradients through time for (a) 'Western' and (b) 'non-Western' cities. (After B. J. L. Berry et al. (1963), Geographical Review, **53**.)

city centre population densities together with an outward spread of settlement into suburban areas made possible by improved transport facilities and motivated by a wide range of social, economic and administrative changes. A generalisation of the changes in residential population density gradients for 'Western' cities through time is provided in Fig. 3.10(a). This indicates three major features:

(a) the initial rise and later decline in population density of the central part of the city;

(b) the outward spread of the urban population through time, and

(c) the consequent decrease in the population density gradient through time.

By contrast, a similar generalisation for 'non-Western' cities (Fig. 3.10b) indicates a continuing rise of densities in the central area and the consequent maintenance of a relatively stable density gradient despite the outward spread of such cities. These differences largely reflect different types of functional zone and the limited development of transport networks. The central areas of 'non-Western' cities tend to retain a major residential function as well as providing a variety of employment opportunities, as in the 'shophouse' core of most Malaysian cities and the *medina* of many Arab cities in North Africa and elsewhere. The suburban areas frequently include extensive, densely populated squatter settlements as well as better-quality housing at lower densities, giving rise to higher *average* population densities than in most 'Western' suburbs. Additionally, the immature development of urban transport systems tends to limit the general outward spread of settlement, thus giving rise to a more compact urban plan than in a 'Western' city of comparable population and to higher overall population densities. In time, the transport systems of urban areas in such cities may become similar to those of 'Western' cities. But this is by no means certain and the pressures imposed on city councils that are already grievously short of money and face a continuing rapid increase in population may well restrict transport development for many years to come. Administrative difficulties like these will tend to perpetuate the differences in population density gradients outlined above.

4 Population and resources

Malthus and after

We have already focused attention briefly on the problem of providing sufficient food and other resources to meet the needs of a growing world population. This is not a new problem. At a local level there have been many occasions in history when a particular group reached a stage where it was difficult or impossible to supply all the subsistence needs of the community. Such situations have often been important motivating factors behind migrations, as was the case in Ireland in the nineteenth century, when some 800,000 people left the country in the space of only five years or so after the potato crop failures of the 1840s. Additionally, many people may die from starvation when inadequate food supplies are available, as happened in India and Ethiopia in the mid-1970s (see Fig. 4.1).

In the early nineteenth century there was some concern that a stage had been reached in Great Britain where the population was likely to grow to such an extent that it would exceed the capacity of the country to supply food for the community. People's ideas were strongly influenced by the writings of the Reverend T. R. Malthus, who in 1798 had published the first edition of his *Essay on the Principle of Population*. This essay and the subsequent writings of Malthus were much discussed when they were first published and have continued to be a source of interest and argument in recent times.

Basically Malthus suggested that whereas food production was likely at best to increase at an arithmetic rate (i.e. by the repeated addition of a uniform increment in each uniform interval of time), population tended to increase at a geometric rate and was likely to double every twenty-five years or so unless certain checks were imposed on it. Thus, while food output was likely to increase in a series of twenty-five year intervals only in the progression:

1, 2, 3, 4, 5, 6, 7, 8, 9, etc.

population was capable of increasing in the progression:

1, 2, 4, 8, 16, 32, 64, 128, 256, etc.

On the basis of a supposed world population of 1,000 million in the early nineteenth century and an adequate means of subsistence at that time, Malthus suggested that there was a potential for a population increase to 256,000 million within 200 years but that the means of subsistence were only capable of being increased enough for 9,000 million to be fed at the level prevailing at the beginning of the period. He therefore considered that the population increase should be kept down to the level at which

35

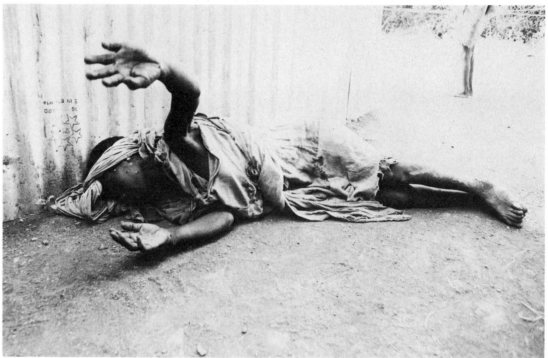

4.1 A starving youngster in Kobbo, Ethiopia, in 1973. In the early 1970s three successive years of drought in the grain-producing area of the Kobbo Valley led to mass migration from the rural areas. Many migrants went to small towns like Kobbo to beg for food but, despite the efforts of international agencies, many died from starvation and disease. Similar situations have been common in much of the Sahel zone of Africa in recent years, though pastoralists have often been the worst sufferers.

it could be supported by the operation of various checks on population growth, which he categorised as 'preventive' and 'positive' checks.

The chief preventive check envisaged by Malthus was that of 'moral restraint', which was seen as a deliberate decision by men to refrain 'from pursuing the dictate of nature in an early attachment to one woman', i.e. to marry later in life than had been usual and only at a stage when fully capable of supporting a family. This, it was anticipated, would give rise to smaller families and probably to fewer families, but Malthus was strongly opposed to birth control *within* marriage and did not suggest that parents should try to restrict the number of children born to them after their marriage. Malthus was clearly aware that problems might arise from the postponement of marriage to a later date, such as an increase in the number of illegitimate births, but considered that these problems were likely to be less serious than those caused by a continuation of rapid population increase.

He saw positive checks to population growth as being any causes which contributed to the shortening of human lifespans. He included in this category poor living and working conditions which might give rise to low resistance to disease, as well as more obvious factors such as disease itself, war and famine. Some of the conclusions which can be drawn from Malthus's ideas thus have obvious political connotations and this partly accounts for the interest in his writings and possibly also the misrepresentation of some of his ideas by authors such as Cobbett, the famous early English radical. Some later writers modified his ideas, suggesting, for example, strong government action to ensure later marriages and, indeed, such action was taken in parts of Germany in the mid-nineteenth century (see Glass, 1953). Others did not accept the view that birth control should not be practised after marriage and one group in particular, called the Malthusian League, strongly argued the case for birth control, though this was contrary to the principles of conduct which Malthus himself had advocated.

Obviously any forecasts concerning future relationships between population and food supply, or the supply of other resources, are based on a number of assumptions concerning rates of consumption, production and population change. The problems of forecasting population changes have already been considered (see Chapter 3). In modern times population growth has rarely been at an even rate for long periods and it is very difficult to anticipate even a few years in advance what growth rates will be. Similarly there are difficulties in forecasting rates of increase in food supply or how consumption will vary. Despite this, the consideration of the future balance between population and food supplies has continued to attract the interest of many people and gloomy predictions concerning this balance are often described as 'Malthusian' or 'neo-Malthusian'.

One assumption in many discussions of the future situation is that there is a definite ceiling to food production from any given area. Thus it can be argued that beyond a certain stage continued population growth will result in less food being available per head until ultimately some people have insufficient to eat. They will then die, either directly from starvation or from disease resulting from a lack of resistance brought about by malnutrition.

This increased mortality rate acts as a 'Malthusian check' on population growth and might be expected also to affect the fertility rate, in at least two ways. First, the deaths of many women of child-bearing age and of husbands of such women would be likely to have an immediate effect on the numbers of children born and the deaths of younger people would reduce the numbers of those available to become parents in later years. Second, it is likely that the situation would encourage deliberate attempts to reduce the number of children being born because of the increasing awareness of the problems caused by continuing population growth. Thus a sequence of events might occur similar to that shown diagrammatically in Fig. 4.2, culminating in a decrease in the rate of population growth and possibly even a decline in total numbers. Migration, too, might become a significant factor in this decline. It is also possible that fertility would decline eventually

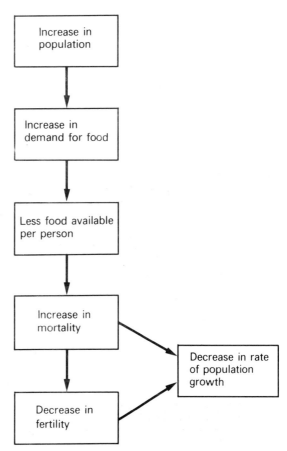

4.2   A possible sequence of events envisaged by some Malthusians (see comments in text).

as a result of a reduction in the physiological capacity to conceive in conditions of malnutrition. (It is worth noting that this appears to have happened in recent years during periods of famine in Bangladesh and the Sahel (sub-Saharan) zone of Africa.)

Looking further ahead, if the decrease in population growth rate gave rise to a decline in the total population to a level where food supplies were again more than adequate it would seem possible that checks on growth would cease to operate and population would again increase. If this were repeated a cyclical pattern might emerge with fluctuations above and below a critical level determined by the food supply ceiling. This type of pattern is illustrated in Fig. 4.3.

The pattern of development outlined above has been clearly observed in animal populations and the limited evidence available suggests that it has probably been a feature of some primitive

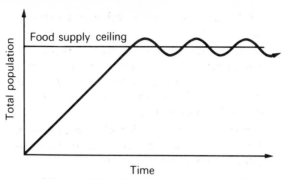

4.3 The possible effect of a food supply ceiling on population growth. (After Haggett, 1975.)

human societies. Some countries (e.g. India: see Case Study 5) have, in recent years, found great difficulty in supplying sufficient food for their populations but, in Great Britain, the gloomy predictions made in the early nineteenth century have not been realised, largely because some of the assumptions on which these predictions were based proved to be invalid.

In fact, population continued to increase in Great Britain after 1800 and, though grave concern about food supplies was expressed by politicians and others for many years, living standards also improved in time. A series of developments based on improved techniques in agriculture, industry and transportation revolutionised the economy of Great Britain and of much of the rest of the world, resulting in great increases in agricultural productivity and the output of manufactured goods in Great Britain and making it possible for much of the food needed by the British population to be obtained from other parts of the world in exchange for industrial goods and services provided by Great Britain. These changes were on a scale unprecedented in history and emphasise the difficulties of forecasting what is likely to happen in the future with regard to population growth and food supplies. So far as nineteenth-century Britain was concerned, the changes in economic structure and productivity meant that population growth was not limited by any food-supply shortages of the type that had been envisaged. The pattern of development which occurred in the nineteenth century may be represented as in Fig. 4.4, though it must also be remembered that during this period many people emigrated from Great Britain and various internal adjustments in population distribution also occurred as a result of migration.

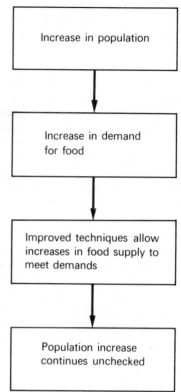

4.4 Population increase and food supply in nineteenth-century Britain (see comments in text).

More recently there has been a reduction in the rate of growth of the British population, especially in the twentieth century (see Case Study 1). The reasons for this are complex and incompletely understood, but seem to be fundamentally related to social attitudes rather than being a result of direct physical controls such as a shortage of food.

An alternative model to that of Malthus has been developed by Ester Boserup, a Danish economist, who has experience as a research worker for the United Nations in several LDCs. She has pointed out (Boserup, 1965) that the Malthusian approach to the relationship between agriculture and population growth is 'based upon the belief that the supply of food for the human race is inherently inelastic and this lack of elasticity is the main factor governing the rate of population growth'. Thus population growth is seen as being dependent upon preceding changes in agricultural productivity.

These changes are themselves seen as occurring in response to various other factors which occur largely by chance, such as particular technical innovations.

Boserup asserts, however, that it is more realistic to suggest that population growth is a major factor in determining the nature of agricultural developments rather than being controlled by them. Her views are sometimes summarised in the phrase 'necessity is the mother of invention', because she argues that in many pre-industrial societies population growth served as the main stimulus to change agricultural techniques and so increase food production. She supports her views with evidence from LDCs and states that few people would wish to suggest, in line with what she sees as the essence of Malthusian thinking, that rapid population growth in these areas in recent years can be explained by reference to changes in the conditions for food production. She goes further, to claim that in agricultural development generally, and not merely in the experience of LDCs in the twentieth century, 'agricultural developments are caused by population trends rather than the other way round'.

Her investigations were based on a range of land-use systems which she classified on the basis of their intensity of production, measured in terms of cropping frequency. In an admittedly simple classification, she identifies five different intensities of agricultural land use recognisable in many parts of Latin America, Africa and Asia. These are:

1 *Forest-fallow cultivation*, in which plots of land are cleared in the forest each year, cropped for a year or two and then left fallow long enough for forest to re-colonise the cleared areas. This implies a fallow of at least twenty to twenty-five years and possibly as long as a hundred years.

2 *Bush-fallow cultivation*, in which the process is similar to forest-fallow but the fallow period is much shorter (normally six to ten years) so the vegetation which develops on cleared land is not forest but bush with possibly a few young trees. These first two groups are sometimes jointly described as long-fallow or shifting cultivation systems.

3 *Short-fallow cultivation*, in which the fallow period is only one or two years so that only

wild grasses are likely to colonise the cleared area.

4 *Annual cropping*, in which land is usually left uncultivated for several months between harvest and planting – a period which can be viewed as a fallow period though it is not normally so described.

5 *Multi-cropping*, in which plots bear two or more successive crops each year so that cropping is virtually continuous.

Boserup points out that during the twentieth century, as population has increased, there has been a change from less intensive to more intensive systems of cropping in many parts of Latin America, Africa and Asia. Thus in some areas forest-fallow cultivation has gradually changed to bush-fallow cultivation or even more intensive systems and in parts of Asia, in particular, the growth of population has stimulated the rapid spread of multi-cropping systems.

Related to these changes have been changes in technique which, in Boserup's view, have developed because of the changes in land use. She points out that forest-fallow cultivation normally involves the burning of trees and other vegetation on a plot before planting or sowing directly into the ashes left after burning. A digging-stick is an adequate tool to make a hole for planting in these conditions and no hoeing is required because the soil is relatively weed-free and of a suitable texture for planting. When the vegetation burnt off is more sparse, however, as in bush-fallow cultivation, hoeing is usually necessary before planting and so the hoe is introduced not just as a technical improvement on the digging stick but because an additional operation is needed when the more intensive bush-fallow cultivation replaces forest-fallow. A further change to short-fallow cultivation would be greatly helped by the use of a plough, for burning is less efficient as a means of preparing land for cultivation when the vegetation is mainly grass and so roots tend to be left largely intact. Boserup emphasises that in cases where a plough is not available at this stage, short-fallow cultivation is often avoided altogether by lengthening the period of cultivation in a bush-fallow system so that the land is cultivated year after year for perhaps as much as eight years. This restricts grass growth and the plot is then left fallow for a further eight or ten years so a bush rather than dominantly grass vegetation develops. If population density continues to increase there may be a 'jump' directly from bush-fallow to annual cropping without an intervening period of short-fallow cultivation.

Boserup suggests that similar patterns of change operated much earlier in time in Europe as population increased. She argues that, unless population increases, intensification of agricultural production and associated technical changes are unlikely and thus population change has stimulated agricultural development in many areas. Her ideas tend to assume that the techniques required for new agricultural systems are known to the societies undergoing poulation growth and she recognises that if this is not the case then the agricultural system is likely to regulate population size. This theory of agricultural and population change has also been criticised because of the simplified description and classification of agricultural systems in terms of intensity of production, when in fact a variety of agricultural types can be recognised at any given intensity. Nevertheless, Boserup's work is a useful and interesting contrast to that of Malthus and clearly casts doubt on some of the basic tenets of Malthusian theory.

Despite this and other criticisms of Malthusian ideas, much recent comment on the topic of relationships between population growth and food supply has been comparable in some ways to that of the Malthusian era. Various forecasts have predicted doom for either the world as a whole or for individual countries such as India and China as population continues to increase and threatens to outrun supplies of food or other resources. Attempts have also been made to estimate the ultimate population that the world can support, one extreme example being that of a physicist, J. H. Fremlin, who in 1964 calculated that the limit would be reached with a population density of approximately 100 persons per square yard of the earth's surface and a total population of 60,000 million million. At rates of increase similar to those of the mid-1960s Fremlin calculated that this population total would be reached in 890 years' time, but he also made a wide range of other assumptions concerning the provision of food and

energy supplies and envisaged the construction of buildings up to 2,000 storeys high on both present land and sea areas to house the world's population. Fremlin saw the ultimate limit to population growth as a 'heat limit'. People and their activities convert other forms of energy into heat and with a population of the size envisaged in 890 years' time, Fremlin suggested that the outer surface of the planet, which he anticipated would be in the form of a 'world roof' covering the planet by this time, would need to be kept at about the melting point of iron to radiate away excess heat being generated by man and his activities.

The nature of resources

Although some of Fremlin's ideas may at present seem more like science fiction than probability, the provision of adequate resources for future populations is clearly as crucial an issue now as it was in the time of Malthus. The term 'resource' is widely used but can be a source of confusion. One fundamental division is between human resources, which can be taken to incorporate the skills and abilities of particular groups of people as well as their total numbers, and natural resources, which man derives from the physical environment. Basically this latter group includes the supply of any items that are regarded as useful or necessary to man, but it is helpful to differentiate, as does Haggett (1975), between stocks and resources. He suggests that 'all the material components of the environment, including both mass and energy, both things biological and things inert can be described as the total stock'. By contrast, resources are seen as a cultural concept, with a stock becoming a resource only when it can be utilised by man to meet his needs for food or for other purposes. Factors affecting this transformation might be technical, economic or social and clearly change through time. Thus many minerals have been transformed from stocks into resources in relatively recent times as man has perceived a use for them and developed a technology capable of providing them in a form in which they are needed at a cost which someone is prepared to pay.

Natural resources fall into two main groups: those which are not renewable and those which are. Non-renewable resources are those which cannot effectively be replaced once they have been worked out except in terms of a geological time-scale (though some can be re-cycled for future use). Most minerals belong to this first category and recent technological developments have been instrumental in these being used at an extremely rapid rate in modern times. Most of this consumption is a result of demand from the more advanced industrial nations. Meadows *et al.* (1972) calculated that in 1970 the population of the United States was consuming resources at a rate per capita seven times that of the world average. They also suggested that as the rest of the world developed economically it was likely to follow a pattern of increasing industrial output similar to that followed by the United States (see Fig. 4.5) and so also increase the rate of resource utilisation. This suggestion, of course, is based on various assumptions concerning future development which may not ultimately prove to be justified. Other nations may follow different patterns of economic development from that implied, while new technological developments may alter the present relationship between industrial output and resource utilisation (e.g. through the re-cycling of resources). The scale of the problem, however, is indicated by the fact that during the last fifty years the quantity of most minerals used by man has exceeded the totals of these minerals used in the whole of man's previous existence.

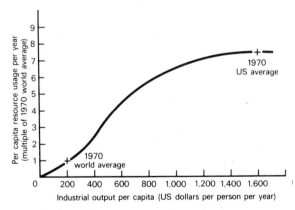

4.5 Industrial output per capita and resource usage (after Meadows *et al.*, 1972). This postulated model suggests that as industrial output increases, non-renewable resource consumption rises rapidly, gradually levelling off at a high rate of consumption, as has happened in the United States (see further comments in text).

Renewable resources, as their name implies, are not used up in the same way. This category includes soil and biotic resources (i.e. resources derived directly from living things) which provide, indirectly or directly, much of the world's food supply. It also includes a group, sometimes separately described as flow resources, which includes running water, ocean tides, winds and solar energy. While the resources in this category are renewable or re-usable in different ways or, in some cases (e.g. wind), available continuously though at a variable level, their use to man is clearly related to his level of technology and management skills. Most biotic resources can be utilised at such a rate that they are effectively destroyed. Examples include the rapid clearance of forest in many areas and the over-fishing of certain zones such as the North Sea in recent years. Soil resources, too, can be harmed by bad management, as was apparent in the notorious Tennessee Valley area of the United States before the 1930s. A similar problem can also be seen in several tropical areas where shifting cultivation is practised. These agricultural methods rely on land being used for crops periodically and then being allowed to 'rest' or lie fallow for a period before being used again (see pp. 39–40). But in some areas of tropical Africa, Asia and Latin America where these methods are practised, the fallow periods have tended to become shorter as more and more land is needed to provide food for the increasing population, and soil quality has declined because of over-use.

Technological innovation can greatly alter the value of flow resources. For example, the opening of the Rance power station in France in 1966 marked a major advance in the use of tidal energy, which had previously been used mainly for very small projects such as the operation of corn-mills on the ebb tide. In a different way, supplies of running water can be greatly affected by man's operations. On the one hand careful control of rates of flow by the construction of dams and similar installations can markedly improve the value of water resources. On the other hand the consumption on a massive scale of groundwater supplies tapped through boreholes can seriously deplete groundwater reserves and so reduce rates of flow of surface water.

Man's way of life and, indeed, his very

survival, are clearly related to the development of these different types of resource. It is also evident, though, that changes in technology may make 'new' resources available to man, or may result in present resources being used in different ways from those common at the present time. The scale of such changes is something we cannot truly comprehend – you will get some idea of the problem if you try to imagine a medieval farmer envisaging the kind of technology that we almost take for granted today – yet it is something which any assessment of future development should try to take into account.

Perhaps the best-known recent attempt to assess the world situation with regard to population growth and resource utilisation has been that by the interdisciplinary team commissioned by the 'Club of Rome', an international group concerned about the problems threatening human society. Some of the conclusions of this team have been published in *The Limits to Growth* (Meadows *et al.*, 1972). They include the following:

1 If the present growth trends in world population, industrialisation, pollution, food production and resource depletion continue unchanged, the limits to growth on this planet will be reached sometime within the next hundred years. The most probable result will be a rather sudden and uncontrollable decline in both population and industrial capacity.

2 It is possible to alter these growth trends and to establish a condition of ecological and economic stability that is sustainable far into the future. The state of global equilibrium could be designed so that the basic material needs of each person on earth were satisfied and each person had an equal opportunity to realise his or her individual potential.

The first of these statements has been widely criticised, largely on the grounds that it is based on a variety of assumptions and generalisations which could be invalid, yet the general point of view expressed reflects the opinion of many people at the present time. Others are more optimistic concerning the future availability of resources or rates of consumption of such re-

sources. These people would therefore disagree fundamentally with Meadows and those who share his views, largely because of the failure of the report to allow for appreciable changes in technology – which could affect resource availability and provision in many ways. A comment in a review of the book (in *The Economist*, March 1972) perhaps sums up this attitude: 'In 1872 any scientist could have proved a city the size of London was impossible, because where were Londoners going to stable all the horses and how could they avoid being asphyxiated by the manure?'

The second statement raises various issues concerning the ways in which man can regulate the use of resources. It also hints at the fact that man's basic material needs are not met in all parts of the world at the present time and that various differences exist which affect population/resource relationships. As long ago as 1959 E. A. Ackerman attempted to categorise the different parts of the world into a series of population/resource regions (reproduced in Zelinsky, 1966). These regions (see Fig. 4.6) pay significant attention to the technological levels of particular societies and, though representing considerable generalisations, are a useful indicator of some of the world's present spatial inequalities.

Type 1 (the United States type) consists of large territories which are well stocked with 'known or probable resources', have populations of small or moderate size in relation to resource potential and also have an advanced, rapidly expanding technology, skilled manpower and 'the social means for maximising national and individual affluence'. This almost-ideal situation is marred only by the rapid and destructive manner in which the populations of these territories have utilised resources so that some may be irreversibly damaged or destroyed (e.g. certain forest and mineral resources). Zelinsky suggests that clear membership of this group of territories belongs only to the United States, Canada, Australia, New Zealand and the USSR (especially its more recently settled central and eastern portions), but that Argentina, Uruguay and southern Brazil perhaps fit this category more closely than any of the others.

Type 2 (the European type) consists of another relatively well-favoured group of terri-

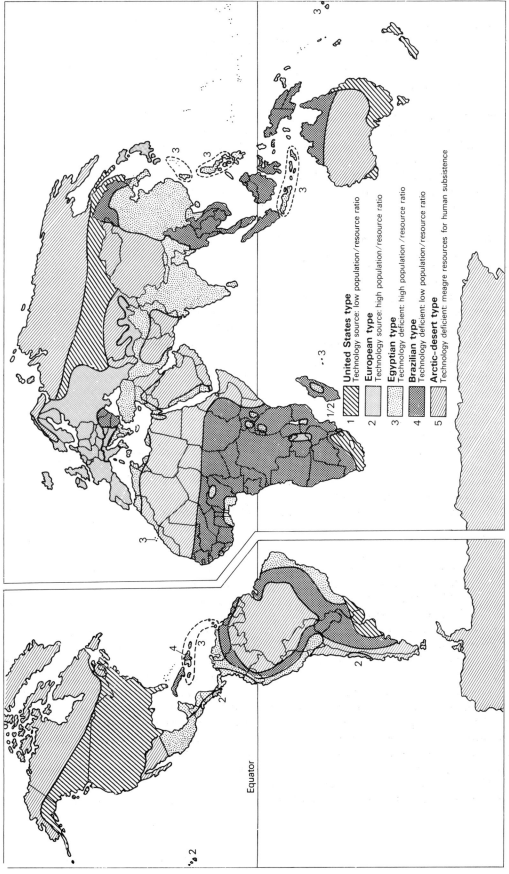

United States type
1 Technology source: low population/resource ratio

European type
2 Technology source: high population/resource ratio

Egyptian type
3 Technology deficient: high population/resource ratio

Brazilian type
4 Technology deficient: low population/resource ratio

Arctic–desert type
5 Technology deficient: meagre resources for human subsistence

Equator

4.6 Population/resource regions from Ackermann's classification. (After Hauser and Duncan.)

tories in which the social and technological skills of the populations are similar to those in type 1 but the resource base is more confined and so a much more careful attitude towards resources is necessary. These territories rely for their prosperity on an elaborate system of trade in which they offer skilled services and advanced industrial products in exchange for other, usually less skilled services and mainly primary products including food, fossil fuels and other raw materials which they cannot supply from within their own territories. Zelinsky emphasises the fluid boundaries of this group and cites Japan as an example of a country which has joined the group in relatively recent times.

Type 3 (the Egyptian type) consists of territories which have a large population in relation to their resources and, in contrast to type 2, are technologically backward. Population continues to increase at a rapid rate in these areas, imposing great strains on their dwindling resource base. By contrast, type 4 (the Brazilian type) consists of territories which, though technologically similar to type 3, have a relatively small population in relation to their resource potential. Development of the stock of resources in these areas has so far been limited, however, and Zelinsky suggests that their situation is a transient one. Most have rapidly expanding populations, so the extent of their resource base provides only a breathing space in which socio-economic and technological changes are possible.

Type 5 (Arctic–desert type) includes principally those areas which, because their physical environments are unattractive to man, are occupied only by primitive societies or relatively isolated groups at a higher level of technological development. At present these areas are relatively insignificant in terms of human occupance or resources, though in future this may not be so and, as Zelinsky has suggested, the same is true of the world's oceans, which form a potential source of major supplies of food and minerals.

It is possible to criticise the categorisation of particular areas within the above scheme (see Exercise 11) but it does, at least, indicate something of the range of population/resource relationships and emphasises the significance of technology as a third, related element.

The concept of optimum population

Technological change is also of great significance in any discussion of the concepts of optimum population, over-population and under-population. There is an attractive simplicity in the idea that for any area there is an optimum population (i.e. a total population which is the ideal size to live and work in such an area) and that a higher total population would result in the area being over-populated and a lower total in it being under-populated. Unfortunately, when considered in detail, this idea is seen to be of much greater complexity. It is easy to appreciate the concept of a population optimum in a very general way, but it is almost impossible to define it precisely in a manner which is universally acceptable, or to suggest a precise number which is the optimum population for a particular area.

Nor is it practical to consider an optimum population as a static feature, for changes in technology, as already suggested, can have a major impact on the capacity of a population to support itself at an acceptable level. For example, the application of modern technological methods to the tapping of underground water, oil and gas supplies in the Sahara since 1950 could perhaps be seen as increasing the optimum population of the region by enabling food production to be increased in some areas and by generating higher incomes in others.

This example suggests that measurement of the optimum population might have an economic basis and, indeed, the concept has most frequently been considered largely in economic terms. In such terms, the optimum population of an area might be defined as 'the number of people that, in a given natural, cultural, and social environment, produces the maximum economic return' (Petersen, 1975). But, as Petersen points out, this is not an entirely satisfactory definition. The basic size of a population is a very crude indicator of its economic potential, for the abilities, health and age structure of a population can greatly affect its value as a workforce. If we consider only age structure, it is obvious that a population with more than half its members over 60 or under 15 has a very different economic potential from one in which less than a third of the total falls into these age categories. The 'maximum economic return' is also difficult to define, although it is often measured simply in terms of the Gross National Product (GNP) per capita (a measure which attempts to represent in monetary terms the total product of a country, including both goods and services). A high GNP does not necessarily reflect a situation in which all members of a society obtain even the basic necessities for life. Some economists would argue that the maximum economic return is not very meaningful unless some attention is also given to the spread of economic benefits throughout the population.

The relationship between demographic variables and the economy has been examined in some detail by Wrigley (1967, 1969), as regards both primitive and more advanced societies. In a book of this kind it is impossible to consider in depth much of Wrigley's work but some aspects of it are particularly helpful in illustrating graphically the concept of an optimum population defined in economic terms. Wrigley developed a series of models based on presumed demographic changes in a society assumed to be at a comparatively primitive level of material culture in a situation where that culture is static 'so that it is not possible to secure a steady increase in the production of food in the community by taking advantage of technical advances in agriculture' (Wrigley, 1967, p. 194).

This implies that the population could not exceed a ceiling determined by the potential food production of the area at the stated level of material culture.

Wrigley suggests, however, that it is wrong to assume that the population would necessarily increase to that ceiling, arguing that an equilibrium level of population might be established at one of several points below the ceiling, in accordance with changing fertility and mortality levels. He indicates three possibilities (see Fig. 4.7 a, b and c) to illustrate this. In Fig. 4.7 (a) the population increases at a uniform rate until point A, with the levels of fertility and mortality remaining constant. Thereafter both mortality and fertility are affected as a critical population density is reached, with mortality increasing and fertility declining until at point B these two are in balance and the population neither rises nor falls. In Fig. 4.7 (b) mortality changes in the same way as in the previous example, rising steadily beyond point A when the critical population density is reached, but fertility is affected much later and to a lesser extent. In this situation the population increases to C, a considerably higher point than B in Fig. 4.7 (a), before fertility and mortality are in balance. In Fig. 4.7 (c) a further case is illustrated, where the pattern of mortality changes is again as in Fig. 4.7 (a) but fertility declines much more

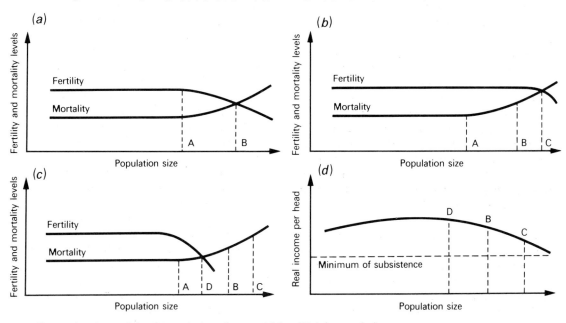

4.7   Some simple models of population change. (After Wrigley, 1967.)

45

rapidly beyond point A than in either of the two previous cases, so that fertility and mortality are in balance at a total well below that reached in Fig. 4.7(a) or (b).

The final graph, Fig. 4.7(d), shows the implications of these three situations in terms of living standards as indicated by real income per head. Clearly, given the assumptions of a limited resource base and a fixed level of material culture, there will be some population total at which real income per head will be at a maximum. Wrigley suggests that it is reasonable to suppose that mortality levels will begin to rise sometime *after* this optimum level has been reached. If the fertility and mortality levels intersect before mortality begins to increase then an optimum level of population might result, 'enjoying the highest standard of living possible in the cultural and environmental context of the day and place'. Points D, B and C in Fig. 4.7(d) all represent later stages of population growth than this optimum, with D (taken from Fig. 4.7c) representing a more advantageous equilibrium level of population than B (from Fig. 4.7a), and B a more advantageous equilibrium level than C (from Fig. 4.7b) – always assuming that the optimum population is that in which real incomes are at the highest level.

Clearly the models of demographic development in this example are based on a series of stated assumptions and Wrigley goes on to examine a range of other possibilities related to different assumptions and more complex situations (e.g. cases where the area of land worked by a group is extended at a particular stage of development and different techniques are utilised to provide a more intensive use of resources). The introduction of such possibilities means that the population ceiling is no longer fixed and attempts to define an optimum population involve much more complex problems, even if such an optimum is considered capable of definition in terms of real incomes or some such economic measure.

Fundamental questions might be posed, however, concerning whether the concept of an optimum population should be seen solely in economic terms at all. Can a population be the optimum for an area, no matter what immediate economic returns it achieves, if it is using up resources in such a way that it is causing massive pollution or depleting soil and biotic resources in a manner that is likely to cause problems for future populations? Is there a population level for an area at which social and psychological stresses become a significant factor to be considered, as can happen with some animal populations? Or should the concept of optimum population be considered more in terms of Southwood's definition (quoted in Taylor, 1972): 'the optimum population of man is the maximum that can be maintained indefinitely without detriment to the health of the individuals from pollution or from social or nutritional stress'?

Clearly no simple definition of optimum population is likely to be entirely satisfactory and the terms under- and over-population should be used with care, if at all. These concepts are extremely complex, involving consideration of a wide variety of factors, many of which are difficult to assess objectively and which may well change through time as a result of technological or cultural developments which are themselves difficult to anticipate. Despite this, many national population policies are implicitly based on the concept of an optimum population. Thus attempts to reduce birth rates in India or Singapore (see Case Studies 5 and 4), for example, imply either that these two states consider themselves to be over-populated now, or that they think they are likely to be so in future if they do not have population policies. Similarly, the opposition of some Latin American governments to family planning policies suggests that they may believe their countries to be under-populated at present, though their attitudes also have religious and political overtones in some cases.

Population and food supply

We have already shown that the population/resource relationship which was uppermost in the mind of Malthus about 180 years ago still gives rise to much controversy and concern today. Food is one of the basic needs of mankind yet food supplies are still inadequate in many parts of the world – at least periodically – and food consumption varies greatly between different areas.

Fig. 4.8 gives an indication of the contrasts in food consumption, expressed in terms of

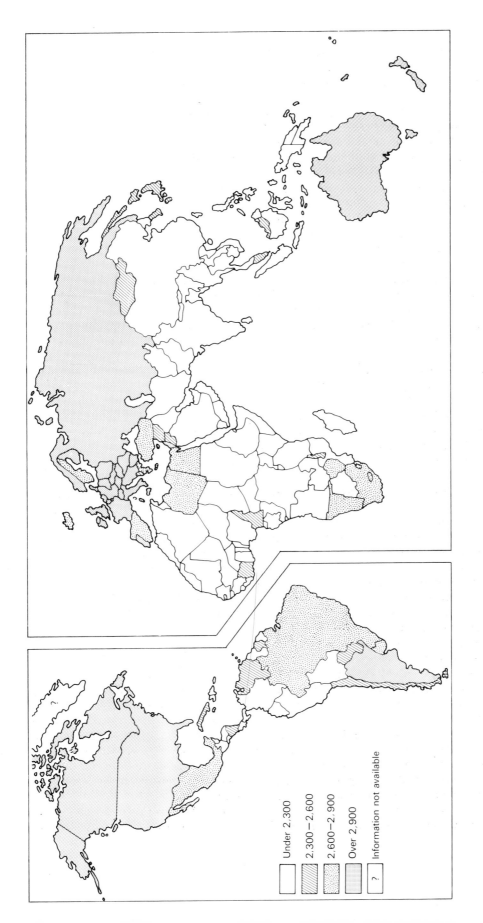

Under 2.300

2.300–2.600

2.600–2.900

Over 2.900

? Information not available

4.8 Daily calorie intake per capita by countries (early 1970s).

calorie intake, which exist between different countries. The basic calorie intake necessary for a person to live in normal health is a matter of disagreement between nutritionists and, of course, differs greatly between individuals on the basis of such variables as age, physique, kind of employment and general living habits. It is usual to suggest, however, that for most communities an average daily intake of at least 2,300 calories is necessary for healthy life, and some experts would suggest a considerably higher figure. An examination of Fig. 4.8 makes it clear that many of the world's people live in countries where the average calorie intake is well below this figure and, even allowing for variations in consumption within individual countries, it is apparent that many people do not receive sufficient food for normal health to be maintained. Investigations carried out by the Food and Agricultural Organisation of the United Nations (FAO, 1975) suggest that in the early 1970s approximately 25 % of the population in many countries in south and east Asia, Latin America and Africa had insufficient diets, compared with only about 3 % of the population in more affluent regions like North America, Western Europe and Australasia. In absolute terms this means that between 450 and 500 million people had an insufficient diet at that date and the available evidence would suggest that the total has probably increased since then. In years when extensive famines occur, as in the Sahel zone of Africa in the mid-1970s (see Fig. 4.1), then totals well above the average result and food shortage becomes a very 'newsworthy' topic but it is important to remember that such famines represent only a marginal worsening of a permanent situation.

While millions of people go hungry every year, food consumption in affluent areas continues to rise. Between 1960 and 1972 the average consumption of grain per head in the United States, including 'indirect' consumption through livestock products, increased by more than the amount currently available per head for consumption in many LDCs. A large amount of grain is consumed by livestock to provide meat in areas like North America and Western Europe (only about one-twelfth of the total cereal consumption of North America is consumed directly by people, the majority being fed to livestock). Some people suggest that dietary changes in such areas that led to reduced consumption of grain could resolve most of the food shortage problems in LDCs. While this is largely true in theory, the problem is in fact more complex. Even if an extra 25 million tonnes of cereals were available annually on world markets, i.e. sufficient to solve most of the basic nutritional needs of the world, it seems highly unlikely that it would find its way to the LDCs. What makes matters worse is that the poorest people in those countries could not afford to buy such food on the open market. In an average year in the late 1960s or early 1970s some 10 to 15 million tonnes of food reached LDCs under food aid programmes of one kind or another, but much of this failed to reach the poorest people, who are normally most in need of it. The problems of increasing food production in LDCs are very considerable (see later comments) and future demands for more food could possibly most easily be met by farmers in North America. Some forecasts suggest that the shortfall in food production from LDCs in relation to their needs will be three times as great in 1985 as it was in 1975. It is difficult to see production on this kind of scale being paid for by LDCs, by international aid organisations or by the more affluent nations unless there is much radical re-thinking at government level before then. Estimates of this kind are notoriously unreliable but it is clear that massive efforts need to be made to increase food production in LDCs wherever possible.

In the past, much attention has been given by nutritionists to the amount of protein needed to maintain normal health and it has been common to suggest that while a basic level of calorie intake is necessary it is essential that a certain proportion of everyone's diet should consist of protein-rich foods like fish, meat and milk. Thus considerable effort has been devoted to attempts to encourage the production of these types of food in areas such as much of the tropics where they form a relatively small proportion of many diets. Recent evidence suggests, however, that in the majority of cases if a person has an adequate calorie intake then he will also receive sufficient protein for basic needs. If this is so, and it is still to some extent a controversial issue, it would imply that future attempts to boost production in LDCs might be concentrated on the traditional grain and root

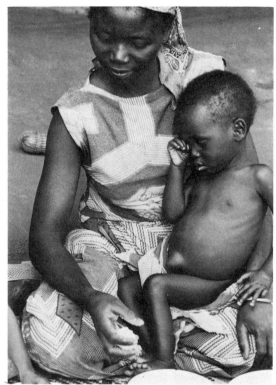

4.9 A child suffering from kwashiorkor. This two-year-old in Malawi was being fed on maize porridge, the staple diet in much of the country. He was so weak from undernourishment that he was unable to stand.

crops rather than involving major changes in crop type.

One of the major consequences of food shortages in LDCs is the presence of nutritional diseases such as kwashiorkor (Fig. 4.9), beri-beri and pellagra. Children tend to be amongst the worst sufferers and many die from under-nourishment when still young, while those who survive may be permanently affected either physically or mentally as a result of dietary deficiencies in their early years. A growing body of evidence suggests that in periods of acute food shortages, of the kind suffered by some communities in Southern Asia and the Saharan margins of Africa in the 1970s, nutritional deficiencies can directly affect population change not only as a result of increasing death rates but also as a result of a decline in fertility through a reduction in the physiological capacity to conceive. Such changes could clearly threaten the existence of whole communities in periods of prolonged food shortage.

As well as giving rise to particular diseases, undernourishment is likely to cause individuals to be more susceptible to a wide range of other diseases. This is particularly true of many tropical areas where climatic conditions encourage insect disease vectors and where the low living standards mean that poor hygiene and a lack of medical facilities tend to make the problem worse. In such circumstances, diseases like malaria, typhoid, cholera, trypanosomiasis (sleeping sickness), smallpox and dysentery are common.

The widespread prevalence of ill-health in tropical areas is thought to have a major effect on the capacity of many people to work effectively and this probably applies to some extent to less developed areas outside the tropics too. A low work input is, in turn, likely to affect productivity and, where the majority of the population are agriculturalists, can clearly give rise to food shortages and hence continuing undernourishment and low resistance to disease. Thus a type of circular causation system occurs (see Fig. 4.10), aptly described by one writer as a 'misery-go-round'. It is extremely difficult for this circle to be broken in many communities and one of the major problems is that a worsening of the situation in any one element tends to have cumulative effects so that the total situation can rapidly worsen.

In recent years some progress has been made in reducing disease, but this does not necessarily

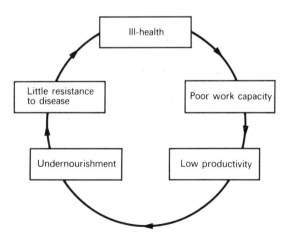

4.10 A circular causation system typical of many LDCs.

resolve the situation for one of the first effects of many medical programmes is to reduce death rates, and especially infant mortality rates, thus altering demographic patterns and often giving rise to a marked population growth that tends to absorb any increases in agricultural output. It is depressing to note that, according to FAO estimates, food production *per head* actually declined in some LDCs during the early 1970s. This, coupled with a general increase in food prices, meant that those who most needed to increase their food consumption found it most difficult to do so.

The most obvious way of improving food consumption in LDCs is by increasing food production in these same areas. Some of the problems involved in doing this have already been mentioned but it is useful to examine the agricultural situation in LDCs in a little more detail as this is clearly so crucial to the overall world situation.

It is first necessary to emphasise that there are many differences between LDCs. The recent development of a group of 'oil-rich' states including, amongst others, Saudi Arabia, Venezuela and Libya, whose national incomes have increased rapidly as a result of increases in oil prices, has emphasised the differences within what has sometimes been referred to as the 'Third World' (in contrast to the other two 'worlds' of the relatively affluent 'western democracies' mainly situated in North America and Western Europe and the communist countries of Central and Eastern Europe, including the USSR). It is not unusual to treat the 'oil-rich' states, most of whom combined politically in the mid-1970s as OPEC (Organisation of Petroleum Exporting Countries), as a separate group from other LDCs, though they still share many of the characteristics of the latter despite their increased national incomes. There are many other differences, however, in terms of physical environment, social organisation, levels of income, etc., both within and between LDCs. Nevertheless, there are also many similarities. Most such countries, for example, are characterised by widespread poverty, low levels of technological development, low levels of education and literacy, limited development of modern manufacturing industries and related low levels of energy consumption, and a poorly developed transport system in comparison with developed countries. Most, too, have a high proportion of their working population in agriculture (sometimes as much as 70% of the total), a dependence on foreign markets for sale of a limited range of agricultural or mineral products, and a rapidly growing population. Many suffer from particular physical constraints, especially those in tropical areas, where soils are often low in plant nutrients, climates unreliable and disease widespread.

Agriculture in LDCs has traditionally tended to be mainly labour-intensive, with little use made of machinery (see Fig. 4.11). Seeds have often been of low quality, fertilisers little used and attempts at disease or pest control limited. The labour force, in addition to being affected by frequent ill-health (see earlier comment), is often also limited in quality by low levels of education and literacy, lack of technical know-how, and poverty, which imposes constraints even when the knowledge needed to make improvements is available. Numerous organisational problems have also limited agricultural development, including the small size and fragmented nature of many landholdings, storage difficulties, lack of rural credit facilities and poor marketing organisation.

In recent years most LDCs have undergone agricultural changes of one kind or another. Many have undertaken some kind of land redistribution or land consolidation programme. The former have often been more significant in terms of social and political development than in economic terms, and as Gilbert (1974) has stated with reference to Latin America 'where land redistribution has been implemented, relatively little impact has been made on the pattern of agricultural production'. Thus in Cuba, where many of the large estates were in foreign hands before Castro's revolution in the 1950s, ownership of farms changed considerably but many farmers continued to work the same land as previously (albeit as owners instead of tenants) and major farm products such as sugar and cattle continued to be produced on large farms organised as state co-operatives instead of as private plantations. Land consolidation schemes such as those in Kenya, where by the 1950s farm fragmentation was extreme in many areas, have probably had some influence in increasing production but this is not always easy to estimate, especially when, as in Kenya,

4.11 Threshing rice in the Yangtze Basin. This scene emphasises that even where mechanisation has been introduced for particular processes, as in the rice-threshing operation shown here, Chinese agriculture still tends to be labour-intensive rather than capital-intensive. Many LDCs, however, lack even the simple machinery being used here.

other changes have occurred at the same time. Re-organisation of landholdings has tended to prove most effective as part of a broader suite of organisational changes, such as occurred in China (see Case Study 6) and, of itself, does not make better farmers of those involved nor, necessarily, bring about increased production.

If such an increase is to be achieved it can, in theory, be brought about either by extending the area under cultivation or by intensifying production from the present cultivated areas. Past experience tends to suggest that though extensions of area may be worthwhile in some countries, such as Brazil, the greater part of any future increase seems likely to come from an improvement of yields in existing cultivated areas. Increased mechanisation has been a means of achieving this in many developed countries but this does not seem a practical proposition for most LDCs except in the form of some kind of intermediate technology which will provide a much easier transition from the primitive implements often used now to the sophisticated machinery used in many developed countries (see Fig. 4.12). Moreover mechanisation, with its implications of decreasing the need for manpower in agricultural areas, would create major difficulties in most LDCs, where unemployment is already a significant problem.

Possibly the most hopeful sign in recent years concerning the increase of output in LDCs has been the development of new high-yielding varieties of cereals, though the introduction of these has been beset with many difficulties. Hybrid varieties are developed by cross-breeding different varieties of the same plant and hybrid varieties of maize were produced over 50 years ago in the USA. In the 1960s, however, experiments with wheat in Mexico and with rice in the Philippines were successful and gave rise to what has, perhaps too optimistically, been called the 'Green Revolution'. The development of new rice varieties was seen as particularly significant in view of the large rice-growing populations of many Asian countries. The new varieties offer the twin advantages of higher yields than traditional varieties and a shorter growing season, so that double-cropping has become a possibility in some areas.

In a few areas the adoption of the new varieties has been generally successful, as in the Muda scheme in the north-west of Peninsular Malaysia (see Fig. 4.13). In this area marked increases in output have been achieved, both as a result of increases in yield and because of the widespread adoption of double-cropping, which increased from 1,200 hectares in 1969 to over 100,000 hectares in 1974. In 1974 the Muda farmers produced almost half of Malaysia's total rice crop and in less than ten years (1965–74) Malaysia's rice production increased from being less than two-thirds of the amount consumed to approximately 90% of the total required, mainly as a result of the Muda scheme. It is significant, however, that the scheme has also provided reliable supplies of water for irrigating one of the two annual crops, effective advice through agricultural advisers and various training schemes, improved banking and credit facilities, efficient marketing schemes and widespread opportunities for agricultural education at different levels. The scheme is, in fact, far more than merely agricultural and this is one of the main bases of its success. The display of a wide range of slogans illustrates some of the thinking behind the scheme: e.g. 'Rural development is about people, their well-being and what they can become', 'Appropriate technology should best be designed through pooled efforts by people who know their own environment extremely well', and our own favourite 'The hardest thing in the world to open is a closed mind'. Additionally the area is one that had a more affluent peasantry than, say, most parts of rural India, before the scheme began.

In India, for whose people the Green Revolution appeared to offer high hopes, most attempts to introduce the new varieties have given rise to very considerable problems. Many of these have arisen because the new varieties can only be grown successfully if they are accompanied by other 'inputs' such as fertilisers, carefully regulated water supplies and pesticides. It is difficult to grow the new crops in most areas which lack irrigation – and only about one-fifth of the rice grown in Asia at present is irrigated. It is also costly to provide the necessary fertilisers and other inputs, and because of this only the wealthier farmers in many areas have been able to adopt the new varieties successfully.

The effects of this situation have varied greatly between different parts of the country. In some areas, such as the wheat-producing district of Ludhiana in the Punjab, where the majority of cultivators have economic holdings in excess of 6 hectares, the benefits of the Green Revolution have been widely, though still to some extent unevenly, shared. In many rice-growing areas, however, the majority of cultivators have basically uneconomic holdings of 1 hectare or less. In these circumstances, though yields have sometimes been increased by the application of small amounts of fertiliser, such increases have usually been insufficient to provide surplus capital for investment in increasing the size of landholdings or in fully utilising the technological changes implicit in the Green Revolution. At best, such farmers have managed to retain stable living standards in the period of inflation and rising costs.

In many cases, however, those who owned only small areas of land have traditionally also leased some land in order to have a large enough area to feed their families and provide for other basic needs. Where this has been so the two factors of:

1 increasing rents for land – a response to the rapid rise in land values which is a direct result of the increased possibility of making a profit from agriculture as a result of the Green Revolution, and

4.12 Changing transport technology in Tunisia. Basic to economic advance in most LDCs is the need for improvements in transport. The donkey-cart in the photograph represents an important intermediate stage between human porterage – the most common form of transport in many LDCs – and mechanised transport. The use of draught animals is, however, restricted in many countries by poverty, animal diseases and the lack of adequate roads or tracks.

4.13 Harvesting rice on the Muda scheme. The increased prosperity associated with this scheme has resulted in some mechanisation but harvesting is still mainly by hand. This situation is likely to change, however, and already several types of small harvester, suitable for use in this area, have been designed.

53

2 the tendency for more wealthy landowners to wish to work more of the land they own – again because of the greater potential for making a profit from it

have often resulted in a dramatic deterioration in the economic conditions of the small farmers. Some such farmers have, in emergency or for short-term profits, been tempted to sell what little land they had and have become landless labourers, increasing numbers of whom are migrating to the urban areas in search of employment.

In some areas, increased prosperity and the need for carefully controlled agricultural techniques on the larger farms where the new high-yielding varieties of grain are being used, resulted initially in an increase in job opportunities for labourers. Often, however, this stage of development has been succeeded by one in which mechanisation has increased and employment opportunities decreased because mechanisation can help farmers to maximise their profits from a particular area of land. For example, the reduced length of time needed for land preparation and other processes because of mechanisation may enable a farmer to produce two crops a year from an area which previously only produced one, so increasing his total profit.

In this kind of situation, farmers with large landholdings have tended to benefit greatly from the Green Revolution but many small farmers and labourers have seen their living standards decline either in absolute terms or relative to their more wealthy neighbours. Frankel (1971) claimed that probably 75–80% of the farmers in the main rice-growing areas of India had suffered a relative decline in their economic position as a result of the Green Revolution. Thus differences in prosperity between farmers have tended to increase and, almost inevitably, this has resulted in considerable unrest and, in some cases, violent conflicts between the different groups.

Moreover, as fertiliser prices have risen dramatically in the 1970s, yields have fallen in some areas as even the more wealthy farmers reduced their fertiliser input. Obviously the Green Revolution is not the panacea that has sometimes been suggested, but it does represent an important step in the fight to increase agricultural production in LDCs. It appears, however, that it needs to be accompanied by many other changes if it is to be successful. It is in this field that governments can possibly be of most value, in such ways as providing rural credit facilities, information services and marketing opportunities, though this is not always easy as many failures of such schemes in India and elsewhere testify.

The experiences associated with the Green Revolution and other agricultural development schemes would seem to imply that it is possible to raise production substantially in LDCs but that rates of increase are likely to be variable and will involve considerable problems, some of which may not be anticipated. Time is obviously a crucial factor and this brings us back to the fact that, at least in the short term, substantial population increases seem likely to occur while agricultural output is being increased. Thus while total food output will probably rise in most LDCs in the near future it is less certain that per capita output of food will also increase. If some way of providing more food in the poorer countries is not found many millions of people will continue to be undernourished, unless a much better system of food distribution is developed than exists in the world at present.

It is this kind of situation which has encouraged the governments of many LDCs to adopt population control measures. These have had varying success (see Case Studies 4 and 5), but most of the evidence seems to suggest that rates of population growth are most likely to decrease if there are changes in social and economic conditions occurring at the same time and especially if general living standards are rising.

Thus there seems likely to be a very real 'food crisis' or 'population problem' – really two aspects of the same problem – for some years to come. The inequalities between developed and less developed countries mean that the problem is much more acute in the latter areas, but within both types of state there are further inequalities. Rich nations or individuals can demand and obtain more than their fair share of the total food supply whereas poorer countries or people lack the wealth needed to make their demands effective. The major producers of surplus food at present are some of the developed, industrialised nations where advanced technology, extensive land resources and large amounts of capital are available. Increas-

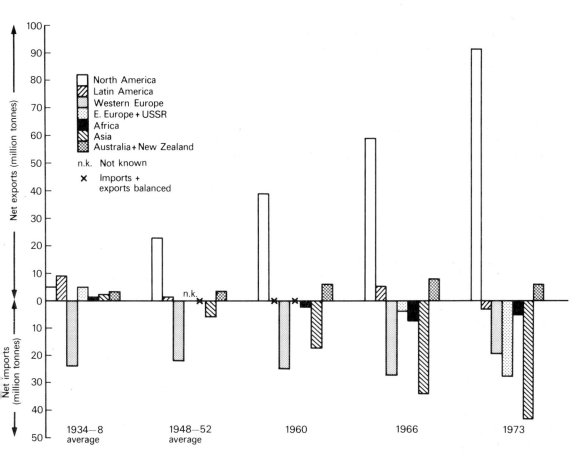

4.14 World trade in food grains for selected years by regions. Note that only North America and Australasia have regularly had an export balance throughout this period and that Western Europe, the only regular net importer in the pre-war period, has since been joined by Asia, Africa, Latin America, and Eastern Europe and the USSR. (Source: US Dept. of Agriculture.)

ingly, North America has dominated the export of world grains (see Fig. 4.14) and further increases in production from this area can perhaps be more easily achieved than from many LDCs.

The relationships between population and food supplies are clearly dependent upon an extremely complex series of factors and processes. Simple forecasts of doom based on extrapolation of present trends or optimistic assumptions that a range of new 'miracle' crops or technological developments will resolve all present problems might be equally misguided. There is, perhaps, no simple solution to these problems unless it is that the world's nations and peoples should put self-interest behind them and be prepared to subordinate their own interests to those of the world as a whole – and perhaps that it is too basic a change to hope for in the near future.

5

Case Study 1
England and Wales:
stages in
demographic evolution

Over the last 200 years the relationship between the rates of fertility, mortality and net immigration in England and Wales has fluctuated periodically, resulting in a rapidly increasing rate of population growth in the second half of the eighteenth century and almost the whole of the nineteenth century, followed by a period of slower growth until about 1920 after which the population grew only very slowly. By the mid-1970s the population was marginally in decline. Population pyramids for 1881, 1931 and 1971 reflect this demographic evolution.

When the first decennial census was taken in England and Wales in 1801 the population was about 9.2 million. One hundred years later it stood at over 32 million and in 1971 it was 49 million. This growth reflects a number of far-reaching demographic changes which were taking place and which in turn influenced and were influenced by economic, technological, cultural and social changes. At first sight the main features of the demographic evolution of England and Wales appear to offer a straight-forward example of progress through the demographic transition. The application of this model to England and Wales is, however, fraught with the problems of sparse and unreliable data before 1837 (when the civil registration of births, deaths and marriages began) and awkward facts before and after that date.

As a result this model has come in for much re-evaluation and criticism by English demographers in the last thirty years.

Fig. 5.1 shows population growth in England and Wales since the beginning of the eighteenth century. Three periods with different rates of change are recognisable: (i) an increasing rate of growth throughout the eighteenth century, followed by (ii) much more vigorous growth throughout the nineteenth century and the first decade of the twentieth century, leading to (iii) a phase of still substantial growth, but of a lesser intensity than in the previous phase. The 1971 census, together with more recent evidence from the Registrar General's quarterly returns, suggest that we may be entering the early stages of a fourth phase in which the population level fluctuates, in some years falling slightly and in others rising slightly. The mid-1970s, for

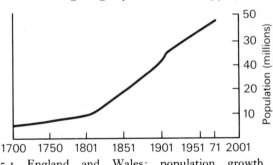

5.1 England and Wales: population growth 1700–1971.

instance, was a time of slight population decline. In the year ending in June 1975 the population of England and Wales dropped by about 10,000. There were only about 38,000 more births than deaths and net emigration continued at the previous year's level of 48,000. In the year ending in June 1976 births fell short of deaths by 3,511, although this was partly due to an increase in deaths over the previous year which was attributed to an influenza outbreak in the late winter.

If changing rates of births and deaths are plotted on the same graph (Fig. 5.2) we can see the relationship between these two demographic variables and total population growth, and the apparently close parallel between the population cycle of England and Wales and the demographic transition model. Fig. 5.2 reveals four stages as follows:

(A) *Stage 1, ending in the 1740s.* This period appears to have been characterised in England and Wales by sharply fluctuating birth and death rates though the long-term trend was for population to increase slowly.

(B) *Stage 2, 1740s–1880.* This long period of development, whose onset coincided broadly with the early years of the Industrial Revolution, witnessed a rise in population from 6 million to 25 million. The acceleration in the rate of growth was a remarkable one and there has been much research in recent years on the causes of this demographic change. The three variables of fertility, mortality and net immigration are all possible determinants of this change. As immigration is generally thought to have been of only minor importance, attention has been focused on birth

and death rates. If reliable statistics were available for the period 1740–1840 much of the problem would be resolved, but this is not the case and researchers have been forced to concentrate on detailed studies at the local and regional levels using a variety of official, semi-official, ecclesiastical, institutional and privately compiled records of varying quality. It is hoped that the accumulation of data from such studies will eventually enable new generalisations to be made at the national level. Meanwhile the argument goes on. Among the unresolved questions about the first 100 years of Stage 2 are

(i)   Was the rise in the rate of population growth the result of a fall in the death rate or was it due to a rise in the birth rate because of the lowering of the average age at which people married? (Recent research indicates that in the period 1750–1845, earlier marriage with a consequent rise in completed family size was a very important factor in Ireland.)

(ii) Were the supposed advances in surgery, midwifery, medicines, hospitals and dispensaries major factors in reducing mortality or were they of negligible importance? There is conflicting evidence here. Indeed some scholars believe that in the short term the supposed advances probably increased mortality.

(iii) What was the contribution of improved public health, through improved nutrition to the changing rate of growth?

(C) *Stage 3, 1880–1920.* Death rates fell steeply for much of this period and, in contrast to the previous period, were accompanied by a sharp decline in birth rates. By the early years of the twentieth century the falling birth rate was reflected in the slowing rate of population increase. Living standards rose during this period, and together with the spread of birth control propaganda came a desire to limit family size. The effect of World War 1 at the close of this period is clearly shown on the graph.

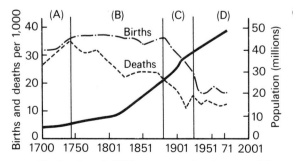

5.2   England and Wales: stages in demographic evolution.

(D) *Stage 4, 1920–1970s.* During this period birth rates and death rates have stayed at a relatively low level and population growth has slowed down. Birth rates have shown most fluctuation, rising and falling again as the depression years of the 1930s and the war years gave way to the post-war 'bulge', followed in the 1960s by the widespread use of 'the pill' and the legalisation of abortion. Fig. 5.3, which appeared in *The Times* in 1974, shows changing birth rates in the United Kingdom in a period of medical advance, medical controversy and changing social attitudes.

As England and Wales passed from one stage in their demographic evolution to another, so the population structure changed. The population pyramids (Fig. 5.4) for 1881, 1931 and 1971 reveal three markedly different populations and show clearly the pyramid shapes associated with different stages of a country's demographic evolution. The 1881 pyramid shows a young population with 70 % of the population under 35 years of age. By 1931 there had been a significant change. The broadest part of the pyramid is no longer at the base, but

among the young adults. In addition there is a broadening in the upper ranges reflecting greater lifespans. The low fertility rates in the 1930s and during World War 2 are reflected in 1971 in the narrowing of the pyramid in the 30–40 age range, and by this date the ageing of the population is very clearly marked, indicating a situation closely comparable with those in France and Sweden as depicted in Fig. 2.7.

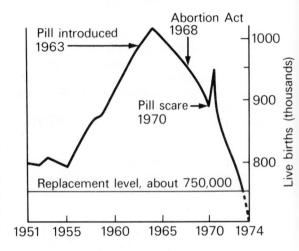

5.3   United Kingdom: live births 1951–74.

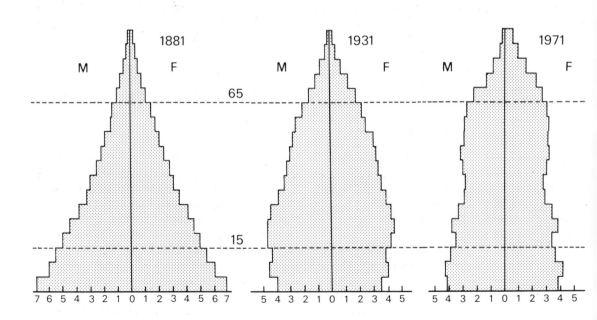

5.4   England and Wales: population pyramids for 1881, 1931 and 1971.

58

6

Case Study 2
USA: aspects of recent population change

The United States, with a population in 1976 estimated at more than 215 million, is the fourth largest country in the world in terms of population size; only China, India and the USSR have larger populations. Its population characteristics, like those of England and Wales, reflect an affluent industrial country at a late stage in demographic evolution. Important distinguishing features of the United States in the most recent period of its demographic history (between the 1940s and the 1970s) are low, stable death rates, declining birth rates, diminishing family and household sizes, an ageing population and marked ethnic and regional demographic differences.

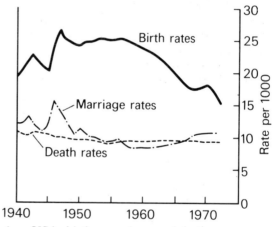

6.1   USA: births, marriages and deaths 1940–72.

Between 1960 and 1970 the population of the USA increased by almost 25 million, an enormous increase in absolute terms (equivalent to half of the present population of England and Wales), but in relative terms (a 13 % increase) representing its lowest inter-censal increase of the twentieth century except for the depression years of the 1930s. It was in marked contrast to the 1950–60 increase of 19 % (28 million) which was the largest inter-censal increase since 1910.

Fig. 6.1 shows the changing birth, death and marriage rates since 1940. The graph clearly shows the stable, low death rate (hovering between 9 and 11 per thousand) and the variability in birth and marriage rates during the

same period. The most interesting feature of the graph is the changing relationship between the marriage rate and the birth rate. At the end of World War 2 the marriage rate rose from 11 per thousand of the population (1944) to over 15 per thousand (1946) and there followed a rise in the birth rate from about 20 per thousand in 1945 to over 26 per thousand in 1947. There was then a continuing relatively high rate until the late 1950s.

This close relationship between marriages and births in the late 1940s and most of the 1950s contrasts markedly with the situation in

59

the late 1960s and early 1970s. After a relative decline in the 1950s the marriage rate rose again in the 1960s and early 1970s as the young men and women born in the first post-war years reached marriageable age. However, except for 1969 and 1970 the birth rate has continued to decline and reached an all-time low of 15.6 per thousand in 1972. The introduction of popular, more effective, birth control techniques such as 'the pill' has been an important factor enabling married couples to delay child-bearing, to control child-spacing and to plan smaller families. Coupled with this has been the changing status of women in American society. In just over twenty years the number of working women has increased by nearly a third. The proportion of married women between 20 and 24 in the labour force jumped from 37% to 48% between 1965 and 1970, again an increase of nearly one-third. This increase was far greater than the increase in the total female labour force and greater than the increase for single (i.e. never married, widowed or divorced) women of the same age. It is also likely that married women will in future account for a larger proportion of employment in traditionally male occupations requiring long-term career commitment, with the probable result of still smaller families.

The declining birth rate, together with longer lifespan, is reflected in the population pyramid (Fig. 6.2) for the United States in 1970. As in England and Wales the pyramid is typified by

a relatively narrow base, a tapering in the 30–40 age range, a substantial proportion of over-60s and an excess of females over males beyond middle age.

The non-White populations in the USA, particularly the Blacks, show variations from the main national trends. In 1970 the Black population of the USA stood at 23 million, an increase of 17% on the 1960 population, compared with the national growth rate of 13%. Thus the Black growth rate is almost one-third greater than the total population growth rate. Table 6.1 indicates how different trends in White and Black birth and death rates during the 1960s are reflected in contrasting age structures. The Black population at the end of the 1960s was much younger than the White population (less than 45% of the White population being below 25 years of age, compared with over 54% of the Black) while the more lowly socio-economic position held by the majority of Blacks is reflected in the relatively small proportion of the Black population in the over-55 age group – 14% compared with nearly 20% in the case of the White population.

Table 6.1. *USA : age structure of the White and Black populations, 1960 and 1970*

Age groups	1960 White	1960 Black	1970 White	1970 Black
Under 5	10.9	14.4	8.1	10.8
5–17	24.0	}37.5	25.1	31.3
18–24	8.6		11.6	12.0
25–34	12.7	12.8	12.3	11.9
35–44	13.6	12.2	11.4	10.6
45–54	11.6	9.9	11.7	9.4
55–64	8.9	6.9	9.5	7.1
65–74	6.4	4.3	6.3	4.6
75 and over	3.3	1.9	4.0	2.3

Source: US Bureau of Census, *US Census of Population* 1960 and 1970.

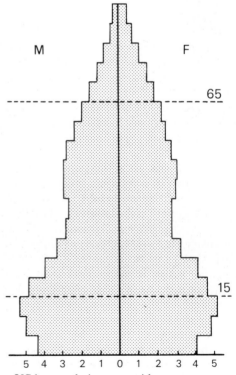

6.2 USA: population pyramid 1970.

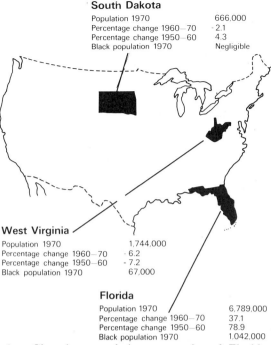

South Dakota

Population 1970	666,000
Percentage change 1960—70	- 2.1
Percentage change 1950—60	4.3
Black population 1970	Negligible

West Virginia

Population 1970	1,744,000
Percentage change 1960—70	- 6.2
Percentage change 1950—60	- 7.2
Black population 1970	67,000

Florida

Population 1970	6,789,000
Percentage change 1960—70	37.1
Percentage change 1950—60	78.9
Black population 1970	1,042,000

6.3 Changing population geography of Florida, South Dakota and West Virginia.

6.4 Senior citizens at a Florida resort. Greater opportunities for outdoor leisure activities, less crime, less pollution, warm winters and, often, lower living costs have attracted large numbers of retired persons from the states of the North-east and the Midwest.

Regional economic growth, stagnation and decline are also reflected in population totals and structures. The three states of South Dakota, West Virginia and Florida afford interesting examples of the impact of economic change on population geography (Fig. 6.3).

South Dakota is a rural state with a small, scattered population. Throughout the last thirty years it has suffered a continuous outflow of its rural population and it is becoming increasingly middle-aged and elderly in terms of its age structure. The state has never been attractive to Blacks and few of them live there.

West Virginia is also suffering from depopulation, this time caused by the decline of mining and manufacturing as well as agriculture. Young adults have migrated to more prosperous areas leaving behind, as in South Dakota, an ageing population. Young Black West Virginians have been part of this continuous out-migration and Black migrants from the Southern States have by-passed West Virginia, resulting in a relatively small Black population.

Florida stands in almost total contrast to both South Dakota and West Virginia. Unlike these two states, Florida is experiencing enormous economic expansion, particularly in the sphere of recreation and leisure. During the 1950s, when it was the fastest-growing state, its population grew by 79 %, and this was followed by a growth rate of over 37 % in the 1960s. The interesting feature of Florida's growth is that because of the importance of resorts, many of them housing large, permanent, retired populations (Fig. 6.4), massive in-migration has not resulted in a youthful population structure. However, because of the great increase of job opportunities the state has attracted large numbers of rural Southern Blacks and they represent a more youthful component of the population.

Case Study 3
Urbanisation in Australia

The Australian population is overwhelmingly coastal and conforms to the three generalisations concerning the distribution of population at the continental scale as suggested by Fielding (see p. 21). Australia has long been characterised by a high degree of urbanisation and the last thirty years has seen a continuation of this trend to such an extent that it is now among the top five urbanised countries, if city states such as Hong Kong, Macao and Singapore are excluded. Immigration has been an important element in the growth of the major Australian cities and population projections suggest that if the present fertility rate is maintained and immigration continues at the present level two vast urban agglomerations will emerge in South-east Australia by the middle of the next century.

In 1940 the Australian geographer Griffith Taylor pointed out the very uneven distribution of population in Australia in a simple but telling map, the main features of which are incorporated in Fig. 7.1. He divided the country into two parts – Empty Australia and Economic Australia – the dividing line on Taylor's map being where the population density fell below one-eighth of a person per square mile. Within Economic Australia he identified five particularly attractive areas: eastern New South Wales, the greater part of Victoria, the south-east

corner of Queensland, the southern Flinders Range in South Australia and the extreme south-west corner of Western Australia. Taylor also commented at some length on the remarkable degree of urbanisation in Australia at that time when only one-third of the population lived in rural areas, in a country largely dependent upon the export of primary produce.

Since the 1940s the Australian population has become even more unequally distributed, its coastal concentration has become more pronounced and it has become even more a country of town and city dwellers. At the end of World War 2 68.8% of Australia's population of 7.5 million was urban and by 1971, when the population had grown to 12.7 million, the population living in urban areas had increased to 85.6% (see Table 7.1). During the same period rural population fell in every state. Nor was the decline just relative; with a few notable exceptions absolute rural decline was general throughout the post-war period. The reasons for the rural population decline include increased mechanisation, the relative decline of rural incomes, especially in dairying areas, the lack of alternative employment opportunities in most of these areas and a recession in the wool industry in the late 1960s which led to substantial out-migration in parts of New South Wales (NSW) and Victoria, where some areas recorded declines of between 5 and 10%.

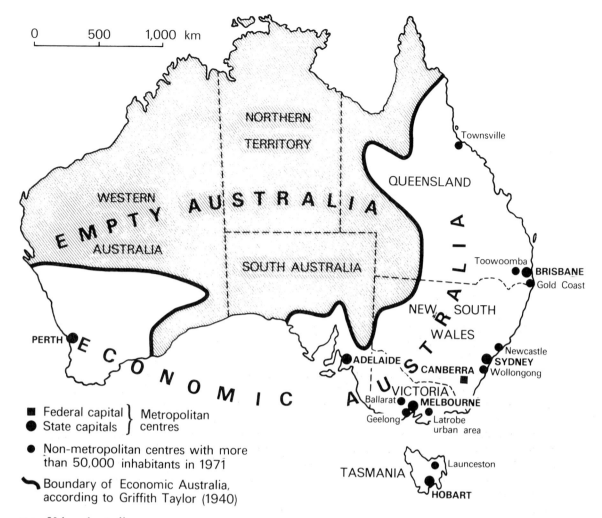

Federal capital ⎱ Metropolitan
State capitals ⎰ centres

Non-metropolitan centres with more
than 50,000 inhabitants in 1971

Boundary of Economic Australia,
according to Griffith Taylor (1940)

7.1 Urban Australia.

Table 7.1. *Australia: rural, urban and metro-*
politan populations in 1947, 1961 and 1971

	1947 (%)	1961 (%)	1971 (%)
Metropolitan	50.72	56.26	60.13
Other urban	18.14	25.88	25.53
Rural	31.14	17.86	14.34
Total number	7,560,755	10,482,900	12,711,574

Source: Censuses of the Commonwealth of
Australia.

As rural decline or stagnation became
common, important urban changes were taking
place. Not only were Australians becoming

increasingly urban, they were also tending to
concentrate in the larger centres. In 1947 56 %
of the population resided in cities of 100,000 or
more persons and by 1971 the proportion had
increased to 64.5 %; during the same period the
proportion living in cities of more than 500,000
(i.e. Sydney, Melbourne, Adelaide, Brisbane
and Perth) grew by over 4 million to nearly
58 %. Even more striking is the fact that 40 %
of the population in 1971 (just over 5 million)
lived in two cities: Sydney and Melbourne.

Some of the most significant urban developments have taken place among the medium and
large non-metropolitan centres. ('Metropolitan
centre' was the official term used prior to the
1971 census for the state capitals and the federal
capital of Canberra.) In 1947 Newcastle (NSW)

was the only non-metropolitan centre with a population of more than 50,000. By the end of the 1960s there were nine centres in this category. These were Newcastle and Wollongong in NSW, the Latrobe urban area and Geelong in Victoria, all industrial towns; Launceston (Tasmania), Ballarat (Victoria) and Toowoomba (Queensland), all regional centres and centres of light manufacturing; Townsville (Queensland) a port and market centre; and Gold Coast, a resort area straddling the NSW–Queensland border. It is notable that five of these growing non-metropolitan centres are located at the coast and two of the remaining four are within 50 kilometres of the coast. Two of the coastal areas have undergone particularly rapid growth, Newcastle having grown from 127,000 in 1947 to 250,000 in 1971 and Wollongong having grown even more rapidly from 63,000 in the mid-1950s to 186,000 in 1971. Thus the already-marked peripheral distribution of population is being reinforced by these changes.

However, in spite of the advances being made by these nine non-metropolitan centres, Australia is still dominated by the state capitals (they contained about 60% of the total Australian population in 1971) and the urban hierarchy of each of the mainland states is dominated by its state capital. In Western Australia, Perth in 1971 was 28 times bigger than its nearest rival. In Victoria, Melbourne was over 20 times bigger than the next biggest centre, as was Adelaide in South Australia. In Queensland, Brisbane was more than 11 times bigger than Townsville. In New South Wales, Sydney was 8 times bigger than Newcastle. In Tasmania the gap was much smaller, with Hobart being only twice as big as Launceston. Only in Tasmania has the proportion of the population in the state capital not increased in the last thirty years.

It was noted earlier that the continuing trend of increased urbanisation in Australia was related to rural depopulation. Another important element in the growth of Australian cities in the post-war period has been immigration. In 1972 there were approximately 2.5 million foreign-born persons in Australia of whom over 2 million migrated to Australia after 1945. Immigrants from both North-west Europe and Southern and Eastern Europe have been overwhelmingly attracted to the occupational opportunities in the metropolitan centres and the fast-growing non-metropolitan centres. Over 70% of the immigrant population lives in the six state capitals and Canberra. In such centres are concentrated the professional and service jobs and the skilled and semi-skilled jobs in the expanding manufacturing sector. This preference for the larger centres is well illustrated from the 1966 census. In that year immigrants made up 18% of the Australian population. Of all the state capitals, only in Brisbane, in 1966, was the proportion of overseas-born less than 20%, and in Perth, Adelaide and Melbourne it was between 25 and 29%. At the other extreme, in the same year, of the 385 urban centres with populations below 5,000, 340 had foreign-born populations of less than 10%.

The attraction of the larger metropolitan centres for migrants from overseas has had the effect of raising the masculinity ratios of their populations. A masculinity ratio is the proportion of males to females in a community. A masculinity ratio of 100 indicates an exact correspondence between the numbers of males and females; a masculinity ratio of less than 100 indicates an excess of females over males; and a masculinity ratio of more than 100 indicates an excess of males over females. The masculinity ratio of the Australian-born populations of the metropolitan centres in 1966 was relatively low at 92. This reflects not only the higher mortality rates and emigration rates of metropolitan-based Australian-born males but also the female-dominated rural–urban migration flow within Australia. In the same year the mean masculinity ratio in metropolitan centres for the overseas-born was 112 and in the case of Yugoslav immigrants it was 149.

One important characteristic feature of large Australian cities at the beginning of the post-war period was their low population density, which was partly explained by the large number of owner-occupiers (upwards of two-thirds), most of whom live in suburban bungalows on fairly large plots. As late as 1954 the density of population in metropolitan Sydney was only 1,034 persons per square kilometre. By 1966, as a result of the continued influx of substantial numbers of rural Australians and overseas migrants to the inner and middle suburban rings, together with the building of low- and high-rise

Table 7.2. *Projected populations of Sydney and Melbourne for 1990, 2000 and 2050*

Year	Sydney				Melbourne			
	1*	2*	3*	4*	1*	2*	3*	4*
1966 (base)	2,541,300	2,541,300	2,541,300	2,541,300	2,230,800	2,230,800	2,230,800	2,230,800
1990	3,288,500	3,094,700	4,127,300	3,893,800	2,934,100	2,758,100	3,786,800	3,570,400
2000	3,648,900	3,246,900	4,950,400	4,443,400	3,273,900	2,910,700	4,596,800	4,127,700
2050	6,413,600	3,585,800	11,021,600	6,897,100	5,848,600	3,214,300	10,482,600	6,608,300

Source: Tables 7.2 and 7.4 in Burnley (1974).
1* Fertility constant, mortality constant, no immigration.
2* Fertility decline, mortality constant, no immigration.
3* Fertility constant, mortality constant, continued immigration.
4* Fertility decline, mortality constant, continued immigration.
The projections for these two cities assume no internal migration net gain.

apartment blocks, the density had increased to 1,895 persons per square kilometre. This density is much lower than in European and North American cities of comparable size. The densities in the mid-1960s in Adelaide (1,382 per square kilometre) and Brisbane (1,135 per square kilometre) were even lower. High population densities approaching those found in the inner and middle zones of European cities are found only in one or two small, centrally located areas in Sydney and Melbourne where there are either three-storey terrace houses or high-rise apartments.

In 1974 two scholars, one a sociologist, the other a geographer, published a series of population projections for the major Australian urban centres (Burnley, 1974). Although surrounded by the same caveats as all population projections their findings pose important questions about future planning policies in the metropolitan areas. The projections are based on a number of different assumptions concerning fertility, mortality and migration. In the simplest terms they assumed the following alternative trends:

(a) the present fertility will *either* remain constant through time *or* it will decline;
(b) the present mortality rate will continue unchanged;
(c) immigration will *either* continue at the present level *or* it will cease altogether.

Thus they assumed there were four possible future patterns, as shown in Fig. 7.2.

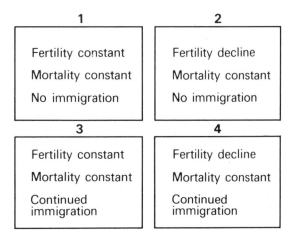

7.2 Component combinations in Choi and Burnley's Australian urban population projections.

Using these criteria they projected forward the populations of the major cities and presented them at five-year intervals up to the year 2000 and then at ten-year intervals up to 2050. Their projections for the two largest cities are summarised in Table 7.2. Their projections suggest that if current fertility and immigration rates continue two huge urbanised regions will emerge in eastern New South Wales and Southern Victoria by the middle of the next century. If this growth takes place it may be accompanied by planning, social, water supply and recreational problems on an unprecedented scale compared with the Australian urban experience so far.

8

Case Study 4
Singapore: a programme
for population control

Many LDCs have rapidly increasing populations as a result of high birth rates and low death rates (see Chapter 2). If the pattern of demographic change followed by many European countries and indicated in the demographic transition model for such areas is also to occur in LDCs, a marked decrease in birth rates is necessary. To date, this has occurred in very few LDCs, but in Singapore strong government policies have enabled family planning programmes to be more successful than in most African, Asian or Latin American countries. This case study examines the nature of these policies and suggests some of the reasons for their success.

The Republic of Singapore had, in 1976, a population of approximately 2.3 million living in an area of 581 square kilometres at an average density of approximately 4,000 persons per square kilometre. This population density is second only to that of Hong Kong and is more than twenty times the density of population in India (see Case Study 5). The vast majority of the people live in urban areas and this, together with the high levels of literacy and education of the Singaporean people, has greatly helped in the spread of new attitudes concerning population control. Economic development in Singapore has been rapid in recent years and official policy is clearly summarised by Dr Margaret

Loh (Executive Secretary, Family Planning and Population Board and Senior Health Officer, Ministry of Health, Singapore), as follows: 'population growth in the Republic has to be carefully controlled if the development efforts are not to be diminished or even negated in the future by excessive demands for more schools, hospitals, social, recreational and public health services by an ever-increasing population and if the quality of life is not to be adversely affected by over-crowding, noise, pollution and social unrest'. Thus population control is seen as a central feature of development planning in Singapore and receives strong governmental backing in a variety of ways.

Between 1949 and 1965 family planning services in Singapore were mainly provided by a voluntary agency, the Singapore Family Planning Association, with some government assistance. In December 1965, however, the government established the Singapore Family Planning and Population Board (SFPPB), a statutory body charged with implementing the first five-year National Family Planning Programme (1966–70), and this Board is now responsible for organising family planning services throughout the country. Table 8.1 indicates something of the effectiveness of family planning policies in Singapore since 1950 in the form of a striking decline in birth rates between

Table 8.1. *Singapore: population trends 1950–73*

Year	1950	1960	1970	1971	1972	1973	1983
Crude birth rate (per thousand)	45.5	38.7	22.1	22.3	23.1	22.1	17
Crude death rate (per thousand)	7.2	6.3	5.2	5.4	5.4	5.5	5
Natural increase (%)	3.8	3.2	1.7	1.7	1.8	1.7	1.2

Sources: Situation Report of International Planned Parenthood Federation, 1974, and Annual Reports, Singapore Family Planning and Population Board.

8.1 Singapore family planning poster.

1950 and 1970 and a corresponding decline in the rate of natural increase despite the extremely low level of death rates in Singapore.

The family planning programme which has achieved these changes is based on the following elements:

1 The establishment of easily accessible advisory and clinical services for family planning. There are more than fifty maternal and child health clinics which also provide family planning services and are situated throughout the Republic, and there is also one clinic specially for men at the National Family Planning Centre. Advisory services provided by the clinics are free of charge and a full range of contraceptives is available at nominal charges.

2 A massive publicity programme aimed at educating and motivating people with regard to family planning. Information is disseminated via radio, television, newspapers, magazines, posters (Fig. 8.1), pamphlets, car stickers, etc., with considerable stress being laid on the social and material benefits which are likely to accrue from having a small family. Complementing this publicity is a motivational programme based on individual interviews with women attending clinics, couples intending to marry, women who have recently lost a child, and women who have had an abortion, in an attempt to see that such individuals are aware of the advantages of family planning and may therefore be motivated to practise it in future.

3 Legislation concerning abortion and sterilisation in the early 1970s. The Abortion Act permits abortion on various grounds, including socio-economic considerations, while under the Voluntary Sterilisation Act persons with two children or even, in certain circumstances, only one child, can apply for sterilisation. Operations are performed for nominal fees in government hospitals so there is no economic bar to people undergoing them.

4 The introduction of social and economic disincentives to the practice of having a large family. These include the abolition of paid maternity leave for women after two children have been born, the provision of income tax relief for only the first three children in a family, increasing fees for medical attendance

at birth as parents have more children and a lower priority of choice of primary school for fourth children and above.

The success of such measures is not easy to judge with accuracy but appears to have been significant. Evidence of crude birth rates alone can be misleading, but in conjunction with a consideration of age-specific fertility rates gives quite a clear picture of the present situation in Singapore. Table 8.1 indicates a decline in birth rate between 1950 and 1970, though in fact the lowest birth rate recorded was in 1969 (21.8 per thousand). Since 1969, as can be seen from the table, there has been some fluctuation in birth rates but this is largely attributable to recent increases in the number of people within the fertile age range (15–44 years) as a result of the increase in births in the period after World War 2. For example, the number of women aged 20–24 years of age almost doubled, from 57,000 in 1966 to 110,000 in 1972, while in the same period the total number of women in the fertile age group (15–44 years) showed an increase of 34%, approximately three times the percentage increase in total population during that period.

In this situation an increase in the birth rate would be inevitable unless the average number of children born to each woman in the fertile age group per year showed a decline. The age-specific fertility rates 1966–73 for Singapore (Table 8.2) indicate that there has, in fact, been such a decline in fertility rates within the Republic during this period, though this has not been at a uniform rate. There was, indeed, a slight increase in 1972 but this was succeeded by a marked decrease in 1973 which would appear to confirm the general pattern of decline.

The ultimate goal of the Singapore government is, however, to reach a situation of *zero population growth*, i.e. one in which *no* population increase occurs, and they are still well away from this. Indeed, the 1.7% annual growth rate in the 1970s is higher than the *maximum* annual growth rate in the United Kingdom during the nineteenth century. A study in 1972 showed that the average completed family size for Singaporeans at that date was 4.3 children. If this family size were maintained, the population would approximately double in a generation, with 4.3 children effectively 'replacing' two parents. The family planning programme aims to achieve a situation where the completed

family size averages only two children, as the poster in Fig. 8.1 clearly indicates. Even if that situation could be achieved almost immediately the population would continue to increase to about twice its present total in the course of the next fifty years because of the present dominance of young people in the age structure (see Fig. 8.2).

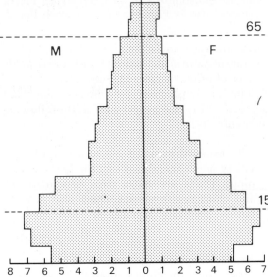

8.2 Singapore: population pyramid 1971. NB Statistics are not available in separate five-year age groups for the population aged over 70.

In the face of this situation the government of Singapore sees the continuation of family planning programmes as essential to the future prosperity of the state. The pattern of family planning programmes in the years ahead seems likely to include a continuation of educational publicity based on the desirability of limiting families to two children together with a possible intensification of socio-economic disincentives to the practice of having larger families than this.

The relative success of family planning programmes to date would seem to be the result of a strong and determined government following clear aims in a situation where the population is easily accessible to advertising and educational programmes because of its concentration in a small area, its relatively high standards of literacy and its relative affluence (see Fig. 8.3) which makes communication by radio, television and newspapers effective. Even without such clearcut policies, however, it is quite pro-

8.3 Orchard Road, Singapore. This busy modern thoroughfare provides a marked contrast to the area shown in Fig. 3.5. The heavy traffic, high-quality shops and advertising are all indicative of the affluence of at least some of Singapore's population.

Table 8.2. *Singapore: age-specific fertility rates 1966–73*

Age group (in years)	1966	1967	1968	1969	1970	1971	1972	1973
15–19	33.1	35.8	30.9	27.1	25.9	25.6	25.5	24.4
20–24	218.5	195.8	165.8	150.1	139.0	138.3	138.0	132.1
25–29	261.2	244.7	236.6	227.8	208.8	214.8	218.8	200.9
30–34	202.0	166.7	152.0	134.3	138.0	137.3	139.1	128.3
35–39	124.8	95.9	85.2	75.2	74.5	68.0	65.5	56.8
40–44	51.7	42.9	35.3	29.4	26.7	21.9	20.8	17.3
Total (15–44 years)	142.9	126.8	114.2	103.5	100.0	98.5	99.9	93.9

Source: Annual Reports, Singapore Family Planning and Population Board.
Rates are expressed as the number of births per thousand women in a particular age group.

bable that the changing socio-economic situation of many Singaporeans would have resulted in a falling birth rate, though perhaps the rate of change would have been slower. This situation is in strong contrast to that of many other countries in Asia, Africa and Latin America where family planning programmes are being recommended by politicians and others at the present time, and Singapore's achievements in the field of family planning are not necessarily an indication that similar results will be obtained elsewhere if similar programmes are adopted.

9

Case Study 5
India: family planning, food production and the Green Revolution

The balance between population and food supplies in India is still precarious despite considerable increases in food production in the period since independence. Rapid population growth has given rise to a wide range of family planning programmes which have, to date, been considerably less successful than those of Singapore (see Case Study 4), a major factor in this being the different socio-economic backgrounds of the two countries. Widespread opposition to family planning has resulted from some aspects of recent policy and, though the Green Revolution has given rise to marked increases in food production in some areas, it has also tended to emphasise inequalities and has often failed to improve the situation of the poorest element of India's rural population. Thus India still faces many of the difficulties typical of LDCs attempting to increase per capita food production but with the added problem of an already massive population.

In the period since independence in 1947, views on India's development prospects have ranged from extreme pessimism to cautious optimism, influenced largely by variations in agricultural output and especially the output of food grains (see Fig. 9.1). The average annual increase in food output of 3 % since the early 1950s has exceeded that of population growth (*c.* 2.5 %), but with a population of more than 600 million by 1976, increasing every year by an increment

equivalent to more than five times the total population of Singapore, there is little margin for complacency. Moreover, inequalities in wealth and distribution mean that possibly a third of India's people receive less than the necessary minimum of food to ensure normal health in any one year. Not surprisingly in this situation family planning programmes of various kinds have been implemented in India as well as attempts to improve food production.

The development of a successful family planning programme in a country like India is a very different problem from that of establishing such a programme in Singapore (see Case Study 4). The total population of India is greater than that of most continents and the ethnic, linguistic and cultural variety is also more like that of a continent than most individual countries. In this situation one of the major difficulties involved in the establishment of efficient family planning schemes is that of motivating so diverse and large a population to practise family planning. This problem is made more difficult because the population is largely composed of rural village dwellers whose levels of literacy and education are relatively low in comparison with a country like Singapore. This is because the basic poverty of the country, with a GNP per capita less than one-tenth that of Singapore, imposes limitations on the amount of money which can be provided to help in family plan-

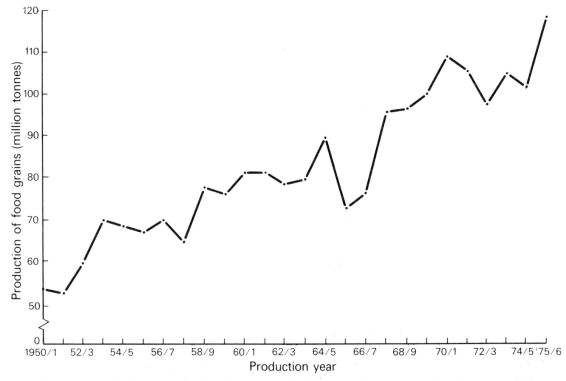

9.1 Production of food grains in India 1950/1 to 1975/6. (Sources: Government of India Annual Economic Surveys and UN Statistical Yearbooks.)

ning programmes, and because in many parts of India there is little economic security in either rural or urban areas (Fig. 9.2).

Some awareness of a need for family planning was apparent in India as early as the 1920s when the first family planning clinics were opened, but the population of India has continued to grow rapidly throughout the twentieth century (see Fig. 9.3). India was one of the first countries officially to acknowledge its commitment to family planning when the first five-year development plan (1951–6) stated that: 'The rapid increase in population and the consequent pressure on the limited resources available have brought to the forefront the urgency of problems of family planning.' Despite this statement, expenditure on family planning was very limited in the first two five-year plans, and though this increased in the third plan (1961–6) it is only since the mid-1960s that government concern has been clearly matched by a large-scale provision of funds for family planning.

Under the Indian constitution, individual states are responsible for the administration

9.2 Rural poverty in India. This child squats on the dry, cracked and useless soil of her parents' farm during one of the recurrent droughts of the 1960s which emphasised the basic insecurity of much of India's agriculture. The food in the child's bowl was made from pounded roots because no grain was available.

71

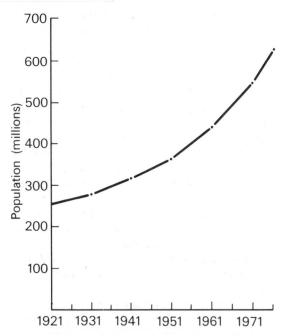

9.3 India: population growth 1921–76. Statistics for the period before 1951 have been adjusted to relate to the area of India as designated in 1947 when the separate states of India and Pakistan came into being.

and implementation of family planning programmes through state family planning bureaux, but virtually the entire cost is borne by the central government. Additionally, a major independent organisation, the Family Planning Association of India, receives financial support from the central government and from the International Planned Parenthood Federation, while several other independent agencies receive aid from home and overseas for their programmes. By the mid-1970s the government was providing family planning advice and services through more than 45,000 clinics, while contraceptives were sold at subsidised rates through a wide range of outlets including postmen, teachers and the wholesale and retail networks of concerns such as Lipton Tea and the Hindustan Lever soap firm, as well as more orthodox outlets such as hospitals and family planning clinics.

Information and education programmes concerned with birth control were widespread. Several unusual approaches had been used to carry the message to India's village populations, including that of decorating an elephant with family planning slogans and using this as the focal point of a tour of India's rural areas. This seemingly bizarre approach to publicity emphasises one of the problems of family planning education, for many Indians are simply not reached by newspapers, radio broadcasts or television and so a wide variety of other forms of advertising have been used. These have included simple posters, wall paintings, matchbox covers, postage stamps, performances of song and dance, films, puppet shows and mobile government publicity units. The basic strategy has been to concentrate on a few statements and to use these repeatedly. Posters bearing the family planning symbol of an inverted red triangle and the faces of two adults and two children with the simple slogan 'Two or three children...stop' appeared on notice boards all over India in the 1960s (see Fig. 9.4). Other slogans included 'A small family is a happy family', particularly designed to appeal to most Indians' love for children, and 'Next child not yet...after third never', designed to emphasise the idea of spacing a family as well as limiting its size.

In terms of the provision of advice, information and services, there was considerable similarity between the approach of the Indian government in the 1960s and early 1970s and that which has proved so successful in Singapore. The major difference, perhaps, was the limited amount of legislation in India which impinged directly on family planning. In April 1972, however, a new abortion law came into effect under which medical termination of pregnancy was allowed on health, eugenic, socio-economic and humanitarian grounds. This law also made abortion legal in cases where pregnancy had resulted from failure of a contraceptive method. Individual state legislation was rather more broad-based in some cases and, for example, in Madhya Pradesh and Maharashtra free government medical facilities were limited to those with three children or less.

The success of family planning programmes in India by this date was difficult to judge but had certainly not been spectacularly successful. Statistical data concerning fertility and mortality rates are not readily available for the country as a whole, though official UN estimates suggest that the birth rate was still in excess of 40 per thousand in the early 1970s while the death rate

9.4 A large family planning poster dominates the scene in a small Indian township.

materials, transistor radios and grants for home improvements. 'Motivators' also received monetary payments but, according to many reports, government or state employees including policemen, teachers, health workers, and civil servants of many kinds, were given 'target figures' of people they should 'motivate' to be sterilised and, if they failed to reach their target, were liable to have their pay stopped or promotion prospects reduced. Some of these reports were possibly exaggerated but there do appear to have been cases of this kind in several areas. The situation inevitably gave rise to great concern and strong opposition. Many observers have seen opposition to sterilisation as being an important issue in causing the defeat of Mrs Gandhi, the then Prime Minister, and her Congress Party, in the 1977 Indian General Election.

It is difficult to anticipate what the long-term effects of this acceleration of the sterilisation programme will be on family planning programmes in India for, despite the results it achieved in terms of the number sterilised, it clearly caused much resentment towards family planning officials as well as the government in power at the time. A further examination of Fig. 9.5 indicates that in 1971 approximately 44 %

had fallen to approximately 16 per thousand giving a natural increase rate of around 2.5 % per annum. Plans to reduce the birth rate to 25 per thousand by 1980 were revised, in the light of the evidence available, to 30 per thousand. Although the population pyramid for 1971 (Fig. 9.5) suggested that family planning might be having some effect (compare the two youngest age groups), and increased sales of contraceptives in the early 1970s pointed to a similar conclusion, more emphasis began to be given to sterilisation as a means of controlling population growth.

Information concerning sterilisation programmes is not entirely clear, but by the early 1970s the number of sterilisation operations in India was probably averaging over 1 million per year and in 1975 reached almost 2 million. In 1976 it increased dramatically to approximately 7 million (*The Times*, 30 December 1976) as a result of a vigorous programme launched in spring of that year with strong government backing. In one state, Maharashtra, compulsory sterilisation was introduced for parents of three or more living children, and elsewhere propaganda was intensified and strong incentives were offered both to those undergoing vasectomy (male sterilisation) operations and to those 'motivating' others to do so. Rewards for those being sterilised included money, food, clothing

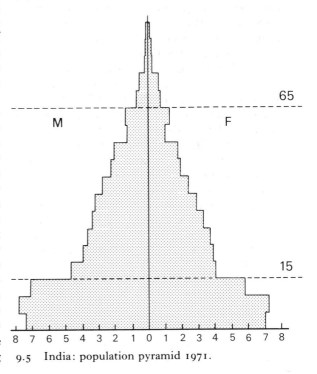

9.5 India: population pyramid 1971.

of the population of India had not reached the age of 15. Their progress through the fertile age range seems certain to give rise to continued rapid growth for some years to come. Most population projections suggest India's total population will exceed 800 million by the mid-1980s. It is easy to see why drastic population control measures have been favoured by some politicians but recent experience suggests that the introduction of such measures is by no means easy and should perhaps be seen as part of a wider programme. In the meantime, it is clear that the possibilities of improving food supplies need attention so that the demands of the growing population in both the immediate and long-term future can be met.

In the thirty years after independence was achieved in 1947, production of food grains (principally rice, wheat, maize and various types of millet and pulses) more than doubled in India, with increases occurring at the most rapid rate during the last decade of this period. Production has varied considerably from year to year even in the recent past (see Fig. 9.1), and is still dependent to a considerable extent on the vagaries of the monsoon rains despite a massive expansion of irrigation facilities, but India has achieved a great deal since independence. However, during the same period the population has increased by between 250 and 300 million and some estimates suggest that as many as 200 million are regularly underfed at the present time.

During the 1950s irrigation potential was considerably expanded, mainly through the development of large-scale schemes, and the cultivated area extended appreciably, but production increases were limited by the continuing use of traditional methods, low-quality seeds and minimal inputs of fertiliser. Government assistance tended to be thinly spread over a wide area in an attempt to aid as many as possible of India's farmers, who make up approximately 70% of the total population. The beginnings of a new approach became apparent in the early 1960s with the introduction of intensive agricultural district programmes (IADP). This was an attempt to increase production by concentrating on areas where conditions seemed most favourable for agriculture – usually those with good irrigation facilities and often areas which were already more prosperous than most. The

results, in terms of increased output, were promising, but marked a change in policy which tended to increase disparities in living standards between different areas, a feature which has been emphasised even more in recent years and which has caused considerable concern.

By 1964/5 food grain production was nearly 90 million tonnes compared to only 55 million tonnes in 1950/1, and in the same period the area under food grain production had increased by over 20% and average yields by over 40%. In the following two years, however, devastating droughts reduced output dramatically (to 72 million tonnes in 1965/6) and approximately 10 million tonnes of grain had to be imported each year. Even this failed to solve the problems of many of India's poorer people, who lacked money to buy grain and tended to be the worst sufferers from deficiencies in the system of aid distribution. The problems of these two years encouraged a drastic reconsideration of agricultural policy and increases in output have since been based largely on the new high-yielding varieties of grain (HYVs) which have recently become available. These have been combined with an increased use of fertilisers and pesticides (both essential if the use of HYVs is to prove successful) and an expansion of minor irrigation works. Thus the so-called Green Revolution began.

In the decade from 1965/6 to 1975/6 the area under HYVs increased from under 2 million to approximately 30 million hectares, the quantity of chemical fertiliser used increased fourfold and irrigation potential expanded by over 5 million hectares. In 1975/6 food grain production reached 118 million tonnes and estimates anticipated a continuing increase to about 125 million tonnes at the end of the 1970s. With only about one-quarter of the area under food grains being occupied by HYVs in 1975/6, there would seem to be scope for further increases in output. Such increases are dependent on a variety of factors, however, some of which are likely to act as major constraints on expansion.

The provision of adequate water supplies is a major difficulty despite the great increases in irrigation facilities. Many parts of India still lack guaranteed water supplies throughout the necessary period of the growing season and periodic droughts are a serious problem. This was apparent in 1972/3, for example, when famine affected much of rural India despite a total food grain production of 97 million tonnes, nearly 35% higher than in 1965/6.

Early difficulties were often based on an incomplete understanding of the nature of the new varieties so that, for example, peasant farmers failed to apply the necessary fertilisers and pesticides and consequently their crops were of low quality and quantity. In at least one area, the Godavari Delta, the rice strain planted (IR8) matured and was ready for harvesting in the middle of the heavy rains of mid-October and so much of the crop was lost. In some areas the new varieties were so unpopular with consumers that they could not be sold and the farmers suffered financial losses. In the longer term, however, other problems have arisen which reflect the socio-economic background of the areas in which the crops are being grown.

Crucial to these problems is the investment necessary to ensure successful growth of the HYVs. Seeds are more expensive than are those of traditional varieties and the necessary fertilisers and pesticides are often too costly for the poorer farmers. Irrigation is clearly advantageous in many areas and is often necessary if double-cropping, a common feature associated with the adoption of HYVs, is to be practised. Yet this too involves considerable expenditure. Double-cropping is also often accompanied by the adoption of mechanised ploughing practices which prepare the land more effectively but involve further expenditure and may also have the side effect of causing unemployment for agricultural labourers who previously worked the land by hand (see earlier comments on pp. 52–4).

Thus the adoption of HYVs has tended to be far easier for more wealthy farmers than for those who lack capital and the Green Revolution has been most successful in those areas, such as the Punjab, where farms are larger and where, by Indian standards, many of the farmers were already affluent before the introduction of HYVs. In other areas the new developments have resulted in a sharpening of social tensions because of the rapid benefits which have accrued to the more wealthy farmers while poorer farmers and landless labourers have failed to benefit similarly.

The need for a more even share in the benefits of increased agricultural output is something of which the Indian government is well aware. After the early problems associated with the Green Revolution, the government has tried to widen the scope of agricultural changes by encouraging the more general use of some aspects of good traditional practice in cases where the use of HYVs has caused difficulties. Thus some traditional varieties of rice which give higher yields than most others, though less high than HYVs, have proved successful because they need less pesticides and fertilisers than HYVs, and intercropping (growing a second type of crop between the rows of the first) has proved a satisfactory way to increase food output in some areas.

Future increases in production are likely to be related to a wider range of changes than those envisaged in the early years of the Green Revolution. Perhaps the two most effective ways for the government to help in this situation are through the provision of further irrigation facilities, providing cheap water supplies to the poorer farmers, and through a much improved supply of rural credit facilities at low interest rates for the least wealthy members of the community. The participation of the poorer members of rural society in the agricultural changes now taking place is essential if the gap between rich and poor in the countryside is not to grow larger. If this can be achieved, and it would be foolish to pretend that it will be easy, then living standards should rise for all Indians and, in addition to the obvious benefits of this, other social changes would be more likely to occur including, perhaps, changed attitudes to family planning. Thus the future of the Green Revolution would seem to be crucial to the population–food supply balance in India in more ways than one.

10

Case Study 6
Population and
food supply in China

This case study provides an example of a contrasting approach to that of India in the attempt to increase food supplies for an expanding population. China has faced many problems similar to those of other LDCs, including India, but has attempted to resolve them in a fundamentally different manner from most LDCs. The basic socio-economic structure of the country has been dramatically altered and farm organisation substantially changed since the 1949 takeover of power by a communist government. Although mistakes have been made, agricultural output has been considerably increased and living standards for the poorest elements of the population improved during a period of marked population growth.

The year 1949 marked a major turning point in China's development, for in that year a new, communist government took power and initiated a whole range of social, economic and political changes that have since radically altered the life of most Chinese people. In this case study we shall concentrate on changes in agriculture, though these cannot be examined in isolation. Agriculture is only one facet of an integrated approach to development which is unique in the world today, though certain aspects of the Chinese approach to development have been adopted in other countries such as Tanzania, Zambia and some of the communist countries of Asia and Eastern Europe.

In 1949 China was suffering from the effects of a long period of war against Japan and from internal strife between the communists and the previous ruling party of China, the Kuomintang. The country was poor by any standard and millions of people in both rural and urban areas existed on the borderline of starvation. Natural disasters such as floods or drought were familiar features of life in much of China before 1949, and in bad years resulted in the deaths of many thousands of people. In 1920, for example, half a million people are believed to have died as a result of famine in much of northern China following a major drought, while as many as 20 million became refugees. Until 1949 most of the agricultural land was in the hands of a relatively small number of people, with the majority of Chinese farmers renting their land from such landlords at crippling rents. The tenants often had to pay more than half their harvests as rent in kind, and they struggled on from year to year with inefficient methods, little equipment, poor seeds and few incentives to improve the land they worked. With a total population probably in excess of 500 million, of whom some 80% lived in rural areas, the new government of China faced problems which many saw as insuperable. Most notable among these was the basic problem of feeding this large population adequately.

The years which followed saw many changes

in agriculture. The first major reform was a re-distribution of land which involved holdings being taken from landlords and rich peasants and shared out so that all heads of families in a particular rural area held similar quantities of land. (The population was categorised into five main groups: landlords, rich peasants, middle peasants, poor peasants and workers (landless).) This re-distribution was not completed until 1953 and, though seen by many of the Chinese people as the fulfilment of their dreams, it marked only the first of a series of changes. The new basis of land-ownership did not solve the problems of agriculture; nor did it provide more capital and fertilisers, better seeds and improved machinery. In fact, by the time the land distribution was complete, other changes were about to take place. These occurred at different rates in different areas and marked a progressive 'socialisation' of agricultural organisation through a series of stages marked by the formation of mutual aid teams, elementary co-operatives and advanced co-operatives.

Mutual aid teams operated on the basis of private land-ownership but for part or all of the year labour, draught animals and sometimes other equipment were pooled so that farmwork was carried out on an exchange basis between different farmers. The *elementary co-operatives* were semi-socialist in that landholdings were also pooled and worked by the members of the co-operative using their combined resources of equipment and draught animals, but in addition to being paid for their work members of the co-operative also received dividends for the land, animals and equipment they had contributed to the scheme. The *advanced co-operatives* moved a stage beyond this with all the means of production – land, animals and equipment – being collectively owned and payment to members of the co-operative being solely in terms of their labour input. The only exception to this was that members of the co-operatives were normally allowed to retain smallholdings on which they grew a few vegetables, raised poultry and possibly reared one or two pigs.

By 1957 approximately 90 % of the farms in China were organised in advanced co-operatives, a tremendous change from the situation less than five years earlier. Inevitably there was some opposition to these changes. In the main though they appear to have been brought about by persuasion rather than compulsion and by obtaining the support of the peasant population for the new forms of organisation. This support was, no doubt, encouraged by the fact that agricultural production continued to rise in most areas throughout the period of change, especially in terms of the yield of basic food grains, which were given the highest priority on most co-operatives. By 1957 total rice production was probably some 70 % higher than it had been in the late 1940s, and wheat production had also been increased, though to a lesser extent.

It is important to note at this point that there are many problems involved in using production statistics (and other data) for China. Official figures have not been made available for many years and, even when they have, there are controversies about their accuracy. We believe the statistics used in this case study give at least an accurate impression of general trends, though some Western experts would argue that the figures themselves are too high. Official Chinese figures for 'food grain' production (i.e. for most basic food crops expressed in terms of grain equivalents) showed an increase from 160 to 200 million tonnes for the period 1953–7, and though some other sources suggest that the 1957 production may only have been of the order of 185 million tonnes it would appear that re-organisation had some immediate beneficial effect.

The advanced co-operatives varied in size but generally consisted of between 100 and 200 families. They were run by elected management committees, including political representatives, but were concerned almost entirely with agriculture. Their size was criticised as being too large to organise the agricultural labour force efficiently and yet too small to carry out effectively large-scale land-management or water-control schemes that were of crucial importance to agricultural development. In April 1958 a group of co-operatives in the province of Honan (see Fig. 10.1) joined together to form a new kind of much larger unit, which was eventually called a *commune*. The possibilities of this new form of organisational unit were rapidly appreciated by the Chinese government, and by December 1958 some 700,000 advanced co-operatives had been re-organised into approximately 26,500 communes.

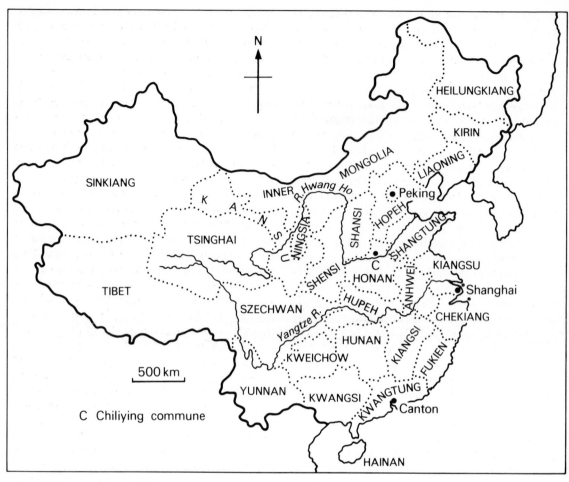

10.1 China: some general features.

This change involved far more than a merely agricultural re-organisation. The commune took over responsibility for all economic activity including industry and trade as well as agriculture, for education, social welfare, local government and even for some aspects of military organisation. It thus represented an integrated economic, social and political unit which could plan and organise all aspects of development within a particular area. The internal organisation of a commune is based on a series of groupings of people at different levels. Thus the commune (usually of from 2,000 to 12,000 families) is subdivided into production brigades of some 150 to 500 families (or occasionally even larger groups) and the brigades are, in turn, subdivided into production teams of about 15 to 30 families. This organisation is flexible so

that, for example, several production teams might combine to carry out tasks which are too large for a single team and several brigades can combine for really major tasks like the construction of a new irrigation scheme.

The communes came into being at a time of great optimism in China. The 'Great Leap Forward' policy, originating in 1958 and followed later in the year by the re-organisation into communes, marked the beginning of a series of developments, some of them ill-founded, whereby attempts were made to bring about economic growth of one kind or another. Typical of this period was the establishment of new industries in the rural areas, including many which failed to survive for very long, the massive extension of irrigation schemes and new measures for flood control. It was a time

78

of great enthusiasm and many errors of judgment, and it was followed by a period which created even greater problems for the communes because, between 1959 and 1961, China suffered a series of natural disasters which at earlier dates would almost certainly have resulted in massive loss of life. As it was, the communes appear to have organised themselves sufficiently well to combat the worst of the problems created by successive droughts and floods and, largely through ensuring a fair distribution of the reduced supplies of food which were available, to avoid famine. Food production seems to have shown little increase in this period, however, and probably did not advance much above the 1957 level until the mid-1960s.

Throughout this period and since, the emphasis has been on self-reliance, with the members of the communes being encouraged to rely on their own efforts and not on the state or other outside agencies. This sort of attitude is fostered by propaganda on a massive scale with slogans like 'The people and the people alone are the motive force in the making of world history'. Attention is also focused on 'pace-setters' who have done particularly well in one way or another. Thus in the late 1960s the Chinese people were enjoined to 'Learn from Tachai' (see Fig. 10.2), the Tachai production brigade having overcome great difficulties to transform an area in the loess mountains of Shansi Province (see Fig. 10.1) that was badly affected by soil erosion into fertile terraced farmland. The members of the brigade now live in proper stone houses, whereas many formerly lived in caves, and they regularly produce sufficient grain to sell a surplus to the state.

The achievements of Tachai have been repeated in many other parts of China largely through self-help projects of one kind or another. The Chiliying commune (described in Chu Li and Tien Chieh-Yun, 1974: see Fig. 10.1), in Honan Province, illustrates the sort of progress made in a successful commune. Chiliying consists of 38 villages to the north of the Hwang Ho or Yellow River, and in 1973 had a population of over 53,000 people organised into 38 production brigades, each of which embraced one village. The brigades were subdivided into a total of 298 production teams. The commune was formed by the amalgamation of 56 advanced

co-operatives in July 1958 and incorporated altogether 6,200 hectares of cultivated land. The brigades own the larger means of production, e.g. tractors and large-scale irrigation and drainage machinery, but the teams own some equipment themselves, such as draught animals, small threshers, reapers and crushers. The yields of grain and cotton have both increased greatly since the commune was established (see Fig. 10.3), and in 1965 Chiliying was self-sufficient in grain for the first time in recent history. The area now regularly produces a surplus of grain. One of the major factors in bringing about these improvements has been the development of an irrigation system which now serves over 90% of the total cultivated area, using water from the Hwang Ho. This compares with a situation where only a small part of the present commune's area was irrigated before 1949 and rather less than 30% by 1957. Part of the work involved the construction of three main canals across the commune, dug by a combined force of over 10,000 people. Other significant changes include major increases in mechanisation so that, for example, more than 90% of the commune's cultivated land is now worked by tractor; the construction of a fertiliser factory which provides cheap supplies of calcium superphosphate to the farmers; and a marked increase in the provision of educational facilities, from six schools of different types in 1948, to fifty-six, including one agro-technical school, in 1973.

Obviously the development of the communes has not been entirely without problems. Some communes have been much more successful than others but most seem to have achieved appreciable economic growth. Many of the problems which have arisen seem to have been in social and political rather than economic fields, though these are more obviously interlinked in China than in most other parts of the world. The Cultural Revolution was a period of massive and sometimes violent re-assessment of attitudes. One of the main effects of this movement, which began in 1965 and ultimately affected virtually the whole of China, was to check any tendencies for a movement back towards capitalist attitudes or a capitalist type of economy in which profit was the prime motivation for economic activities. In so doing, the period of the Cultural Revolution clearly

10.2 Learning from Tachai. Visitors from other parts of China (in the background) watch female members of the Tachai production brigade hauling rocks in hand-carts and doing other heavy work. It is hoped that when the spectators return home they will encourage their own brigades to adopt similar methods with equal enthusiasm.

re-emphasised the belief of the Chinese leaders that development involves political and social as well as economic aspects. After the early years of the Cultural Revolution the educational system was even more firmly integrated with the political ideology and economic system of the country (thus university students, for example, normally studied politics as part of their course and also spent periods of time working in factories or on farms), though since the death of Mao Tse-Tung in 1976 a further period of re-thinking of these inter-relationships has begun.

Whatever problems the communes have faced or created, there is little doubt that they have been instrumental in increasing food production in China. Official statistics suggest that food grain production more than doubled between 1949 and 1974 from around 110 million tonnes to around 250 million tonnes. (Most non-Chinese estimates suggest that production for 1974 was rather less than 250 million tonnes, but nearly all would agree that it was in excess

of 200 million tonnes.) In the same period population increased by approximately 60 % to a total of approximately 800 million. Thus, despite a massive population increase, China appeared to be in a considerably better situation in 1974 in terms of food supply per head than was the case in 1949. Official attitudes to the 'population problem' seem to have fluctuated during this period, ranging from optimistic suggestions that China could feed her population however rapidly it might grow to the introduction of intensive family planning schemes.

In the later stages of the Cultural Revolution a firm acceptance of the value of family planning emerged and has since been strongly supported. In particular, China's 'barefoot doctors', young people with rudimentary medical training who participate generally in the work of the communes where they live yet also act as doctors and health visitors, seem to be responsible for birth-control education in the rural areas. Their efforts would appear to be a crucial

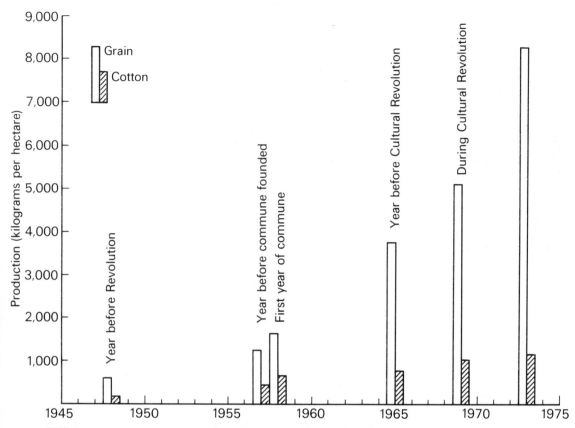

10.3 Chiliying commune: average grain and cotton yields in selected years.

element in China's attempts to increase the material welfare of its people. Improvements in medical facilities and general living standards must almost inevitably reduce death rates, so that unless birth rates also decline the rate of population growth will increase. Even if birth rates decline dramatically in the next decade or so, China's population will still almost certainly exceed 1,000 million by the end of the century, possibly even by 1990, so the need for further increases in food production is obvious. Only time will tell how successful the Chinese people will be in their attempts to balance food supply and population growth, but the massive transformation of agriculture and of many other aspects of life which has occurred already makes the outlook far more optimistic than some neo-Malthusian forecasts have suggested in the past.

Part Three

Population migration and
circulation: some
general considerations

11 Definition of terms

In its widest sense, human movement may be
defined as a temporary, semi-permanent or
permanent change of location. In this definition
no restriction is placed on the distance of the
move, its duration, or upon the voluntary or
involuntary nature of the act, and no distinction
is made between movements within countries
and movements between countries. Thus a
move across a landing from one apartment to
another would count as an act of population
movement just as much as the seasonal wanderings of the Bakhtiari peoples of Iran (Fig.
11.1) or the journey of a Pakistani family from
Kashmir to a permanent home in Leicester,
England – though, of course, the backgrounds
and consequences of such moves are vastly
different. Another group of human movements
includes the continual moves of migratory
workers such as the 2,000 wheat-cutting combine harvester crews who, each year, travel
progressively northwards across the United
States, starting in Texas in May and reaching
the Canadian border in Montana or North
Dakota in September – a distance of some 2,800
kilometres. Another example of this kind of
movement is the itinerant construction gang,
such as the workers who have built Britain's
motorway system. The daily movement of
workers from their homes in the suburbs and
in the countryside to their work-places is yet
another type of movement which has been

investigated by geographers and planners, especially since World War 2.

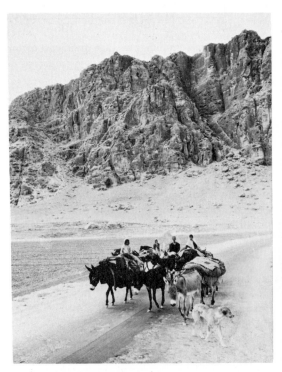

11.1 A Bakhtiari family group during the annual
migration from the Zagros Mountains to the
coastal plain in Iran.

It is plain from the examples above that it is unsatisfactory to include the great diversity of human movement under the one umbrella term of migration, and that it is unwise to label all movers as migrants. Mindful of this the United Nations in 1958 published a multilingual demographic dictionary in which a wide range of terms used in the study of population geography, including studies of human movement, was defined. It is important to know the meaning of the most widely used of these internationally recognised terms, but it will become clear that in practice it is not always possible to draw a sharp distinction between one type of movement and another.

The term *mobility* is all-embracing and includes both *circulation* and *migration*; all the cases cited in the opening paragraph of this chapter, therefore, are examples of the spatial *mobility* of population. *Circulation* has been defined as 'a great variety of movements usually short-term, repetitive or cyclical in character, but all having in common the lack of any declared intention of a permanent or long-standing change of residence' (Zelinsky, 1971). Thus, the movements of the Bakhtiari, the American wheat-cutting teams and the motorway construction gangs, as well as of daily commuters, would be considered by many scholars to be examples of circulation rather than migration. *Migration* is a much more restricted term than circulation in that it is normally used only to describe a movement from one administrative unit to another that results in a permanent change of residence. There is, however, no general agreement about the lowest level of administrative unit which should be considered for the purposes of migration studies. In developed countries it is possible to obtain data for very small areas, such as enumeration districts in England and Wales and census tracts in the United States, the former often containing only a few hundred people, but such detailed information is rarely available in LDCs. Whatever level of administrative unit is considered, the apartment dweller mentioned in the opening paragraph cannot 'officially' be called a migrant. Some scholars would term such a person a *mover*. But are distance or the crossing of an administrative boundary the most appropriate criteria? An American geographer, Zelinsky, an international authority on population geography has recently re-stated the problem in this way: 'Which family is more migratory, the one transferred 3,000 miles across the continent by an employer to be plugged into a suburb almost duplicating its former neighbourhood, or the black family that moves a city block into a previously white district?'

There is yet another practical problem connected with the application of the term migration. The United Nations definition of permanent change of residence is 'having a duration of one year or more'. In practice, many geographers and other social scientists pursuing migration studies in those regions where census data are unreliable or unavailable have been forced to collect their own data in the field and have often ignored official definitions of permanence. In any case there are many examples of long-term circulation involving absence from home for a period of longer than one year. In such circumstances individuals and groups may, despite their prolonged absence, maintain very close economic and social links with their homelands. Cases of this kind can be found, for example, in the Republic of South Africa, where several million 'migrants' of this type work in mines and factories and on plantations (Fig. 11.2).

Migrations involve interactions between peoples and the displacement of populations and there is a whole host of terms related to these characteristics. Persons moving across internal administrative boundaries are either *in-migrants* (and the process is called *in-migration*) or *out-migrants* (*out-migration*). *Immigrants* (*immigration*) and *emigrants* (*emigration*) are persons who cross international boundaries. Migrations are embarked upon from an area of *origin* and are completed at an area of *destination*. Migrants sharing a common origin and destination form a *migration stream* or *migration current*. Normally, wherever there is a stream there is a *counter-stream*, which is the reverse of the stream at a lower volume. Where a study is solely concerned with migration between two areas, whether at the inter-regional or international level, the aggregate of stream and counter-stream is termed the *gross interchange* between the two areas and the difference between the two is called the *net interchange* or *net stream*. In investigations restricted to the effects

11.2 A 'migrant' Bantu worker in a gold mine in the Republic of South Africa. The gold mines have traditionally recruited labour on short-term contracts from neighbouring countries such as Botswana and Malawi as well as from most parts of the Republic.

of migration on a single area it is usual to refer to the total movement of population (in-migration plus out-migration or immigration plus emigration) as the *gross migration*, whereas the difference between in-migration and out-migration (or immigration and emigration) is the *net migration* or *balance of migration*. This may be a positive or negative amount. The relationship between gross and net migration is expressed in terms of the *efficiency of migration*. An attempt is made in Fig. 11.3 to illustrate quantitatively a number of these terms.

Internal migrations in nation B

Montana province is mountainous and sparsely populated. There is little in- or out-migration. Piedmont province has witnessed heavy de-population during the past decade. It is a region of marginal farms and declining mineral resources. Some hydro-electric power schemes have been initiated during the past five years. The map shows a migration stream of 40,000

out-migrants from Piedmont province, who have become in-migrants of Central province. There is a counter-stream of 10,000 from Central to Piedmont province. The gross interchange between the two provinces is 50,000 persons and the net interchange is 30,000. Treated separately, the gross migration for Central and Piedmont provinces is 50,000 in each case, but there is a marked difference in the balance of migration: in Central province it is +30,000 and in Piedmont it is −30,000. If we look next at the efficiency of the migrations between the two provinces we can see that it is relatively high in that the ratio of stream to counter-stream is 4:1 and there has been a net re-distribution of 30,000 people.

Turning next to migration between Central province and Northland province we see a rather different picture. Both of these provinces are relatively affluent industrial regions with a high degree of urbanisation. Migration levels between the two provinces are high. The gross interchange is 100,000 persons, but the net

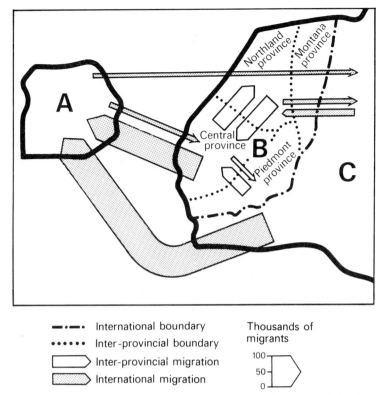

—·—·	International boundary
••••••	Inter-provincial boundary
▭▷	Inter-provincial migration
▨▷	International migration

Thousands of migrants

100
50
0

11.3 Migration patterns for three hypothetical nation states. Island nation A is separated by a narrow sea from continental nations B and C which are themselves separated by a high mountain range. State B is composed of four provinces whose boundaries are shown. The map shows selected migration streams for the most recent five-year period. For the purposes of the accompanying analysis it is assumed that migration between the three nations and other nations is negligible and is therefore ignored.

interchange is zero. Viewed from Northland province, the gross migration is 100,000 and the balance of migration is zero. Migration has not been efficient in that the ratio of stream to counter-stream is 1:1 and the net re-distribution of people effected by the two streams is again zero. Low efficiency is a usual occurrence if the conditions at the sources of origin and destination are similar.

International migrations between nations A, B and C

The migration streams are uneven. Nation A, which has undergone a period of spectacular economic growth in the last five years, accompanied by chronic labour shortages, has received 100,000 immigrants from nation C and 80,000 immigrants from nation B during that time. During the same period 15,000 persons have migrated from nation A to nation B and 10,000

have migrated from nation A to nation C. If we consider the migrations between nation A and nation C (a relatively undeveloped and densely populated country) we can see that there is a major migration stream from C to A and a relatively small counter-stream from A to C. (It is interesting to speculate about the nature of the counter-stream. A good proportion of the 10,000 persons migrating from A to C may, in fact, have originated in C and may be taking part in long-term circulation rather than international migration.) The gross interchange between A and C is 110,000 persons and the net interchange is 90,000. From the point of view of nation A the balance of migration is 90,000, and from the point of view of nation C it is −90,000. The efficiency of the migration is high in that the ratio of stream to counter-stream is 10:1 and there has been a net re-distribution of 90,000 people.

12 Processes and patterns of migration

One of the characteristics of modern geography is the quest for and formulation of models to represent or predict man's spatial behaviour. Such models are well represented in the field of migration studies. Two of the most widely quoted and used conceptual reference points are the 'push–pull' concept and Ravenstein's 'Laws of Migration'. The first is concerned with reasons for migration and the second with the selection of migrants and the development of migration patterns. These two generalisations, although they are continuously being modified and refined, are the cornerstones of much modern theoretical work.

Reasons for migration: the decision-making process

The push–pull concept simply states that for any individual the decision to migrate results from the interplay of two forces: pressures at his permanent place of residence (pushes) and inducements from a number of potential destinations (pulls). Examples of push factors are low wages, unemployment, political, racial and religious oppression, and natural disasters such as drought, famine and flood. Pull factors include employment offers and opportunities, better medical and social provision, and political and religious tolerance. It is clear that in some cases only pushes will be present (for example,

when unforeseen natural disasters occur), in others pulls will be of overwhelming importance (as in the case of a professional person who may find great job satisfaction in one place and then suddenly be confronted by a challenging new opportunity elsewhere), while in a third instance there may be both strong pushes and pulls (as in the case of Puerto Rican migrants who have been pushed from their homeland by unemployment, poverty, overcrowding and poor living conditions and pulled towards the United States by a favourable migration policy, the wide range of employment opportunities, better levels of living and social welfare provisions).

Two further dimensions of the basic push–pull concept are worth noting. First, migration is selective: in certain circumstances and at certain times particular persons or groups are more likely to migrate than others. Such selectivity is sometimes known as *differential migration*. Important differentials are age, sex and socio-economic status. For example, large numbers of the migrants to coastal resort areas in England in the mid-1970s were retired persons. People aged over 65 (who comprise 13.07 % of the total UK population) represent more than 20 % of the population of the South-coast resorts of Worthing, Hove, Hastings and Eastbourne. Modern migrations are overwhelmingly of an economic nature, however, and in the vast majority of these, persons in the young adult age group of 20–34 years are predominant. Sex selectivity appears to vary according to the stage of development of the society concerned. In the very broadest terms studies tend to suggest that in advanced industrial countries females are predominant in short-distance migrations while males are predominant in long-distance migrations. Conversely, in LDCs males are normally in the majority in short- and long-distance internal migrations and in international migrations. In the case of socio-economic (occupational) selectivity, professional people – referred to by F. Musgrove as 'the migratory elite' – are proportionally far more migratory than skilled or unskilled workers.

Another aspect of differential migration is that the age, sex and occupational structures of migration streams vary in response to changing conditions in the area of origin and at potential destinations. In certain conditions (e.g. specific labour requirements in another region) only particular age groups may elect to migrate. In others (e.g. in times of earthquakes or floods), whole communities may move. In the former case the migrants may be said to be positively selected, in that they move to a particular destination in search of betterment, whereas in the latter the migrants may be said to be negatively selected in that there may be little choice involved in the decision to move and in the selection of their destination in the first

(a)

The *New York Times* said that in Kilkenny even the dogs had deserted: also the legal profession had been annihilated, because where there were no people left, there could be no litigation.[8] In 1841 the population of Ireland had been 8,175,124, and Disraeli said it was the most thickly populated country in Europe. According to the 1851 census the population was only 6,552,385. The commissioners of the census remarked that at the normal rate of increase the population should then have been over nine millions, so the real loss was about two and a half million people in ten years. And in the years between 1851 and 1854 another 822,000 left.[9]

Many sailed directly from Irish ports. In starving Limerick most ships were advertised as sailing not just for New York or Quebec but 'for the flourishing city of New York'; 'for the flourishing city of Quebec'. But most people went first to England and sailed from Liverpool. Others stayed in England, not because they had any love of that country but because they had no money to go further. They were not welcome. One family got as far as Cheshire and camped near the house of Thomas Murdoch, chairman of the emigration commissioners. The moment his servants noticed the Irish they considered them a pestilence to be driven away. Murdoch went down to the camp and found a poor family of four children, and their mother, father, and grandmother. The mother said they used to live fifteen miles from Athlone. They had brought over a tattered blanket with them, took sticks out of a hedge and propped the blanket up like a tent, and slept under it on the bare ground. Murdoch saw smoke, and a kettle boiling, and asked what they had there. They said nettles. For three years before this, they had existed on three acres of potatoes, in Ireland, but this year they had none to plant, the workhouse was overflowing, so their master said there was nothing for them but to leave, and if they did leave he would give them a pound note. With this they begged their way to Dublin and paid their fare to Liverpool, and then walked to Murdoch's place, thirty-six miles from Liverpool.[10]

12.1 (See legend over.)

120,000 Somali nomads settled on the land

From Our Correspondent
Nairobi, Aug 22

The resettlement of some 120,000 Somali nomads whose former livestock herds perished in the drought-affected areas of Somalia has been successfully accomplished, President Siad Barre has announced in Mogadishu.

The operation to settle them in farming areas in the south and in fishing settlements and along the coast has been accomplished several months ahead of schedule. It represents a tremendous achievement, of which the Somalis are proud.

The Soviet Union provided 16 aircraft, which carried nearly 110,000 people to resettlement areas over the past two months, often using improvised airstrips built in a matter of days by the people themselves. Others were carried in lorries, most of which were again provided by the Russians.

There are still problems in providing food until crop production can be fully developed. It appears, however, that large numbers of Somalis have accepted the need to change their nomadic way of life, and to concentrate for the first time on agriculture.

12.1 Two examples of negatively selected migration.

instance. Two widely different migrations, both exhibiting the characteristics of negative selection and indifference to age and sex, are described in Fig. 12.1.

A second important corollary of the push–pull concept is *migration elasticity*. This concept acknowledges the fact that individuals react differently to the pressures and inducements which lead to the decision to migrate. In some cases very little stimulus is required before an individual migrates; in other cases pushes and pulls have to be exerted either with great intensity or for a long time before migration takes place. Cases have been reported of disappointed migrants from the United Kingdom to Australia, who, after a short stay, have returned to the UK, and then, after another unsettled period, have embarked upon a second migration to Australia. In such cases the attractions and drawbacks of the two places must have been under constant review before the final decision was made.

E. S. Lee (1966) has recently re-stated the basic push–pull concept in the terms outlined in Fig. 12.2. Instead of isolating the pressures and stimuli confronting particular individuals or groups, Lee presents a reality in which a place of origin is characterised by a number of attributes. Lee states that each individual will perceive these attributes differently according to, for example, sex, age, education or marital status. A particular individual will see some of these factors as advantages and these will discourage migration (plus factors at origin) while others will be seen as disadvantages and will encourage migration (minus factors at origin). The same individual will be indifferent towards a third group of factors (neutral factors at origin). A similar picture of positive, negative and neutral factors is present at a potential destination.

To translate this into individual terms, consider the case of a middle-aged bachelor, working as a relatively poorly paid farm labourer (minus factor at origin) in a declining rural area, who has a consuming interest in salmon fishing. He may view the salmon rivers of his home region as important reasons for staying there (plus factor at origin), while at the same time being attracted by offers of well-paid factory employment in a nearby industrial region (plus factor at destination). The fact that flexible shift

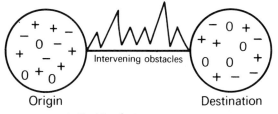

+ Positive factors

− Negative factors

O Neutral factors

12.2 E. S. Lee's theory of migration. (After Lee, 1966.)

work (to fit in with domestic commitments) will be available for wives of employees will not enter his calculations (neutral factor at destination). Another farm labourer with no outdoor hobbies and with a grown-up family and a wife keen to supplement her husband's income would see the situation in a rather different light.

Having established the idea of the evaluation of perceived advantages and disadvantages at the place of origin and a potential destination,

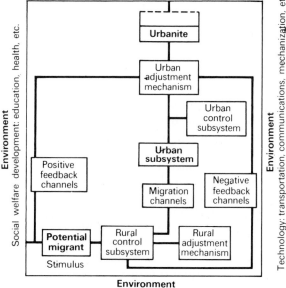

Environment
Economic conditions: wages, prices, consumer preferences, degrees of commercialisation and industrial development

12.3 Mabogunje's rural–urban migration system. (After Mabogunje, 1970.)

Lee then introduces a further component: the potential migrant is confronted by one or a number of real or perceived obstacles which must be overcome before migration can take place. These may be physical (the Berlin Wall, the Rockies), financial, medical, academic or legal (immigration quotas, work permit regulations). Thus Lee sees migration in terms of four related groups of factors: factors associated with the area of origin, factors associated with the area of destination, intervening obstacles and personal factors.

So far migration has been viewed as a one-way, start and finish relationship between an origin and a destination. Mabogunje (1970), an African scholar writing with particular reference to Africa, has approached rural–urban migration from another point of view: that of a system which is undergoing continued modification as events in one part cause repercussions elsewhere. (In the simplest terms a 'system' may be defined as a complex of interacting elements.) Mabogunje's ideas are summarised in Fig. 12.3. The diagram shows the African rural–urban migration system operating within an economic, social, political and technological environment. This environment is one of change: of increasing degrees of commercialisation and industrialisation, of rising health and education standards, of changing government policies and of better transportation links and increased mechanisation. The system and the environment act and react upon each other continuously.

Having been stimulated to move by the environment, the potential migrant then comes under the influence of what Mabogunje calls the rural control subsystem, which in the African context is the family and the rural community, whose attitudes will determine the volume of rural–urban migration. These attitudes will in turn be influenced by the ability of families and communities to adjust to migration loss. When migration takes place the rural dweller passes from the rural control subsystem to an urban subsystem with its own control subsystem (e.g. housing and job opportunities) and adjustment mechanism (e.g. an expanding labour market) which may transform the rural dweller into an urbanite. If the migrant maintains contact with his home area as the adjustment to urban life takes place, he sends back information which modifies the system. This information may be of difficulties, setbacks and frustrations (negative feedback), which will discourage further migration, or of successes and opportunities (positive feedback), which will encourage further migration.

Although this systems approach is specifically related to African rural–urban migration, it is relevant to the study of migrations in general. Besides highlighting the self-modifying nature of a migration system, Mabogunje's study emphasises the threefold effect of migration: on the area of origin, on the area of destination and on the migrant himself. This is an aspect of migration which will be returned to in the case studies which conclude this part of the book.

Who migrates where?: the generation of migration patterns

As long ago as the 1880s an English demographer, E. G. Ravenstein, in a study based on the birthplace data in the 1881 census of England and Wales, formulated what he called seven 'Laws of Migration', and, as was noted earlier, these have remained remarkably useful as starting points for the investigation of modern migrations. Ravenstein's laws are as follows:

1 We have already proved that the great body of our migrants only proceed a short distance and that there takes place consequently a universal shifting or displacement of the population, which produces 'currents of migration' setting in the direction of the great centres of commerce and industry which absorb the migrants...

2 It is the natural outcome of the movement of this migration, limited in range, but universal throughout the country, that the processes of absorption go on in the following manner: The inhabitants of a country immediately surrounding a town of rapid growth, flock into it; the gaps thus left by the rural population are filled up by migrants from more remote districts, until the attractive force of one of our rapidly growing cities makes its influence felt, step by step, to the most remote corner of the Kingdom. Migrants enumerated in a certain centre of absorption will consequently grow less with the distance proportionately to the native population which furnishes them...

3 The process of dispersion is the inverse of that of absorption and exhibits similar features.

4 Each main current of migration produces a compensating counter-current.

5 Migrants proceeding long distances generally go by preference to one of the great centres of commerce and industry.

6 The natives of towns are less migratory than those of rural parts of the country.

7 Females are more migratory than males.

The fourth generalisation has already been noted in the discussion of stream and counter-stream (see Chapter 11). Similarly, Ravenstein's sixth and seventh laws refer to differential migration, which has been discussed elsewhere. The remaining generalisations (1, 2, 3 and 5) are, however, of central importance in the explanation of patterns of migration and they have been confirmed, restated and modified in a large number of studies in recent years. The essence of Ravenstein's first, second, third and fifth laws is embodied in the modern concepts of distance-decay, intervening opportunities and stepwise movement.

Distance-decay

On the influence of distance on migration, Ravenstein was very explicit in the last sentence of his second law. He argued that the volume of migration is inversely related to distance in that areas adjacent to a centre of absorption will normally provide more migrants than distant areas. On a graph with arithmetical scales, this relationship between volume of migration and distance produces a reverse-J (Fig. 12.4a) curve, thus showing that the volume of migration does not fall off regularly with increasing distance but tends to decline at a decreasing rate. This is called a *negative exponential relationship* and when plotted on logarithmic graph paper it appears as a straight line (Fig. 12.4b). The relationship is called *distance-decay* and is analogous to Newton's law of universal gravitation; it is therefore, an example of a *gravity model*. The basis of the gravity model in a geographical context is that two places interact with each other in proportion to the product of their 'masses' and inversely according to some function of the distance between them. The 'mass' of a place may be expressed in various ways according to the problem under investigation. It may, for example, be the population of the place, or the number of its retail outlets, or the number of job opportunities.

An example of the distance-decay relationship is illustrated in Fig. 12.5 using birthplace data from the 1861 census of England and Wales. The table and graphs show the number of migrants enumerated in Sheffield in that year who had been born in five increasingly distant counties to the south of the (then) town. The graphs show a falling off by a multiple of the distance rather like the gravity model, but they must be treated with some caution. The simple relationship shown in the graphs did not obtain in every direction. If the 'slopes' of decreasing numbers of migrants in all directions from a centre of absorption are seen, in the mind's eye, as a cone, with the centre of absorption at the peak, then small subsidiary cones may appear on the slopes. In the case of Sheffield in 1861, London formed such a cone. Although smaller in area than Warwickshire and more than 90 km further away from Sheffield, it furnished 227 more migrants. Plainly, migration does not just fall off with distance; it is also necessary to take into account the population of the places concerned. The volume of migration between two large towns is likely to be greater than the volume of migration between one of the towns and a sparsely populated rural area as distant as the other town. Thus, if account is taken of population levels, the gross migration between two places may be expressed by a gravity model in the form:

$$M_{ij} = \frac{P_i P_j}{d_{ij}}$$

where M_{ij} = gross migration between places i and j
P_i = population of place i
P_j = population of place j
di_j = distance between places i and j

Intervening opportunities

So far two factors which influence the generation of migration patterns have been isolated: first, distance between an area of origin and a potential area of destination, and secondly, population levels, which determine the number of potential migrants in one area and the number of opportunities at a potential destination. At this point a third factor must be recognised, that of intervening opportunities between an area of origin and a potential destination. This concept was introduced by an American scholar, Stouffer, in 1940 and refined by him in 1960. In his original article Stouffer wrote that 'the number of persons going a given distance is directly proportional to the number of opportunities at that distance and inversely proportional to the number of intervening opportunities'. A reconsideration of the nineteenth-century Sheffield example will illustrate this concept. It was noted earlier that only thirty-

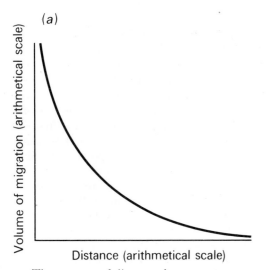

(a)

Volume of migration (arithmetical scale)

Distance (arithmetical scale)

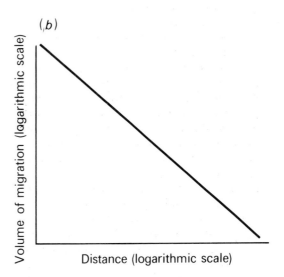

(b)

Volume of migration (logarithmic scale)

Distance (logarithmic scale)

12.4 The concept of distance-decay.

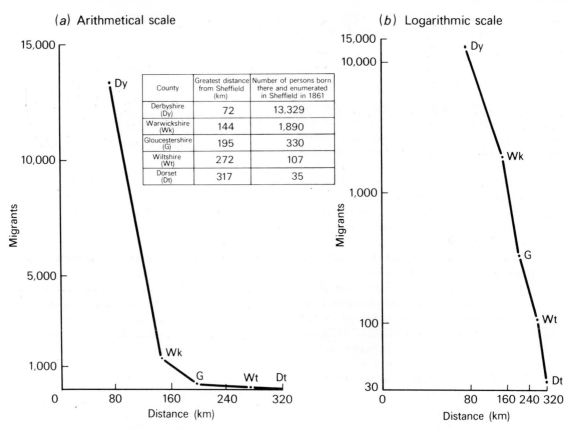

(a) Arithmetical scale

(b) Logarithmic scale

County	Greatest distance from Sheffield (km)	Number of persons born there and enumerated in Sheffield in 1861
Derbyshire (Dy)	72	13,329
Warwickshire (Wk)	144	1,890
Gloucestershire (G)	195	330
Wiltshire (Wt)	272	107
Dorset (Dt)	317	35

12.5 Migrants in Sheffield in 1861 who were born in Derbyshire, Warwickshire, Gloucestershire, Wiltshire and Dorset.

five persons who had been born in Dorset were living in Sheffield in 1861 and this has been partly explained in terms of distance and the relatively small population of Dorset. What, then, were the destinations of the people leaving Dorset in the first half of the nineteenth century? Many moved to Bristol and the industrial towns of the Midlands. In terms of opportunities, Sheffield did not differ markedly from Bristol or the Midlands towns, but the latter places were nearer to Dorset than Sheffield and, other things being equal, the migrant would settle as soon as he had found an appropriate opportunity. Thus viewed as opportunities, Bristol and the Midlands towns intervened between Sheffield and the Dorset migrant.

A study completed in the United States in the 1950s (Rose, 1955, in Jansen, 1970) took the concepts of distance-decay and intervening opportunities a step further by testing the hypothesis that persons of higher status (in occupational

terms) seeking better positions (opportunities) must move further to find them than persons of lower status. The author recorded the previous place of residence and the new address in the city of a sample of 1,221 people who moved to Minneapolis, Minnesota, between the middle of March and the beginning of July 1955. Previously he had compiled a map of Minneapolis in which each census tract was ranked from I to V according to the socio-economic status of its population. Tracts in the first rank were those which contained the highest aggregate scores based on the proportion of highly rated houses, the proportion of well-educated inhabitants, the proportion of professional workers and the proportion of White people. The tracts ranked fifth had the lowest aggregate scores based on these characteristics. Having compiled this map it was possible, by plotting the new addresses of the sampled population, to assign the migrants to one of five socio-economic groups (Class I to Class V). The places moved from were classified into concentric rings centred on Minneapolis (Fig. 12.6a). In addition each place of origin was classified into east or west of the Mississippi (on which Minneapolis stands). The southern states were classified separately. The findings of the study were as follows:

(i) The distance moved decreased steadily as the status of the neighbourhood declined. Thus the original hypothesis was generally confirmed (Fig. 12.6b and c).

(ii) Class V migrants proved to be an exception. This was partly accounted for by the number of Blacks included in this class who had migrated greater distances than the Whites in the same class.

(iii) While most migrants in Class I were from the east (urban professional people moving from large cities in the industrial Midwest), the opposite was increasingly true in Classes II to IV where most migrants originated from the west – from rural areas in Minnesota, and neighbouring North and South Dakota.

In terms of Stouffer's concept, this study suggested that people in low-status occupations were finding many more intervening opportunities in a given distance than people with high-status occupations, and that geographical position has an important influence on opportunities for migration. Although Rose's assumptions and techniques have been heavily criticised, his study throws interesting light on the related concepts of distance-decay and intervening opportunities.

Stepwise movement

The germ of this concept is incorporated in Ravenstein's second generalisation where he states that 'The inhabitants of a country immediately surrounding a town of rapid growth, flock into it; the gaps thus left...are filled up by migrants from more remote districts, until the attractive force...makes itself felt, step by step, to the most remote parts of the Kingdom.' Fig. 12.7(a) shows, in its simplest terms, the type of hierarchical stepwise movement hinted at by Ravenstein and since investigated by many scholars.

The difficulty of assessing the validity of this

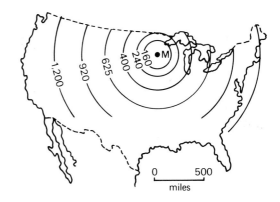

(a) Location of Minneapolis

(b) Median distances (miles) travelled (by census tract class)

200	100	West	East	100	200
			I		
			II		
			III		
			IV		
			V (White)		

(c) Percentage of migrants (by census tract class) originating from within 240 miles of Minnesota

	West		East
I	26.08	I	24.20
II	29.44	II	30.56
III	34.69	III	28.38
IV	38.65	IV	36.20
V (white)	28.81	V (white)	47.62

12.6 Distance and direction travelled by 1,221 migrants to Minneapolis, Minnesota, 15 March to 1 July 1955. (After Rose, 1955.)

concept lies in the problem of obtaining migration case-histories. Even where such data are available or have been obtained through questionnaire surveys the evidence is often conflicting. All that can be safely concluded is that stepwise movement up a hierarchy from a rural-farm environment to the national metropolis is just one of many types of movement which include short-circuits of the hierarchy and reverse movements (Fig. 12.7b).

A study completed in New Zealand (Keown, 1971) in which migrations in the predominantly rural western Southland region of South Island were investigated, showed that the stepwise

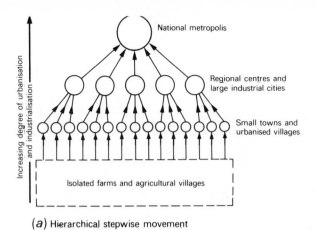

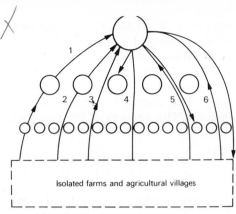

(a) Hierarchical stepwise movement

(b) Six types of migratory movement originating from rural areas

12.7 Stepwise migratory movements.

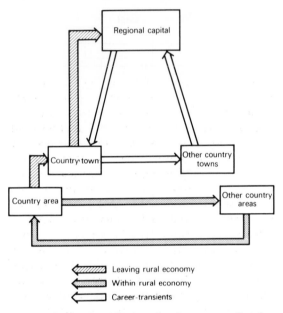

Leaving rural economy

Within rural economy

Career-transients

12.8 A model of rural migration for western Southland, New Zealand. (After Keown, 1971.)

model failed to account for all the migrations which had taken place. Instead the study suggested that a stepwise movement up the urban hierarchy is just one of three types of movement, each of which is related to occupational characteristics (Fig. 12.8).

The author recognises three groups of migrants in western Southland as follows:

(i) A group of migrants who work in farming, forestry and mining in the study area and who move over short distances within the area.

(ii) Another group of persons who are changing their occupation. They are generally leaving farming, forestry and mining and seeking different types of employment in larger towns and cities. Their movements fit the stepwise concept of movement up the urban hierarchy.

(iii) A third group termed *career-transients*, who move through the area for promotion within a regional or national context and whose moves are in no way related to distance or a stepwise progression. Such migrants include government officers, post-office workers, bank and railway officials and teachers. Whether they are moving up or down the urban hierarchy or laterally within it depends to a great extent on whether they began their careers in a large city or country town and on the location of opportunities for promotion within their chosen careers.

This chapter has ranged widely over a large field of study and a substantial number of concepts and models has been introduced. These concepts and models will be further illustrated in the case studies of migration in England and Wales, Western Europe, the United States, Brazil and East Africa in Part IV.

13 Circulation

We introduced and briefly discussed the idea of circulation in Chapter 11, but the significance of such temporary, often short and repetitive movements in all societies demands more detailed treatment. Not only is a study of circulation important because of its economic and social significance, but also because of the planning problems which it brings at local, regional and national levels in many countries. There are great varieties in type, frequency of return to the same point and intensity of circulation, and it is beyond the scope of this chapter to deal with every aspect. What we will try to provide is a review of the changing form and function of circulation as the modernisation of societies takes place. Particular emphasis will be placed on the journey to work in developed countries.

Circulation in primitive and less developed societies

In many sedentary peasant societies, both in the historic past in what are now developed countries, and at the present time in large parts of the less developed world, patterns of work, thought and daily movement were, or are, rigidly circumscribed. Inherited class, occupation and gender were, and still are in many societies, formidable barriers to personal mobility. In such societies *fields of information* are usually small and ideas and attitudes change only slowly. (An information field is the area from which a sedentary individual receives information. Such fields normally show the effects of distance-decay. In addition they tend to vary in size in relation to the degree of modernisation of the society to which the individual belongs.) In such circumstances circulation is often restricted to movements concerned with tilling the land, pasturing animals, trips to local markets and visits related to religious observance. Local communities, especially in broken country, may in such conditions have relatively little contact with their neighbours except in times of inter-community disputes and at marriages. Such relatively immobile peasant societies are still common in isolated regions in Latin America, Africa and Asia.

Another important type of circulation in primitive societies is nomadism and its variants. The movements of primitive food gatherers such as the Semang and Sakai of the Malay peninsula, the Eskimo seal and caribou hunters of Arctic North America, shifting cultivators such as the Boro of the Amazon Basin and the Land Dyaks of Sarawak and Sabah, as well as the camel and goat herders of North Africa and the Middle East, the horse and sheep herders of Central Asia and the cattle herders of East Africa, may all be included in this broad group. As in sedentary peasant societies the movements of such groups have a basic regularity and orderliness. In the case of shifting cultivators, movement from one area to another takes place at fairly regular intervals. This can be every year, or at the end of two or three years, or sometimes every four or five years. Most, but not all, of these movements take place within fairly well-defined territories, and groups often return after long intervals to land previously cultivated and abandoned. Similarly, the movement of nomadic livestock herders is marked by a seasonal or yearly rhythm. There are no property lines but traditional pastures are fixed according to water supply and grass growth, and particular areas are the exclusive property of certain groups. Another characteristic common to the gatherers, hunters, shifting cultivators and nomadic herdsmen is the relative impermanence of the homestead, which may be a hastily improvised shelter of branches and leaves, a mud house with a roof of thatch or dung (Fig. 13.1), a tent of some kind, or even a dwelling made of ice, as in the case of the Eskimo igloo.

Only in the most remote regions do societies of the kind described above continue to live in isolation from the outside world. De-colonisation (including the re-drawing of political boundaries), the rise to power of new political regimes, wars, agricultural development and re-organisation, mineral exploitation, road construction and military considerations have all brought such groups into contact with modern society to a lesser or greater extent. In extreme cases groups have been forced to settle permanently, either through environmental deterioration as in parts of the Sahara or by government direction as in parts of the USSR. Even where traditional ways of life persist, they are much infiltrated by outside influences and circulatory movements have often been severely curtailed. A good example of circulatory curtailment is provided by the Kirghiz peoples of the Wakhan Corridor in the highlands of Afghanistan (Fig. 13.2). During the 1920s and 1930s the Soviet Union to the north closed its boundaries to them, and this was followed in the 1940s and 1950s by similar treatment from India and Pakistan to the south and China to the east. Thus these peoples have found their former grazing and trading territories gradually diminished in this century so that they are now confined to the upper reaches of the valley of the Amu Darya (River Oxus) at altitudes over 4,000 m. In the early 1970s there were some 2,700 Kirghiz nomads in the eastern half of the Wakhan Corridor tending 3,000 yaks and 30,000 sheep. Their summer encampments lie near the two lakes on the broad valley floor, but in autumn when the valley lands become damp

13.1 A traditional dwelling of the semi-nomadic Maasai. Many of the younger Maasai no longer live in the traditional wattle and dung dwellings of the type shown here but build houses of concrete blocks with corrugated metal roofs.

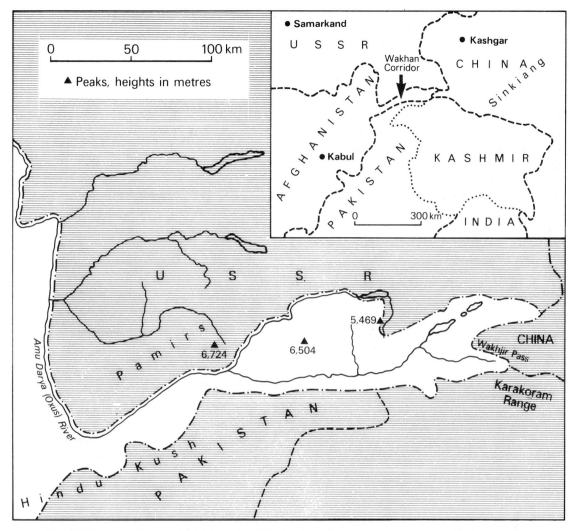

13.2 The Wakhan corridor in the highlands of Afghanistan.

and communications difficult, they dismantle their *yurts* (a kind of tent made of skins) and move to the edge of the south-facing uplands on the USSR border and near to the Wakhjir Pass.

Another example of the decline of nomadism in very recent times is furnished by the Tuareg of the Ahaggar Massif in southern Algeria. Until as recently as the early 1960s, on the eve of the declaration of Algerian independence (1962), Tuareg social, political and economic life remained remarkably intact. It was based on a hierarchical structure composed of camel-owning nobles whose main function was raiding. There were also vassal tribes who guarded the encampments and the herds of goats which were the lifeline of the nobles and also engaged in caravan trading. A third group consisted of slaves (called *iklan*), who had been brought from the Sudan or taken from caravans. Finally there were sedentary farmers who cultivated irrigated areas under a kind of contract system from Tuareg landowners and who lived in many cases in wretched poverty.

In the last decade this traditional system has undergone immense change as the result of the actions of the Algerian government and because of deteriorating climatic conditions. The sedentary cultivators have been encouraged to claim and farm their irrigated 'gardens' as their own property. The Tuareg slaves have been given

97

13.3 Advertisements for overseas posts.

their freedom by the government, encouraged
to leave the goat camps and given the opportunity to work on agricultural co-operatives
which have been created throughout the region.
During this period of political, social and economic upheaval the region, at the best of times
one of small and irregular rainfall, has undergone a protracted drought which has substantially reduced the contribution of nomadic
goat-herding to the subsistence economy of the
Tuareg. At the same time the caravan trade with
Niger to the south has dwindled into insignificance. Thus the loss of slaves, loss of ownership
of irrigated gardens and the decline in caravan
trade, together with the drought-induced reduction of nomadic pastoralism, have brought to
an end many aspects of traditional Tuareg life.
The Tuareg are becoming increasingly dependent upon the tourist trade, producing leather
goods and acting as guides and providing
camels for mountain treks. Gradually they are
becoming 'sedentarised', with numbers of
them working on the agricultural co-operatives
alongside their former tenants and slaves. It is
not expected, however, that nomadic pastoralism in the Ahaggar will disappear completely,
because pastoral co-operatives may be created
in artificially irrigated zones between the centres
of sedentary cultivation.

As communities modernise there are significant changes in circulation patterns, including
changes of type, duration and selectivity. In
many cases the early stages of modernisation
occurred during the days of colonial empire-
building, and this often resulted in the creation
of various kinds of long-distance and long-term

13.4 Traffic on the Exeter by-pass. In developed countries, 5-day working weeks, annual holidays of 3–4 weeks or more and widespread car ownership allow a much wider variety and a much greater volume of leisure and recreation-orientated circulation than ever before – with its attendant problems.

circulation related to labour requirements on plantations, in mines, in factories and on railways. This has been particularly important in the past in Africa, and is still important in much of that continent. In some cases in this category, absence from home is so long, despite continued economic and social ties with the area of origin, that the distinction between circulation and migration is difficult to make.

During the period of modernisation in developing countries another kind of long-term circulation is often in evidence, this time not practised by the indigenous population but by aliens. This is the long-distance circulation of foreign skilled workers, technicians, scientists and teachers on 'short-term' contracts. At the present time, for example, there is a strong demand for skilled workers and professional people in the oil-rich countries of the Middle East, and in one of these, Saudi Arabia, there are now about 2,000 Britons working in a wide range of occupations including medicine, accountancy and skilled construction trades. Few will remain there permanently. Two examples of this form of international circulation are illustrated by the advertisements shown in Fig. 13.3.

The traffic, however, is not all one way; there

is a strong counter-current of students from developing countries pursuing courses in educational establishments in developed countries. There were, for instance, more than 95,000 foreign students in the United Kingdom during 1973–4, many of them from developing countries. On some courses foreign students far outnumber British students. In a report in the *Times Higher Education Supplement* on 16 January 1976 it was reported that of the forty-six students taking the master's degree in hydrocarbon chemistry at the University of Manchester Institute of Science and Technology, only two were British. On the master's course on the transmission of electric power there was only one English student out of twenty-six. Among the top ten countries sending students to the United Kingdom in 1973–4 were LDCs such as Malaysia (10,582), Iran (4,696) and Nigeria (3,426).

Circulation in developed societies

Circulation in advanced nations has reached unprecedented levels in recent years. Much of this is economically motivated, with trips to and from work and during the course of work accounting for a large proportion of adult cir-

Table 13.1. *Journeys in Great Britain, by age and sex of travellers, 1973* (%)

	All persons aged 3–15	Males				Females			
		16–29	30–59	60–64	Over 65	16–29	30–59	60–64	Over 65
To work or in course of work	3	42	53	50	16	28	31	13	6
Education	34	5	—	—	—	4	—	—	—
Shopping	16	7	9	12	25	18	24	35	37
Personal business	7	6	6	8	13	7	8	10	15
Eating/drinking	1	5	3	3	2	4	2	1	1
Sport	4	3	2	2	2	1	—	—	—
Entertainment	8	5	3	3	4	6	5	6	6
Social visit	16	18	12	12	19	21	16	21	24
Holiday	2	1	—	1	1	1	—	2	1
Day trip	7	3	3	5	11	4	4	7	7
Other	3	5	7	4	6	7	9	4	1

Source: *National Travel Survey*, and given in *Social Trends No. 5* (HMSO, 1974).

culation. In addition the number of trips made to shops, to hotels and restaurants, to sports stadia, to friends and relatives and to holiday resorts (Fig. 13.4) is also significant. Table 13.1 shows the result of a sample survey carried out in 1973 to find out the relative importance of various types of journey in Great Britain. Besides showing the prominence of work journeys, the table also shows the significance of sex-selectivity and stage in the *family life-cycle* in many circulatory habits. (It has long been recognised that each individual's life is marked by a number of distinct stages and that each stage is characterised by different patterns of behaviour and activity. In this context, childhood, early maturity, maturity and old age, for instance, are marked by circulatory patterns differing in function, frequency and distance.) One thing that the table does not show is the relative importance of internal and international circulation, the latter type being an increasingly important element of the total circulatory pattern in advanced countries. Entertainers, politicians, athletes and certain types of businessmen spend hundreds of hours each year journeying around the world, and at certain times of year these regular international travellers are joined by holidaymakers. In the third quarter of 1974, for instance, 3.3 million tourists from the United Kingdom went to foreign destinations.

Internal circulation is, however, a far more general feature of modern life than circulation at an international level. Widespread car ownership, high-speed railways (see Fig. 13.5) and increased levels of affluence coupled with shorter working days and weeks and longer annual holidays have all contributed to the high level of circulation in advanced countries. In the last thirty years car ownership has been a particularly potent force (except in the largest urban areas where rapid rail transport is very important) in allowing a wider separation of place of residence from place of work. This has resulted in the relative decline of population in large metropolitan areas and a corresponding population growth in small towns and villages. During this period of *decentralisation of population*, employment opportunities have remained predominantly in the largest metropolitan areas, thus causing a marked increase in the number of *commuters* who live in one community but travel regularly, often daily, to work in another. In terms of circulation this has increased the significance of the journey to work and in settlement terms has resulted in the growth of large numbers of commuter towns and villages at varying distances from the major metropolitan areas. (Commuter villages are also called dormitory villages, suburbanised villages, metropolitan villages, incipient suburbs and discontinuous suburbs.)

The distinction between self-contained communities on the one hand and predomi-

13.5 Tokyo: underground train in rush hour. Although private cars play an increasingly significant role in commuting to small and medium-sized towns, rapid public transport systems, either underground as in this case, or at or above ground level are the most important means of travelling to work in many of the largest metropolitan areas. The white-gloved 'pushers' who help to pack people tightly into the Tokyo trains emphasise the intensity of use of this means of transport.

nantly dormitory settlements on the other is sometimes quite clear, but in many cases communities fall neither into one group nor the other. One method of identifying dormitory settlements and gauging the degree of decentralisation of population is to calculate *job ratios* using the following formula:

$$\frac{\text{People } working \text{ in the area}}{\text{(both residents and commuters)}} \times \frac{100}{1}$$
$$\frac{}{\text{Total number of employed people}} \times \frac{100}{1}$$
$$living \text{ in the area}$$

Job ratios calculated for the boroughs of Greater London in 1966 are shown in Fig. 13.6. The pattern which emerges is not simply one of centrally located employment opportunities and a decentralised commuting population. While, as would be expected, the City of London and Westminster have exceptionally high ratios and boroughs such as Bromley and

Bexley have correspondingly low ones, the impact of the Ford motor works is shown in Barking, and the importance of London airport and its adjacent industrial areas is reflected in the high job ratios in the outer boroughs of Hillingdon and Hounslow. Similarly, the effects of office relocation in Croydon differentiates that borough from Sutton to the west and Bromley to the east.

Journey-to-work patterns are, however, not confined to movements into towns and cities from outside. Complex intra-urban (within cities) patterns of circulation are also characteristic of large urban areas. These patterns are in part the result of intra-urban migrations by individuals and families who when they change their place of residence often retain their previous employment and shopping and leisure patterns (see pp. 108–9). Such migration is predominantly outward to the periphery of the city – although there may also be significant inward movements especially among older, intra-urban migrants – and is usually connected with the life-cycle (see p. 100 for a discussion of this term) as individuals and families adjust to changing circumstances (e.g. income) and demands (e.g. family size). As intra-urban migration takes place houses tend to 'filter down' and people tend to 'filter up'. When first built a new neighbourhood contains housing units of basically similar style and quality and is usually located near the edge of the built-up area (exceptions to this are, for instance, re-development schemes and some fashionable apartment developments). As time passes the houses and the neighbourhood become older and less fashionable compared to newer developments. At the same time, the incomes of many of the original inhabitants increase and family sizes change. Many families move to newer, often larger houses in more fashionable neighbourhoods further out. Families of relatively lower income move into the housing in the initial neighbourhood and for most of these families this area represents an improvement on the housing and neighbourhood from which they have moved. In time the once-new neighbourhood may filter down through the urban income groups from near the top to the bottom.

Obviously not all moves conform to the pattern outlined above but several detailed stu-

13.6 Job ratios for the boroughs of Greater London.

dies in this country and overseas have confirmed the general tendencies. Lansing (1969) in a major study in the United States found that 55 % of in-migrants had lower incomes than the out-migrants and that only 25 % had higher incomes. He also found that 64 % of the houses moved into had more rooms than the houses left. In terms of relationship to the life-cycle he found that 41 % of the families moving into a house were at an earlier stage in the life-cycle than the families moving out and only 28 % were at a later stage.

So far, attention has been focused on the nature of population decentralisation and on the emergence of commuting on a large scale. We must now consider the question of why people commute. Although some people enjoy a long journey to work, many commuters resent the loss of time involved, and investigations suggest that substantial numbers of residents of commuter villages – particularly non-working

wives – dislike many aspects of their lives. Why then do people commute? Surveys conducted in various parts of the United Kingdom suggest the existence of at least four groups of commuters as follows:

(i) Some commuters travel long distances to live in what they believe are better environments. Journey time may be a limiting factor to them but cost (of travelling and house purchase) is not. Such people may travel, for example, from Kent and Sussex to Central London, or from the Peak District to Sheffield, Nottingham, Derby, Stoke or Manchester.

(ii) Another group consists of young commuters, usually young married couples, who commute because housing is cheaper in the outlying towns and villages than in the cities.

(iii) A third group consists of commuters nearing retirement who buy a house in the country or at the seaside and commute until they retire.

(iv) Finally there are those commuters who have not moved from large cities but commute from their life-long place of residence, because of lack of employment opportunities in the local area. Some of these may plan to do this indefinitely, and others, particularly young single people living with their parents, only until they marry.

The term *voluntary commuters* is used by some scholars to describe those in groups (i) to (iii), and the term *inertia commuters* is sometimes used to describe those in group (iv). In those areas where employment as well as population has been decentralised a further group of commuters may be identified who are called *reverse commuters* (Fig. 13.7). These workers, who live in the inner parts of large cities, may need to make a long journey to work every day from the centre to the periphery of the urban area. Indeed in a large number of cities in the United States where the decentralisation of both population and employment has reached an advanced stage, many middle-class people make shorter journeys to work than those in the lower socio-economic groups who still live in inner urban areas.

One outcome of this mixing of urban and rural life is that there is now often no clear break between town and country. Indeed in many areas only the landscape remains truly rural. Because of this it is no longer realistic in many regions to speak of urban industrial areas as opposed to rural agricultural areas. An alternative approach is to view areas in terms of cities and their *commuting hinterlands*. Commuting hinterlands are also called urban fields, although the latter are not based solely on commuting patterns. The term 'daily urban system' has been used in the USA to describe a city and its commuting hinterland. Fig. 13.8 shows the commuting hinterlands of the major cities of England and Wales in 1961. Some of these hinterlands, as in South-west England, South Wales, East Anglia, Humberside and northern England are, in the main, separated from each other and from other commuting regions by rural areas. But the main body of hinterlands stretching from South-east England across the

Midlands to industrial Lancashire and West Yorkshire forms one mass and this has been called the English *megalopolis*. Megalopolis is usually associated with the vast interlocking region of cities and their hinterlands on the north-eastern seaboard of the USA, but it is increasingly used as a general term to describe large urban and urban-orientated regions. (The term megalopolis was originally popularised by Lewis Mumford to describe any large shapeless urban area. The term was then used by Jean Gottmann in his book *Megalopolis: the Urbanised North-eastern Seaboard of the United States* (1961) to describe a specific urbanised region.) Such regions do not constitute vast zones of houses and factories; indeed in most megalopolises only a small proportion of the

13.7 The morning rush hour at Liverpool Street Station, London. Voluntary and inertia commuters leave the train after travelling to Central London from the Essex towns of Chelmsford, Colchester, Frinton, Walton and Clacton. Reverse commuters wait to board the train for its return journey.

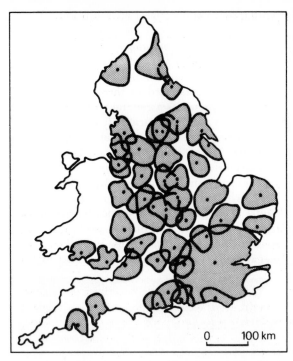

13.8 Generalised commuting hinterlands in England and Wales, 1961. (After Clout, 1972.)

local government areas did not fit the pattern of life and work in the country. The division of England into 79 county boroughs and 45 counties, exercising independent authority and dividing urban areas from rural areas (and hence the places of residence and places of work of millions of people), made physical, social and economic planning very difficult. As a result of this a Royal Commission was set up in 1966 to make recommendations on local government reform, and the report (popularly known as the Redcliffe–Maud Report) was published in 1969. The main conclusions of the report were that the county boroughs and counties (excluding London which was outside the terms of reference of the enquiry) should be replaced by 61 new local government areas, each covering town and country. Three of the largest areas – centred on Birmingham, Manchester and Liverpool – would be called metropolitan areas and would be further subdivided into metropolitan districts. A major criticism of the recommendations was that population size rather than the extent of commuting and service hinterlands

land is truly urban – about 18 % in the case of the English megalopolis. They are, however, urban in a functional sense, i.e. those parts which appear at first sight to be rural are urban in that they act as dormitories for urban employees, they are supply areas for commodities such as dairy produce and water consumed in the urban areas and they are recreation areas for urban people. Such is the degree of decentralisation of both employment and population in the United States, and such is the interrelatedness and overlap between daily urban systems, that it has been postulated that by the year 2000 more than half of the United States' population will live in three giant megalopolises, rather unhappily named Boswash (from Boston to Washington, DC), Chipitts (Chicago to Pittsburgh) and Sansan (San Francisco in Central California to San Diego on the Mexican border).

At the beginning of this chapter it was hinted that problems often arise as circulation becomes more complex. Brief descriptions of post-war developments in England and the United States will illustrate clearly the need for careful planning. It became increasingly obvious in England after World War 2 that the pattern of

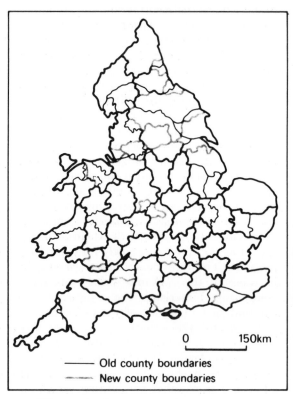

13.9 The new local government map of England and Wales, April 1974.

Old county boundaries
New county boundaries

Table 13.2. *Re-distribution of the total and Black population of the United States, 1960–70*

Type of area	Re-distribution of the total population (%)		Re-distribution of the Black population (%)	
	1960	1970	1960	1970
Large cities	33	31	53	58
Suburban townships outside city boundaries	33	37	15	16
Rural areas	34	32	32	26

had formed the basis of the new administrative structure. Indeed one member of the Commission wrote a minority report suggesting a two-tier system of thirty-five new local government areas (to be called provinces) based much more closely on present and possible future hinterlands, and subdivided into 148 districts.

In the end the government of the day opted for a compromise solution (Fig. 13.9) of 47 counties and 333 districts, and 6 metropolitan counties which are subdivided into metropolitan districts. This system came into operation in April 1974. The new local government map has disappointed most applied geographers because of the failure, for the most part, to match county boundaries with existing and possible future commuting and service hinterlands, thus restricting the effectiveness of planning.

In the United States the problems associated with high levels of circulation are further aggravated by racial strife. Between 1960 and 1970 fifteen of the country's twenty-one largest cities lost population, and much of this loss was the result of the out-migration of families who were, in the main, White and in the middle and upper income brackets. Rapid-transit railways, widespread car ownership, complex motorway systems and decentralisation of employment and retailing have all combined to encourage such residential dispersal. At the same time the large cities have attracted substantial numbers of Black and Spanish Americans and their arrival has tended to accelerate the out-migration of Whites. Thus in the mid-1970s the old cities which grew up in the nineteenth and early twentieth centuries house large numbers of Blacks, while the politically independent suburban communities are predominantly White and middle class (Table 13.2). The Black population of Washington, DC, was 71.1% in 1970. In Detroit it was 43.7%, in Newark 34.1%, Chicago 32.7% and New York City 21.2%.

This residential segregation has given rise to a number of severe problems. The affluent middle classes who use the city's highways, museums, art galleries, golf courses and other institutions and amenities often do not pay city rates. This is a particularly crippling problem to the cities because the relatively poor and often ageing populations demand a high level of health and welfare services. Similarly the cities have been deprived of rates and rents from industry as a result of factory re-location in the suburban communities. If the remaining industry is more heavily taxed to make up this deficit, then accelerated industrial decentralisation is likely to ensue. On the other hand, lowering of taxes to induce industry to stay inevitably leads to reduced city health and welfare services. Another problem arises from the stringent land-use regulations which operate in the suburban communities. By zoning potential residential areas into one-acre and half-acre plots, the lower income groups are effectively excluded through their inability to secure sufficient capital.

It is evident from these brief summaries of trends in England and the United States that sensible physical, economic and social planning can only take place when local government responsibilities are rationalised and the areas which these bodies serve correspond more closely with current or predicted patterns of work and leisure. It is also clear that local government boundaries and responsibilities need to be kept under continuous review.

14 Typologies of migration

Advances in the understanding of the processes and patterns of migration based upon detailed investigations at different scales and in widely different regions have been marked by attempts to summarise these findings in large-scale classificatory models. Such classifications of data into types are called *typologies*. As research has progressed and data have increased in volume, detail and reliability, old typologies have been modified or discarded and others have been proposed.

Most, but not all, typologies take the form of a 'multi-dimensional matrix with some cells empty and some occupied by distinguishable types' (Kosinski and Prothero, 1975, p. 7). In Table 14.1, for instance, two criteria are used: on one axis boundaries crossed are employed and on the other the voluntary or involuntary nature of migration is used. This provides six cells; whether or not all six would be filled by distinctive types would depend upon the region or country under investigation. Besides boundaries crossed and the voluntary or involuntary nature of migration, the following criteria have all been used at various times in constructing typologies:

(i) the temporary or permanent nature of migration;
(ii) the distance of migration;
(iii) the nature of migration (e.g. individual, family, clan, mass);
(iv) the political motivation of migration (e.g. forced, impelled, sponsored, free);
(v) the causes of migration;
(vi) the aims of migration, i.e. whether it is undertaken in order to retain a traditional way of life or to achieve a new way of life;
(vii) the selectivity of migration.

The question naturally arises: why construct typologies? This may be answered from two viewpoints. For the individual scholar they may constitute summaries of the findings of his own investigations, and for planners and politicians they provide the raw materials and guidelines for the drafting of national and regional plans. Detailed proposals in such plans may capitalise on known migratory or circulatory trends; they

Table 14.1. *A simple typology of migration*

	Voluntary	Forced
Intra-regional		
Inter-regional		
International		

Table 14.2. *Petersen's 'general typology of migration'*

Relation	Migratory force	Class of migration	Type of migration	
			Conservative	Innovating
Nature and man	Ecological push	Primitive	Wandering Ranging	Flight from the land
State (or equivalent) and man	Migration policy	Forced Impelled	Displacement Flight	Slave trade Coolie trade
Man and his norms	Higher aspirations	Free	Group	Pioneer
Collective behaviour	Social momentum	Mass	Settlement	Urbanisation

may attempt to contain, slow down or stop them or they may encourage such movements. (See, for instance, Case Study 7 in Part IV.) The examples which follow are selective and emphasis is placed on the most recent classifications.

Examples of typologies

The best-known typology is Petersen's 'General typology of migration', which dates from 1958. (It originally appeared in the *American Sociological Review* but is reprinted in Jansen, 1970.) It is summarised in Table 14.2. This typology hinges on the identification of five broad classes of migration: primitive, forced, impelled, free and mass. Each class of migration is seen to be related to general and specific activating forces and each class of migration is sub-divided into two types: *conservative*, when migrants move in order to retain their previous way of life, and *innovating*, when migrants move in order to achieve a new way or standard of life.

Petersen sees primitive migration as the outcome of man's relationship with his natural environment, in particular his inability to cope with natural forces because of his limited technology. This leads to two types of migration: on the one hand, the conservative wanderings of cultivators and the conservative ranging of gatherers and nomads, and on the other, innovating flight from the land. Petersen cites the Irish migration to the United States following the famine of 1847 as an example of flight from

the land of a 'primitive' people. He points out that they steadfastly avoided the extremely cheap methods of purchasing for farming purposes the publicly owned land in the United States; instead they overwhelmingly went to the great cities and became urban Americans. They stand in contrast to the many rural folk who took part in the mass migrations from Sweden to the United States in the last four decades of the nineteenth century. Many of these went to the northern Midwest, to the states of Minnesota and Wisconsin, and theirs was a conservative migration in that they farmed or became small-town craftsmen and merchants.

Petersen analyses politically motivated migration in the same way. In this case he recognises two classes: impelled migration when the migrants, although under great pressure to migrate, have the power to decide whether or not to leave, and forced migration, when the migrants no longer have that power (see Fig. 14.1). Petersen illustrates the difference between the two by the example of Jewish migration in and from Germany between 1933 and 1945 (and after 1938 in other German-occupied lands). Between 1933 and 1938 the Nazis impelled Jews to migrate from Germany by means of anti-Semitic legislation; between 1938 and 1945 Jews were systematically rounded up and forced to migrate to work-camps and concentration camps. Both of these migrations, using Petersen's criteria, were conservative; the 1933–8 migrations would come under the head-

14.1 Uganda exiles arriving in Britain. Some 30,000 Asians were forced to migrate from Uganda in 1972 as a result of a decision by President Amin. Most were British passport holders and many have settled in Britain.

ing of flight and the later forced migrations are examples of what he calls displacement (see Fig. 14.2). His innovating types of politically motivated migrations are interesting in that the innovating agent is not the migrant himself but the individuals or agencies who, with the backing of prevailing laws and attitudes concerning labour recruitment, organise the migrations. Thus the plantation owners, the colonial powers and their officials were, among others, the innovators in the impelled coolie migrations and the forced slave migrations. Petersen designates these types of movement as innovating because they resulted in changes in work patterns and social patterns.

The vast majority of modern migrations are included in Petersen's last two classes of migration, free and mass. In his definition, free migration consists of individuals and small groups moving of their own free will. There is an element of risk involved in the early stages of such migrations (risk of starvation, non-assimilation, death and so on) and so such migrants set examples for others, who may

eventually transform these small-scale migrations into mass migrations. During periods of mass migration the propensity to migrate appears to be almost inborn in particular groups. Again Petersen differentiates between conservative and innovating migrations. In the case of mass migrations he gives the name settlement to those conservative movements which result in modes of life similar to those at the areas of origin, and he designates as urbanisation those migrations which result in an urban life-style taking the place of a former rural one. The movement of persons from certain Caribbean islands and parts of the Indian sub-continent to the United Kingdom between the end of World War 2 and the first of the Commonwealth Immigrant Acts in 1962 is an example of what began as an innovatory free migration but which was beginning to assume the characteristics of a mass migration until legislation was introduced to reduce the flow of migrants.

A rather different approach to migratory classification is that of Roseman (Roseman, 1971), who places all human movements into

14.2 Displaced persons in the USA after World War 2. These migrants had spent several years in concentration or labour camps during World War 2 and after a further period in displaced persons' camps were finally allowed to settle in the United States.

just two broad classes. The first he calls *reciprocal movements*, and these are circulatory movements such as the journey to work, shopping trips, leisure trips and so on. The second class of movements consists of *migratory movements*, in which Roseman recognises two subtypes: *partial displacement migration* and *total displacement migration*. In a partial displacement migration the location of the home changes but other areas of activity (e.g. place of work, shopping centres visited, and so on) remain largely as before. This is true of much intra-urban migration. In total displacement migra-

tion a move is made to a new location which results in the creation of a completely new set of reciprocal movements.

So far the typologies described have been of general application. There are others which relate to specific continents, countries or regions. A recent attempt to clarify the complexities of human mobility in a particular region has been made for tropical Africa by Gould and Prothero (in Kosinski and Prothero, 1975). In their typology they use the two variables of *space* and *time* (Table 14.3). Space is seen in terms of 'urban' and 'rural', and movements

The vital transition	The mobility transition	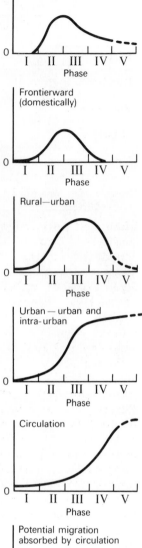

The vital transition

Phase A: *The pre-modern traditional society*
(1) A moderately high to quite high fertility pattern that tends to fluctuate only slightly
(2) Mortality at nearly the same level as fertility on the average, but fluctuating much more from year to year
(3) Little, if any, long-range natural increase or decrease

Phase B: *The early transitional society*
(1) Slight, but significant, rise in fertility, which then remains fairly constant at a high level
(2) Rapid decline in mortality
(3) A relatively rapid rate of natural increase, and thus a major growth in size of population

Phase C: *The late transitional society*
(1) A major decline in fertility, initially rather slight and slow, later quite rapid, until another slowdown occurs as fertility approaches mortality level
(2) A continuing, but slackening, decline in mortality
(3) A significant, but decelerating, natural increase, at rates well below those observed during Phase B

Phase D: *The advanced society*
(1) The decline in fertility has terminated, and a socially controlled fertility oscillates rather unpredictably at low to moderate levels
(2) Mortality is stabilised at levels near or slightly below fertility with little year-to-year variability
(3) There is either a light to moderate rate of natural increase or none at all

Phase E: *A future super-advanced society*
(1) No plausible prediction of fertility behaviour are available, but it is likely that births will be more carefully controlled by individuals – and perhaps by new socio-political means
(2) A stable mortality pattern slightly below present levels seems likely, unless organic diseases are controlled and lifespan is greatly extended

The mobility transition

Phase I: *The pre-modern traditional society*
(1) Little genuine residential migration and only such limited circulation as is sanctioned by customary practice in land utilisation, social visits, commerce, warfare, or religious observances

Phase II: *The early transitional society*
(1) Massive movement from countryside to cities, old and new
(2) Significant movement of rural folk to colonisation frontiers, if land suitable for pioneering is available within country
(3) Major outflows of emigrants to available and attractive foreign destinations
(4) Under certain circumstances, a small, but significant, immigration of skilled workers, technicians, and professionals from more advanced parts of the world
(5) Significant growth in various kinds of circulation

Phase III: *The late transitional society*
(1) Slackening, but still major, movement from countryside to city
(2) Lessening flow of migrants to colonisation frontiers
(3) Emigration on the decline or may have ceased altogether
(4) Further increases in circulation, with growth in structural complexity

Phase IV: *The advanced society*
(1) Residential mobility has levelled off and oscillates at a high level
(2) Movement from countryside to city continues but is further reduced in absolute and relative terms
(3) Vigorous movement of migrants from city to city and within individual urban agglomerations
(4) If a settlement frontier has persisted, it is now stagnant or actually retreating
(5) Significant net immigration of unskilled and semi-skilled workers from relatively underdeveloped lands
(6) There may be a significant international migration or circulation of skilled and professional persons, but direction and volume of flow depend on specific conditions
(7) Vigorous accelerating circulation, particularly the economic and pleasure-oriented, but other varieties as well

Phase V: *A future super-advanced society*
(1) There may be a decline in level of residential migration and a deceleration in some forms of circulation as better communication and delivery systems are instituted
(2) Nearly all residential migration may be of the inter-urban and intraurban variety
(3) Some further immigration of relatively unskilled labour from less developed areas is possible
(4) Further acceleration in some current forms of circulation and perhaps the inception of new forms
(5) Strict political control of internal as well as international movements may be imposed

(a) The phases of the mobility transition and their relationship to the phases of the vital transition

14.3 Zelinsky's hypothesis of the mobility transition.
(Source: Zelinsky, 1971.)

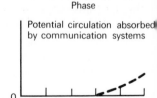

(b) Changes in the volume of different kinds of mobility during the five phases of the mobility transition

Table 14.3. *Gould and Prothero's typology of African population mobility*

Space	Time					
	Circulation				Migration	
	Daily	Periodic	Seasonal	Long-term	Irregular	Permanent
Rural–rural						
Rural–urban						
Urban–rural						
Urban–urban						

Source: Kosinski and Prothero (1975).

within and between each of these spheres are considered. Time is considered in terms of periodicity, ranging from circulatory movements of a few hours' duration to those resulting in a permanent change of residence. In all, the authors recognise four types of spatial movement and six types of temporal movement, thus giving twenty-four separate categories within the typology.

Perhaps the most provocative of recent typologies is Zelinsky's so-called hypothesis of the *mobility transition* (Zelinsky, 1971) shown in Fig. 14.3. Zelinsky summarises his hypothesis in the following terms: 'There are definite patterned regularities in the growth of personal mobility through space–time during recent history, and these regularities comprise an essential component of the modernization process.' Basically he considers that changes in personal mobility through time consist of a number of stages, and that these stages (the mobility transition) closely parallel the stages of the demographic transition, or as Zelinsky terms it, the vital transition. As a nation or region progresses through the various stages of the demographic/ mobility transitions, Zelinsky argues that there are orderly changes in the type as well as the amount of spatial mobility, including chan-

ges in function, frequency, duration, periodicity, distance and types of migrants. As these changes take place they are accompanied by changes in the flow of information and technology so that in the later stages of the transition, potential circulation is cancelled out by improved inter-personal communications such as the telephone, and potential migration by improved commuting opportunities. Zelinsky further suggests that when a country begins to move through the mobility transition at a late date, then (as in the demographic transition) the progression tends to be more rapid than in countries where this happened in the relatively distant past. The author cites Japan as an example of a nation which was in the late stages of Phase I of the mobility transition as late as 1920. Evidence suggests that Taiwan was still in Phase I in 1930 and Sri Lanka as recently as the late 1940s. These countries contrast markedly with England and Wales where the onset of Phase II of the mobility transition began in the second half of the eighteenth century. Although Zelinsky's hypothesis remains largely untested it provides yet another landmark in the attempts to reduce to some semblance of order the apparently chaotic nature of man's spatial mobility.

15

Case Study 7
Regional and local migration in England and Wales, 1851-1971

The growth of population in England and Wales during the nineteenth and twentieth centuries has already been described in Case Study 1 in Part II. As this growth took place there was a substantial re-distribution of the population, and it is the aim of this study to outline the broad migratory trends at regional and local levels since 1851. Obviously this will involve some over-simplification of what were, and continue to be, exceedingly complex processes and patterns. In large areas over relatively short periods of time the trend has not been one of either continuous net in-migration or out-migration but one of fluctuation, as stagnation has succeeded growth and expansion has been followed by decline. The study is in three parts : the period from 1851 to 1911, which was one of rapid rural loss and urban gain ; the period from 1911 to 1951, which saw a reversal of some of the earlier trends ; and the period between 1951 and 1971 in which certain of the trends of the first half of the century accelerated and other trends appeared for the first time.

Migration 1851–1911

During the second half of the nineteenth century the rural areas suffered almost universally from prolonged and heavy depopulation, and gains by migration were recorded only in those rural areas which lay very near to growing urban areas and which became suburbanised.

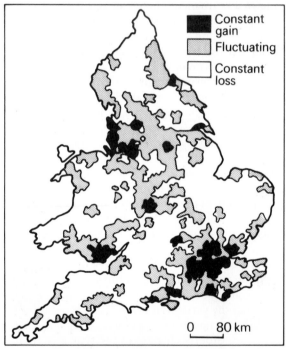

15.1 England and Wales: migrational change 1851–1911. (After Lawton, 1967.)

Fig. 15.1, based on aggregates of migrational changes by decade between 1851 and 1911, shows large areas of severe out-migration stretching across South-west England into the South Midlands, occupying much of East

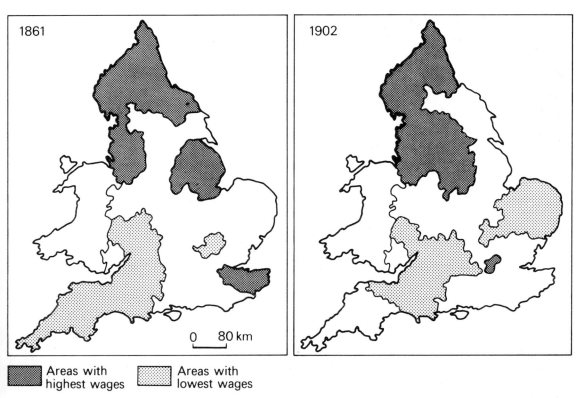

15.2 Weekly wages of agricultural labourers in England in 1861 and 1902. (After Lawton, 1967.)

Anglia, covering Wales outside the coalfields and including large areas in Lincolnshire, the Yorkshire Wolds, the Vale of York and the northern Pennines.

The causes of this heavy out-migration were varied and included both push factors in the rural areas and pull factors at potential destinations. One very important push factor was the decline in the demand for farm labour. During the late eighteenth century and the first half of the nineteenth century, acts of enclosure, reclamation schemes and the more intensive use of farmland actually increased rural population in some areas and kept it stable in others, but after the 1840s the demand for labour for hedging and draining declined. After the 1850s increased mechanisation further reduced the need for manual labour, though, ironically, after 1870 when rural depopulation reached particularly high levels, more mechanisation was called for because of labour shortages.

Not only did agricultural employment opportunities decline but the farmworker was amongst the lowest paid workers. Moreover,

there were marked regional disparities in wage levels. Fig. 15.2 shows broad regional differences in average weekly wages in England in 1831 and 1902. The two maps show clearly that weekly earnings at both dates were lowest in the most remote areas and that wages tended to be higher in the north than in the south. Around the industrial towns and cities, which were predominantly in the Midlands and the north, the intensification of farming for market garden and dairy products also helped to slow down rural decline.

Another aspect of working conditions which prompted out-migration in many rural areas was the decline, as labour surpluses increased, of the old systems of employment. Where this took place, yearly contracts were reduced to monthly, weekly or daily ones, resulting in reduced job security.

Continuously declining rural populations and the penetration of factory-made products into rural areas also caused the out-migration of rural craftsmen, tradesmen and professional people, not only from the villages but also from small country towns. The decline of rurally based trades and professions increased the isolation of the farm labourers among the residual rural population and this provided a further stimulus for out-migration, particularly among the young.

The net result of the prolonged presence of these negative factors was that the number of agricultural labourers (including shepherds) aged over 20 fell (according to calculations made by Lawton, 1967) from 809,000 in 1861 to just over 498,000 in 1911. During the same period the total rural population fell absolutely and proportionally from 9.1 million (45.4 % of the total population) to 7.9 million (21.9 % of the population).

The areas which attracted the rural migrants were London, the fast-growing coalfield industrial areas especially in South Wales, the West Midlands, South Lancashire, West and South Yorkshire, Northumberland and Durham, and the ports of Humberside and Merseyside (Fig. 15.1). All these areas combined the advantages of rapidly growing and varied employment, improved living conditions (especially after the Public Health Act of 1875) and greater opportunities for educational and social advancement. The vast majority of the rural migrants were young and this rapid urban population growth was the result of both in-migration and high birth rates. The combined effects of heavy in-migration and high birth rates resulted in the urban population increasing from just under 9 million in 1851, when it accounted for 54.2 % of the population, to just under 28 million in 1911, by which time 80 % of the population was classified as urban. London, Birmingham, Liverpool and Manchester were the cities in which the greatest absolute population growth took place, followed by Leeds, Newcastle and Sheffield. Among other rapidly growing urban areas were seaside resorts such as Blackpool, Bournemouth and Brighton, inland resorts such as Bath, Cheltenham and Harrogate, 'new towns' such as the industrial creations of Middlesbrough, Scunthorpe and St Helens, and the railway towns of Crewe and Swindon.

Superimposed upon this inter-regional, rural–urban movement was another, the movement of the Irish into the industrial towns and cities of England and Wales. Between 1841 and

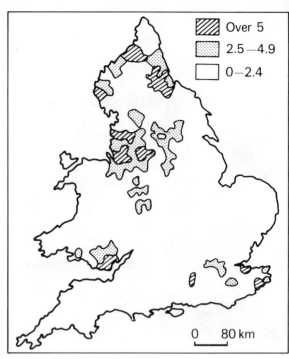

15.3 Distribution of Irish-born persons (as percentage of total population) in England and Wales in 1861. (After Lawton, 1959.)

1851, mainly as a result of the famine of 1847, the Irish-born population in England and Wales grew from 290,000 to 520,000. The next decade also saw a massive immigration and in 1861 the Irish-born population, standing at 602,000, represented 3 % of the total population. After that date, through a decline in immigration and the emigration of substantial numbers of English-domiciled Irish people, particularly to the United States, the Irish-born population steadily declined so that by 1911 there were only 375,000 Irish in England and Wales. Fig. 15.3 shows clearly the preference of the Irish for the industrial districts, particularly those of the west, close to the ports where they had landed. Thus the distribution of the Irish immigrants suggests that they were influenced by distance-decay and by intervening opportunities.

Migration trends between 1911 and 1951

The forty years between 1911 and 1951 saw the continuation of a number of trends from the nineteenth century, and the reversal of a

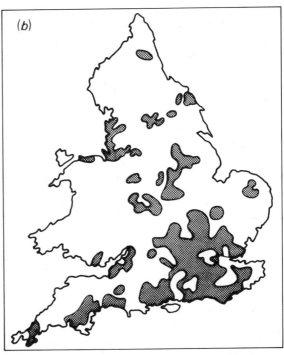

15.4 (a) Population losses by migration, England and Wales 1921–47. (b) Population gains by migration, England and Wales 1921–47. (Simplified from Willatts and Newsom, 1953.)

number of others. Fig. 15.4 (a), showing population losses by migration between 1921 and 1947, indicates clearly the continued depopulation of the remotest and most purely agricultural of the rural areas. Exmoor, Central Wales, northern East Anglia, the Fens, large parts of rural Lincolnshire, the Vale of Pickering, the North York Moors and the northern Pennines all recorded overall net migrational losses during this period. Increased mechanisation, low earnings and isolation continued to be important push factors.

In addition to the rural areas, out-migration became a feature of a number of areas which in the preceding sixty years had been areas of massive and almost continuous population increase. These were the conurbations and the coalfield industrial towns. The migration from the conurbations, which tended to slow down the overall increase of population rather than cause absolute decline, was in large part due to the relocation of population in adjacent rural districts and small towns outside the conurbation boundaries. This took the form of voluntary movement by those seeking rural residential locations while continuing to work in the conurbations, and planned rehousing of populations from inner-city slums. This was a marked feature around London, the West Midland conurbation and Merseyside, especially after 1945. The out-migration from the coalfield towns, which was especially severe in South Wales, Lancashire and North-east England, resulted from the stagnation or decline of the staple industries of these regions, namely cotton spinning and weaving, textile machinery, shipbuilding, coal mining and heavy engineering. Not only did employment fail to expand in the staple industries, but many towns in these regions were dependent upon a narrow range of occupations, often all declining. The contraction of employment opportunities, coupled with continued high levels of natural increase, inevitably led to widespread unemployment and heavy out-migration. The designation in 1934 of three *Special Areas* (the North-east, West Cumberland and South Wales) in which government assistance was available for industrial development, war-time measures to direct industry to new locations, and the reconstitution of the Special Areas as *Development Areas* in 1945 (with the addition of Wrexham, South

Lancashire and North-east Lancashire between 1947 and 1953) all reduced outward migration from the declining areas to some degree although it continued to be important both relatively and absolutely throughout the period.

The most notable features of the map showing areas of net gain through migration in the period 1921–47 (Fig. 15.4*b*) are the concentrations of such areas in the Midlands and, particularly in South-east England. This was the result of the so-called 'drift to the South' from the declining industrial regions. The industrial structure of the towns and cities of the Midlands and South-east England was strikingly different from that of the towns of South Wales and Northern England in two respects. Since the end of the World War I growth industries such as electrical engineering, the manufacture of electronic and radio apparatus, motor vehicle assembly and component manufacturing, aircraft manufacturing, paper making and printing and food products had greatly increased and one-industry towns were far less common. Additionally, service industries such as banking, finance and insurance were overwhelmingly concentrated in the South-east.

Two other features of migration between 1911 and 1951 are worth noting. First, there were significant net gains in rural coalfield areas where deep, concealed coal measures were being exploited for the first time. This was particularly marked in the eastern parts of the Yorkshire, Derbyshire and Nottinghamshire coalfield. Secondly, there were important rural and urban gains, including many retired people, in the coastal areas of Kent, Sussex, Hampshire, Devon, Cornwall, North Wales and Lancashire.

Migration between 1951 and 1971

Since 1951 the most remote Welsh counties and the most northerly English rural counties have continued to suffer migrational losses. Northumberland had the greatest population loss among English counties between 1961 and 1971 and Montgomery and Radnor in Central Wales, which had suffered from severe and continuous out-migration for well over a century, were by 1971 the most thinly populated counties in England and Wales.

There have also been continued losses from the old industrial regions of Northern England and South Wales and from the conurbations and largest cities. Successive British governments since the mid-1940s have initiated and pursued planning policies designed to slow down and eventually eradicate the large-scale migration from the old industrial regions (*Assisted Areas policy*) and to relocate population and industries outside the largest conurbations (*Green Belt and New Town policy*).

Fig. 15.5 shows the distribution of assisted areas and new towns in England and Wales in the early 1970s. By that date, the whole of Wales, almost the whole of Northern England north of Nottingham and much of South-west England were included within the assisted areas. These vary from *Intermediate Areas*, which are growing only slowly economically and are considered to be potential problem areas, to *Development Areas*, which have bad economic and social problems, and *Special Development Areas* in which the economic and social problems are particularly severe. In all these areas government subsidies are available, varying in size according to the type of area and including grants for new industrial buildings, new plant and machinery, capital loans on favourable terms for expansion schemes and grants towards the costs incurred when a business moves to a new area. In addition there are government-built factories for sale or rent at specially reduced rates. Outside the assisted areas industrial development has been restricted by use of the *Industrial Development Certificate* (IDC) policy. This policy, which has operated since 1945, stipulates that new industrial buildings or extensions exceeding a certain size (this has varied over the years as have the areas in which it has been applied) cannot be built without the issue of an IDC by the government, which has powers to refuse certificates in congested areas or areas which it regards as having sufficient industrial development already.

These measures have been successful in promoting industrial development and in slowing down out-migration, but unemployment, substandard housing, derelict land and levels of out-migration are all above the national average in assisted areas, and these areas still lag behind the rest of the country in terms of the rate of creation of new jobs (especially in the service industry sector) and personal income levels.

| New towns | Population (thousands) | | |
Name and date of designation	At designation	1971	Projected total size
1 Stevenage (1946)	7	67	105
2 Crawley (1947)	9	70	79
3 Hemel Hempstead (1947)	21	70	80
4 Harlow (1947)	5	58	90
5 Hatfield (1948)	9	25	30
6 Welwyn (1948)	19	40	50
7 Basildon (1949)	25	77	134
8 Bracknell (1949)	5	34	60
9 Aycliffe (1947)	0	20	45
10 Peterlee (1948)	0	22	30
11 Cwmbran (1949)	12	41	55
12 Corby (1950)	16	48	83
13 Skelmersdale (1961)	10	27	80
14 Redditch (1964)	32	38	90
15 Runcorn (1964)	30	37	90
16 Washington (1964)	20	25	80
17 Newtown (1967)	6	6	13
18 Milton Keynes (1967)	44	46	250
19 Peterborough (1967)	83	87	187
20 Northampton (1968)	131	134	260
21 Warrington (1968)	122	130	202
22 Telford (1968)	70	76	250
23 Central Lancashire (1970)	250	235	500

Special Development Areas
Development Areas
Intermediate Areas
Derelict Land Clearance Areas
Conurbations

15.5 Assisted areas (1972) and new towns (1971) in England and Wales.

The New Towns Act of 1946 was also an important means of regulating population movement and distribution. The towns built during the first phase (1946–50) are overwhelmingly concentrated in the south-east and, with one exception, Corby, they are concerned with either the planned decentralisation of population and employment from Greater London or with the creation of growth points in the assisted areas. The new towns of the second phase (1961–7) are fewer in number, more widely distributed and more diverse in function. Skelmersdale and Redditch are overspill towns, Runcorn is a comprehensive re-development scheme and Washington and Newtown are regional growth centres. The third phase new towns (1967–70) are all expansions of existing medium-sized or large towns and their projected sizes are much greater than those of the towns of the first two phases. Milton Keynes, Peterborough and Northampton are designed to act as counter-magnets to conurbation development in the south-east, and Warrington, Telford and the Central Lancashire new town combine urban renewal schemes with overspill and counter-magnet functions.

The planned relocation of urban populations and voluntary out-migration resulted in a marked decentralisation of population from the conurbations and large cities, particularly in the period 1961–71. In the 1960s, Greater London lost more than 600,000 people and losses were also recorded in the Tyneside conurbation (from 0.86 million to 0.80 million), West Midlands (2.38 million to 2.37 million), South-east Lancashire (2.43 million to 2.39 million) and Merseyside (1.38 million to 1.26 million). Only the West Yorkshire conurbation (1.70 million to 1.73 million) recorded a population increase in the 1960s and significantly this has no related new towns.

In spite of regional and urban planning on a large scale, population and employment have continued to increase most rapidly in the Midlands and South-east England. Between 1951 and 1961 and between 1961 and 1971 the greatest growth of population was recorded in the area south and south-east of a line from the Wash to the mouth of the Severn. One significant difference between the 1950s and the 1960s in this area of marked growth was that the rates of growth of those counties nearest to London which grew very rapidly in the 1950s were lower in the 1960s than those of the outer parts of the region in the East Midlands, East Anglia and the South-west. This change in growth rates suggests that the planned and voluntary population and industrial decentralisation from the inner parts of the Midlands and the South-east is gradually diffusing outwards.

As planned and voluntary dispersal reduced the population of the inner residential districts of the largest cities during the 1950s and 1960s, these areas became increasingly dominated by the least privileged sections of the British population and by immigrant groups. Included in the first group are many infirm and aged persons, unstable and broken families and the homeless. The immigrant groups are dominated by the Irish, whose numbers have risen again in this century and in 1971 stood at just over 675,000, and by coloured immigrants from the so-called New Commonwealth countries, particularly the West Indies, India, Pakistan and Bangladesh. The coloured immigrant population of England and Wales was about 1,120,000 in 1971. In addition, it has been estimated that in 1971 there were about half a million children born in this country of coloured immigrants. At the beginning of the 1970s the West Indians made up the largest coloured immigrant group in the whole of Great Britain (347,000 – including British-born children), followed by Indians (264,000), and Pakistanis including Bangladeshis (173,000). Immigrant arrivals from New Commonwealth countries reached a peak in 1961–2 and were then severely restricted by the Commonwealth Immigrant Acts of 1962, 1965 and 1971. Although push factors such as poverty, overpopulation and unemployment have all been locally important, most experts (see, for instance, Peach, 1968) believe that the demand for labour in Britain has been the dominant reason for most New Commonwealth immigration. These immigrants have avoided the regions of high unemployment in Wales and Northern England and the largest concentrations of both Asian and Caribbean immigrants in 1971 were in London and the West Midlands. In that year London contained 55.5% of the West-Indian-born population and Birmingham a further 13%.

One fear that has been expressed since coloured immigration assumed significant proportions in the late 1950s is that ghettoes will be created of the type and size of those in the United States. In spite of discrimination in the selling of homes and in the allocation of council housing there is clear evidence that West Indian segregation, at least, decreased in the 1960s. The Asian immigrants' attitude to property and community self-sufficiency has, however, meant that they have moved into council housing in only very small numbers and the degree of their segregation within the inner city appears to be increasing.

16

Case Study 8
Migration in the
conterminous
United States, 1960-70

Migration trends in the conterminous United States (the United States excluding Alaska and Hawaii) in the latest inter-censal decade represent a continuation of trends which have been apparent since at least 1930 but which have accelerated markedly since 1950. This study, which complements Case Study 2 in Part II, portrays a country at a late stage in the mobility transition, and shows the influence of the presence of a substantial racial minority on migrational change at regional and local levels.

A close study of Fig. 16.1 and Table 16.1 reveals a number of broad trends. It is clear that there was an enormous amount of rural depopulation during the 1960s which contributed to the absolute population decline in two mainly rural states (North and South Dakota) and below-average population growth in a large number of others. Table 16.1 shows high levels of out-migration from all seven of the mainly agricultural states of the West North Central Division, from five of the eight Mountain states and from Maine, the most northerly and the most rural of the New England states. These states have all been affected, in varying degrees, by farm abandonment, by increased mechanisation and by the consolidation of farm units. For instance, it has been estimated that between 1950 and 1965, 24 million hectares of farmland, an area almost half the size of France, were abandoned for a variety of physical and social reasons. The number of farm workers in the United States has also declined rapidly, from 10 million in 1950 to 4 million in 1970. Similarly, in 1935 there were 6.8 million farms in the country but by 1969 there were less than 3 million and farms over 400 hectares accounted for more than half of the land in farms. These changes in the farm economy have not only resulted in the out-migration of large numbers of farm workers to other regions but have also given rise to a number of important migratory and circulatory movements within the affected states. One result of the decrease in the size of the agricultural labour force has been the decline of large numbers of rural service centres throughout the agricultural interior. As farms have been merged and production methods modernised, rural population densities have fallen dramatically and this, together with the high level of mobility of the residential rural population, has meant that many small-town stores and services have been unable to stay in business. Some of the business people have gone into early retirement and have moved to the outskirts of larger towns. Other rural people, both business men and small farmers, continue to run their farms and businesses on a part-time basis and commute to a second job. It is not unusual, during working hours in agricultural areas within commuting distance of

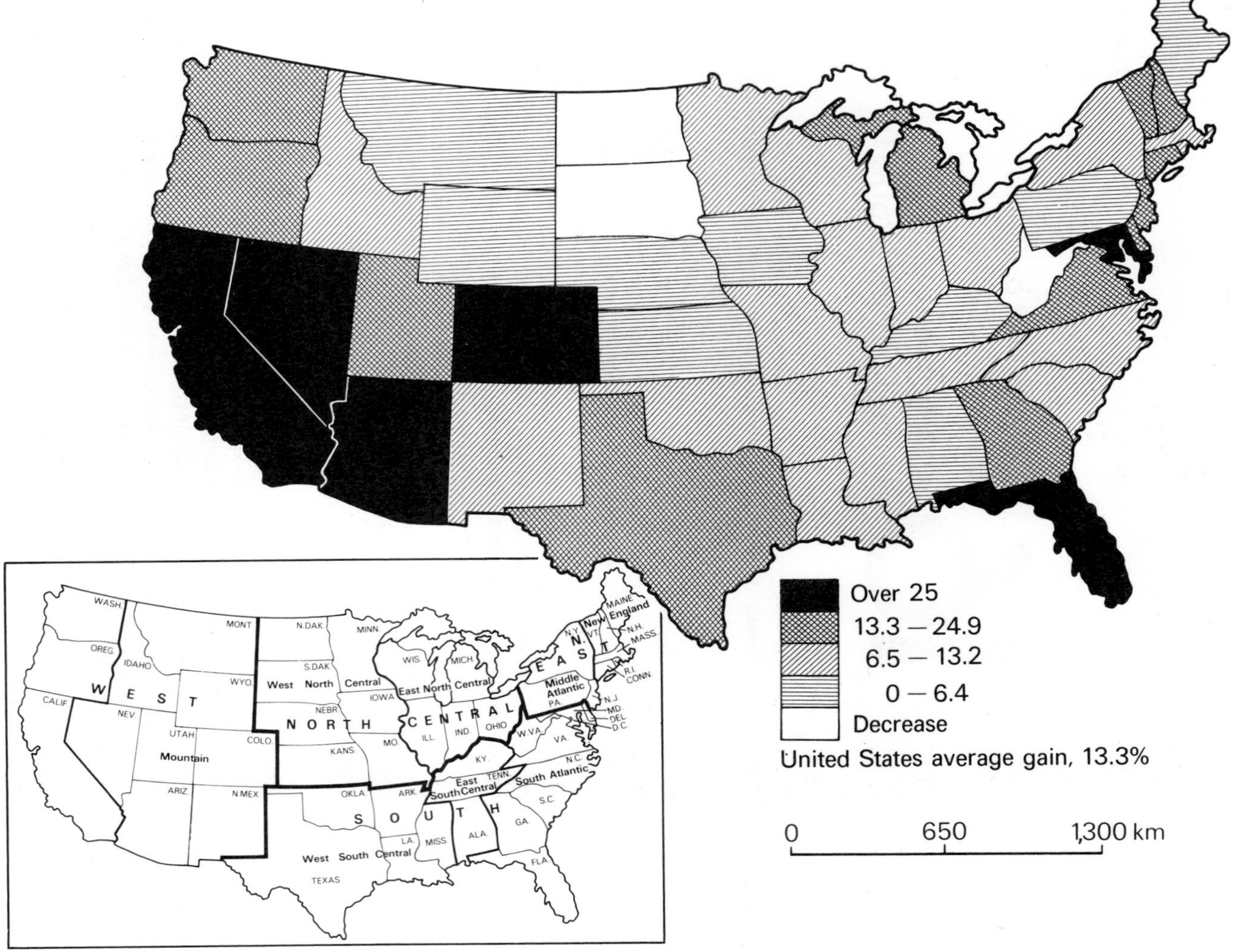

16.1 USA: percentage population change 1960–70, by states. (Sources: US Bureau of the Census, and Davis, 1972.)

Over 25

13.3 — 24.9

6.5 — 13.2

0 — 6.4

Decrease

United States average gain, 13.3%

0   650   1,300 km

Table 16.1. *Net migration*[a] *in the USA 1960–70, by states, divisions and regions*

State	White Number (thousands)	%	Black Number (thousands)	%	State	White Number (thousands)	%	Black Number (thousands)	%
United States	2,234	1.4	−85	−0.5	Maryland	290	11.3	79	15.2
Regions:					District of Columbia	−137	−39.7	36	8.7
Northeast	−520	−1.3	612	20.2	Virginia	206	6.5	−79	−9.7
North Central	−1,272	−2.6	382	11.1	West Virginia	−247	−14.0	−20	−22.2
South	1,806	4.2	−1,380	−12.2	North Carolina	81	2.4	−175	−15.7
West	2,269	8.8	301	27.7	South Carolina	44	2.8	−197	−23.8
New England	205	2.0	72	29.5	Georgia	198	7.0	−154	−13.7
Maine	−69	−7.2	−2	0	Florida	1,340	33.0	−32	−3.6
New Hampshire	68	11.2	0	0	East South Central	−153	−1.6	−560	−20.8
Vermont	14	3.5	0	0	Kentucky	−158	−5.6	1	0.5
Massachusetts	23	0.5	33	29.5	Tennessee	1	0	−51	−8.7
Rhode Island	4	0.5	2	12.2	Alabama	−5	−0.2	−231	−23.6
Connecticut	166	6.8	38	35.4	Mississippi	10	0.8	−279	−30.4
Middle Atlantic	−724	−2.3	510	19.4	West South Central	152	1.1	−282	−10.2
New York	−638	−4.2	396	27.9	Arkansas	38	2.7	−112	−28.7
New Jersey	336	6.1	120	23.3	Louisiana	26	1.2	−163	−15.7
Pennsylvania	−423	−4.0	25	2.9	Oklahoma	−4	−0.2	−3	−2.1
East North Central	−617	−1.9	356	12.3	Texas	92	1.1	−4	−0.3
Ohio	−191	−2.1	45	5.8	Mountain	295	4.5	16	12.6
Indiana	−58	−1.3	32	12.0	Montana	−57	−8.7	0	0
Illinois	−215	−2.4	127	12.2	Idaho	−44	−0.6	0	0
Michigan	−124	−1.7	124	17.3	Wyoming	−39	−12.2	0	0
Wisconsin	−29	−0.8	27	36.1	Colorado	187	11.0	16	40.9
West North Central	−655	−4.4	26	4.6	New Mexico	−120	−13.8	−4	−24.7
Minnesota	−39	−1.2	7	33.3	Arizona	248	21.2	−4	−10.2
Iowa	−189	−6.9	2	6.0	Utah	−16	−1.9	1	0
Missouri	−25	−0.6	14	3.7	Nevada	136	51.5	6	48.0
North Dakota	−94	−15.2	1	0	Pacific	1,974	10.2	286	29.7
South Dakota	−92	−14.0	0	0	Washington	220	8.0	10	20.0
Nebraska	−76	−5.6	2	7.3	Oregon	145	8.4	4	20.9
Kansas	−139	−6.7	−1	−0.9	California	1,528	10.6	272	30.7
South Atlantic	1,807	9.0	−538	−9.2	Alaska	22	12.0	0	0
Delaware	32	8.4	4	6.6	Hawaii	58	28.8	1	0

Source: US Bureau of the Census.
[a] Net migration comprises both net immigration from abroad and net inter-regional, inter-divisional and inter-state migration according to area shown. Minus signs denote net out-migration. In column 3, 0 = less than 1,000; in column 4, 0 = less than 0.5%.

towns and cities, to see clusters of cars parked at the intersections of minor and major roads. These indicate the existence of car pools formed by former full-time rural workers. Each man drives his car to the main highway, parks it, and the whole group travels in one car for the remainder of the long journey to work.

Another interesting outcome of the changing farm economy has been the emergence of the so-called 'sidewalk farmer' and the 'suitcase farmer'. The former is the result of the acqui-sition (by purchase or by rent) by one farmer of a number of scattered areas of farmland. When this occurs there is no longer a clear optimum location for his farm residence and in such circumstances many farmers – particularly in the Great Plains where most of the year's work in wheat farms may be com-pleted in a two-month period – prefer to live in towns (hence the expression sidewalk farmer) and travel to their scattered holdings. The suitcase farmer is essentially a long-distance version of the sidewalk farmer. When farm units are held in different counties or even in different states the farmer will visit his distant holdings, often by light private aeroplane (Fig. 16.2), perhaps only two or three times a year, to supervise operations such as planting, spraying and harvesting.

Another region which has suffered greatly from rural depopulation is the South. From Louisiana and Arkansas eastward to Georgia and the Carolinas rural populations, in this case mainly Black, have left the countryside in large numbers. Several factors have combined to initiate and maintain the high level of Black outmigration from the region. Important push factors are the open discrimination practised against the Blacks and the grinding poverty of the rural slums in which large numbers of southern Blacks live. At the end of the Civil War in 1865 many Blacks became share-croppers or share-tenants on smallholdings which were created from the former plantations. (Share-croppers receive land, seed, fertiliser and implements from the landlord and in return pay him up to half of the value of the cash crop. Share-tenants provide their own seed, fertiliser and implements and pay a smaller proportion of the value of the cash crop.) They had little agricultural education or capital, and in most areas successive generations of Black farmers fought a losing battle against the damage done by heavy rains on farms where no cover crop was grown and against the ravages of the boll weevil. In the face of such difficulties many farmers continued to live on under- or unfarmed smallholdings and commuted to non-agricultural employment. Others gave up their tenancies or sold or rented their freeholds, and migrated.

These rural migrants have, since about 1900, been attracted in large numbers to urban centres within the South and in other parts of the country. Within the South, the industrial cities of the Gulf Coast of Texas and Louisiana have

16.2 A farmer in a light aeroplane over farmland in Iowa.

been and continue to be important magnets, as are the growing towns and cities of Florida and the textile, timber-processing and tobacco-curing towns of the Piedmont and inner coast plain of Georgia and the Carolinas. Industrial regions outside the South have also exerted a considerable pull, and Table 16.1 shows that the period 1960–70 saw the continued migration of large numbers of Blacks to the industrial states of the Middle Atlantic, East North Central and Pacific divisions. One particularly interesting feature of the northward and westward movement of southern Blacks is that the area of origin has had a marked effect on migratory direction and destination. Movements from the South Atlantic division have been predominantly to the cities of the north-east coast, while those from the southern parts of the East South Central division have been mainly northward to the industrial cities of the Midwest. Similarly many Black migrants from the West South Central division have headed for the west coast (see Fig. 16.3). These preferences suggest that,

although all the migration distances are long, distance-decay operates to some degree in Black migration and that the cumulative effects of positive feedback influence the direction and strength of migration streams from the region.

The Appalachian states of West Virginia, Kentucky and Pennsylvania are also in varying stages of population decline and stagnation and Table 16.1 reveals that these states experienced substantial net losses by migration between 1960 and 1970. Large areas within these states and parts of adjacent states lying within the Appalachians suffer from the classic symptoms of economic decline. Their economies are too dependent on occupations in which the demand for labour and/or their products is sluggish or actually declining. In Appalachia these industries are agriculture, coal-mining, steel-making and timber-processing. This problem is compounded by poor communications. Appalachia is a region of long, narrow valley lowlands separated by high, sinuous ridges. In the past traffic has tended to move round the region

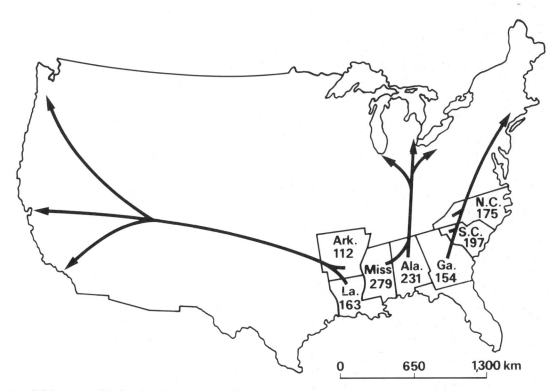

16.3 USA: major Black migration streams. Figures denote net out-migration (in thousands) from seven southern states 1960–70.

rather than through it even though it lies between the prosperous regions of the north-east coast and the Midwest. The problems of Appalachia were brought to the notice of millions of Americans during John F. Kennedy's presidential primary campaign in West Virginia in 1959. The region's problems had a lasting effect on Kennedy and during his presidency and that of his successor President Johnson a series of Acts of Congress were passed, designed to combat the problems of regions of marked poverty and unemployment. The early acts were of a general nature but in 1965 the Appalachian Regional Development Act was passed. Most of the federal funds made available by this Act have been used on highway construction to break down the isolation of the region. The remainder of the money has been used on a variety of projects including the rehabilitation of scarred coal-mining landscapes, water resource surveys and soil erosion control. Since the first acts of the Kennedy administration in 1961 there has been less unemployment, less poverty and less out-migration, but these are still severe and mark out Appalachia as one of the most severely distressed areas in the United States.

So far several broad regions of population decline have been identified. Migrants from these regions together with migrants from other regions joined to form the important seaward and southward migrations which characterised the 1950s and which continued at a high level in the 1960s. One of these movements was to the cold northern states of the Manufacturing Belt. (The Manufacturing Belt, a term coined by Sten de Geer in 1927, refers with minor exceptions to the industrialised parts of the East North Central, Middle Atlantic and New England divisions. In 1969, 55.5% of the employment in manufacturing in the United States was in those three census divisions.) Large numbers of Black migrants, in particular, entered these states, but in most cases there were even higher rates of out-migration among the White population, resulting in slight overall net migration losses. Black migrants have been attracted to these northern states because of the scale and diversity of manufacturing and service employment and the earning potential which accompanies such a concentration of employment opportunities. Indeed, nowhere else in the United States is there a region of comparable size in which the average earnings of the inhabitants are so consistently high. This is partly explained by the fact that the so-called growth industries are strongly represented here, particularly the electrical equipment, rubber and plastics, transport equipment and machinery industries. (Growth industries in the United States at the end of the 1960s, defined by such measures as rate and size of employment growth and rate of growth of value added by manufacturing, were ordnance and accessories, electrical equipment, transport equipment, chemicals and allied products, rubber and plastics products, instruments and related products, and machinery manufacture.) In fact, six out of every ten American workers in growth industries are in the states which make up the Manufacturing Belt. The consequences of the northward and city-ward movements of millions of Blacks were discussed in Chapter 13.

In spite of the great attractions of the Manufacturing Belt, the greatest net migration gains occurred in the Pacific coast states, in Florida and in the mountain states of the south-west, including Colorado. All these states combine environmental and economic advantages which have attracted both people and industries. Of these states, Florida had the second greatest net migration gain (1,308,000 or 26.8%), attracting almost two-thirds of the 2 million White Americans who migrated from the northern states to the South. Among the migrants were many retired persons and in 1970 in twelve of Florida's sixty-seven counties, persons of 65 years or over constituted 20% or more of the population – twice the national average.

The large number of migrants who have gone to the Pacific coast states reflects their rapid advance in national importance since 1940. Since that date the expansion of employment has been continuous and significantly it is in growth industries that the largest developments have taken place. However, the growth and continued importance of manufacturing, which is overwhelmingly concentrated in Seattle, San Francisco and Southern California, is closely related in many cases to government contracts. This is particularly true of Southern California where there is a strong dependence upon ordnance and aerospace industries. Government support for the expansion of these industries began in the years immediately before World

War 2, and the related research and development activity, skilled labour, almost unlimited space for expansion and good flying weather have continued to attract government contracts and so the process of expansion in manufacturing and related service industries has continued. The concentration of highly technical industries on the Pacific coast has meant that since the 1940s thousands of scientists, technologists and engineers have migrated there. In 1968, for example, there were more scientists employed in California (13.7% of the national total) than in any other state. Outstanding career prospects in research and in industry, high salaries and an attractive climate have pulled migrants, particularly to Southern California, from all parts of the USA and Canada and from many other parts of the world.

Regions of continuously expanding employment inevitably attract the poorest and least-skilled members of society, and California in particular has become a magnet for many thousands of America's poor. Spanish-Americans, including both native Americans from the south-west (called Chicanos) and legal and illegal immigrants from Mexico, form a substantial minority in the state. Since the 1920s they have been the mainstay of California's 'army' of itinerant fruit and vegetable pickers (Fig. 16.4) and such workers were estimated to number 250,000 in 1975. Another important group of mainly poor migrants to California in the 1960s were, as already mentioned, Blacks from the western parts of the South. Only New York state had a larger net in-migration of Blacks in the 1960–70 intercensal period. Like the Black migrants to New York, those moving to California have settled mainly in the large metropolitan areas, especially Los Angeles county which in 1970 contained more than half of the state's Black population.

One very significant type of migration which continued at a massive level in the 1960s was the

16.4 Farm labourers of Spanish-American descent harvesting celery near San Diego, California.

movement of Americans from the biggest cities to suburban and rural communities at and beyond the urban periphery. The major causes and consequences of the migrations from cities to suburbs in the United States have already been discussed in Chapter 13, but urban-to-rural movements have so far received no attention. In the continental interior and in large parts of the South where urban influences are relatively remote, most counties have usually gone through three major phases of population change: an early stage of pioneer settlement and population growth, followed by a period of population stability, sometimes short and sometimes protracted, and finally a period of population decline varying greatly in its severity. It is now clear that many rural counties within commuting distance of the largest cities have entered a fourth phase in which substantial population growth has taken place (Fig. 16.5). Rural counties which have entered this fourth phase are particularly numerous in the southern half of New England, in Upper New York state, Indiana, Ohio, southern Michigan and north-eastern Illinois. The extent of this urban–rural migration is further underlined when it is realised that while the total rural population has remained remarkably stable at between 50 and 54 million for the last 50 years, the farm population (as opposed to the non-farm population) within the total rural population has fallen from 60 % to 20 % in the same period.

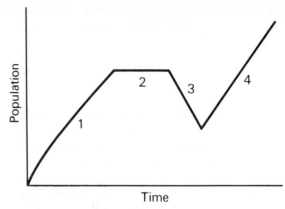

1. Rapid early growth
2. Stability
3. Decline (rural depopulation)
4. Substantial growth of non-farm population

16.5 USA: rural counties: stages in the population cycle. (Source: Zelinsky, 1962.)

The period 1960–70 was one of great migratory change in the United States and the flows outlined in this study constitute only the most striking of many complex and often counter-balancing movements. The problems of classifying the major migratory streams which have been identified and described in this chapter will be posed in one of the exercises in Part V.

17

Case Study 9
Some aspects of population migration in East Africa

A basic problem in discussing patterns of migration in many parts of the world, as has already been indicated, is the limited amount of information available. Detailed population data concerning the major countries of East Africa – Kenya, Uganda and Tanzania (see Fig. 17.1) – are confined mainly to the period since 1945, and even these provide only limited information concerning migration. Thus comment on this area must often be couched in qualitative rather than quantitative terms and conclusions drawn from available evidence can, in some cases, only be tentative. In this study, attention is focused on some aspects of the migrations which have occurred in colonial and more recent times in the context of more general changes in East Africa, in an attempt to indicate something of the significance of migratory movements in the overall economic and social development of this group of LDCs.

The present population of East Africa is a complex mixture of peoples, including significant minority groups of European and Asian origin who moved into the area mainly after the beginning of the colonial era in the late nineteenth century. The African population is generally considered to derive from four main ethnic sources: the Bantu, Nilotic, Nilo-Hamitic and Hamitic peoples who occupied the East African area as a result of migrations from other parts of the continent in the pre-colonial period. These ethnic divisions are based primarily on linguistic differences and provide broad, rather vague groupings within a population which has a very complex cultural background.

The most important group numerically, the Bantu, today occupies most of Tanzania, much of southern Uganda and extensive areas of south and central Kenya, and includes many of the main tribal groupings such as the Kikuyu, Kamba and Luhya of Kenya, the Sukuma and Chagga of Tanzania and the Ganda and Kiga of Uganda. The Bantu peoples appear to have moved into East Africa from the west, possibly as shifting cultivators, prior to the fifteenth century. The other major groups all migrated southwards into the area from a broad zone stretching from the White Nile basin to the Horn of Africa. These southward-moving groups probably all had pastoral economies at some stage but, whereas pastoralism is still dominant amongst some groups such as the Nilo-Hamitic Maasai of central Kenya and northern Tanzania, and the Hamitic Rendille-Galla peoples of northern Kenya, other groups such as the Nilotic Luo of western Kenya have adopted cultivation as a major part of their economy.

Thus, by the late nineteenth century, when European powers were attempting to acquire territory in Africa to develop their colonial

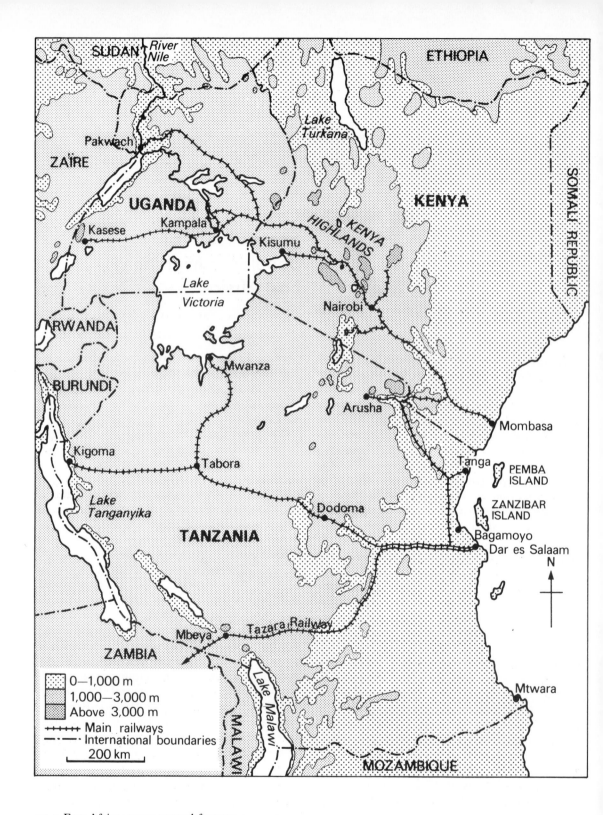

17.1 East Africa: some general features.

empires, most of East Africa was settled by groups of people in a pattern which, though strongly influenced by physical factors such as the need of cultivators for a fairly permanent water supply, was closely related also to the history of migratory patterns in the area. Fig. 17.2 indicates the migration routes within one East African state, Kenya, and shows the present location of some of the main tribal groups.

The situation at this time was by no means stable, however, and though movement has been restricted in more recent times, border conflicts between Somalia and Kenya and Somalia and Ethiopia in the post-colonial period largely reflect the continuing migration of the Hamitic Somali.

Some international influences on migration

One of the most striking features of the pattern of settlement which had developed by the nineteenth century was the massive area of central Kenya and northern Tanzania dominated by the Maasai, sometimes described as a Maasai sea washing against the islands of land dominated by other groups such as the Kikuyu, Kamba and the Chagga peoples, who occupied areas of higher, more easily cultivable land marginal to the drier plateaux of the Maasai area. It is interesting to speculate to what extent the warlike Maasai pastoralists formed a major obstacle to the development of another type of migration in this period. Arab traders, long established in the coastal regions, developed important routes inland for the forced migration of slaves, as well as for other profitable items such as ivory, but appear to have favoured routes which avoided the Maasai lands. The most important route from the coast to the interior in the mid-nineteenth century was from Bagamoyo and neighbouring coastal villages to the territory of the Nyamwezi, near the present town of Tabora, to Lake Tanganyika (see Fig. 17.1). Even the powerful state of Buganda to the north-west of Lake Victoria seems to have been linked to the coast principally by the 1,600 km-long route from Bagamoyo through Nyamwezi territory rather than by a more direct route through Maasai territory, so obviously the Maasai formed at that time a very significant obstacle to movement.

Towards the end of the nineteenth century major changes began to occur as a result of increased European interest in the area. These changes included the development of more modern communication links between the coast and interior, one of which was the railway from Mombasa to Kisumu on Lake Victoria (see Fig. 17.1) which was completed in 1902. This followed a route directly through the previously avoided Maasai territories. These posed few problems for the European partly because the Maasai were troubled by the effects of major rinderpest epidemics affecting their cattle, by smallpox and by internal strife at the time railway construction began. Other railways were constructed further south, in what is now Tanzania (see Fig. 17.1), but none of these had quite the same impact as the Mombasa–Kisumu line, which led to the transformation of the economy of the Kenya Highlands. These highlands, with a climate pleasantly modified by their elevation and with areas of fertile volcanic soils, offered a considerable attraction to European farmers once the railway had been constructed to provide an outlet to world markets for agricultural products like coffee and sisal. The colonial government's action in alienating land for European settlers, much criticised in more recent times, provided a further strong pull factor, and in the early twentieth century European migrants moved in to begin farming here in considerable numbers. Not all of them came directly from Europe and a noteworthy migration stream was that of Boer farmers from South Africa, for whom the positive factors at their Kenyan destination were supplemented by a strong negative factor in South Africa; the discontent occasioned by the political situation following the Boer War. At the end of the First World War additional incentives were offered to demobilised British soldiers who could receive farms of up to 160 acres on a 999-year lease at a minimal rent and this occasioned a further stream of immigrants.

By 1920 a situation had been reached in Kenya whereby the ebb and flow of traditional African migration had been largely restricted as the result of the creation of 'Native Reserves' for the different tribal groups. The formerly powerful Maasai had been confined to an area much smaller than that they had previously dominated and the stream of European migrants

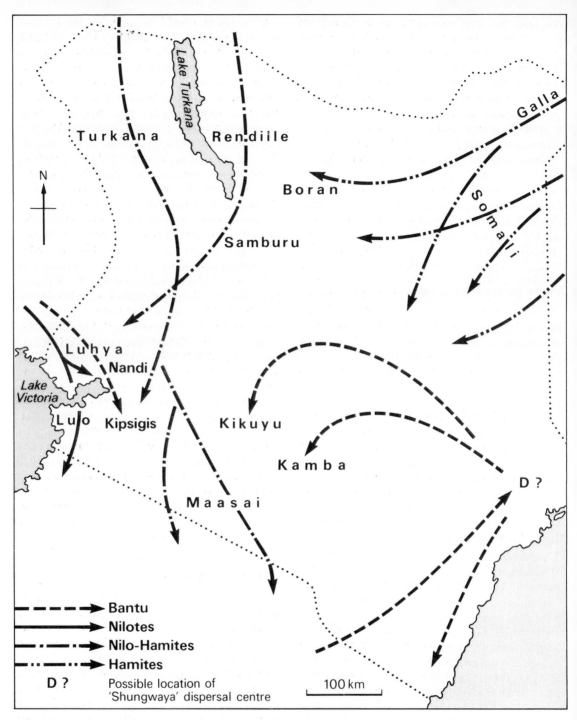

17.2 Kenya: migration routes of main ethnic groups and location of some tribal groups. (NB Lines of migration and location of tribal groups are all approximate.) 'Shungwaya' is thought to have been a secondary dispersal centre for Bantu groups who had moved north into that area but later moved either west into the present Kikuyu–Kamba areas or south again towards Tanzania, possibly as a result of contact with Hamitic groups.

had occupied much of the best agricultural land in the Kenya Highlands and initiated the development of large-scale commercial agriculture. This has since affected both the general economy of the country and, less directly, the lives of many Africans who were previously involved in subsistence activities.

Railway construction also resulted in the migration of many Asians to Kenya. The term 'Asian' as used in East Africa normally denotes people originating from the Indian subcontinent, and labourers were brought in by the British from that area to work on the Mombasa–Kisumu railway. The terms of their indenture gave the labourers the option of being returned to India or discharged in East Africa when they completed their term of employment. The great distance between India and Kenya, the cost of travel and the mental obstacles raised by the considerations involved in travelling to a distant and largely unknown land would normally have provided major barriers to a migration of this distance, but the provision of transport and the terms of employment persuaded more than 30,000 to travel to Kenya to work as railway labourers. Approximately 6,700 of these remained in East Africa when their term of employment ended, about 2,000 continuing to work on the railway but many becoming traders and so filling an economic and social niche between the European and African communities. Other Asians later joined the migratory stream from India to Kenya without similar incentives, being attracted by the opportunities for economic advancement. By 1913 there were some 25,000 Asians in Kenya, a total which had reached more than 175,000 by the time independence was achieved in 1963. Asians also migrated to Uganda and Tanzania but in smaller numbers.

In more recent years many Asians and Europeans have emigrated from Kenya and the other East African countries, particularly in the period immediately before and since independence. (Uganda became independent in 1962. Tanzania was formed in 1964 by the amalgamation of Tanganyika (independent since 1961) and Zanzibar (independent since 1963).) Much of this emigration has been motivated by strong negative factors in the zone of origin rather than positive factors at the destinations of the migrants. These negative factors have included fear of what would happen in the changed political situation after independence, the problem for many farmers of European origin in Kenya that their land was likely to be taken away from them for re-allocation to African farmers, and the general economic changes incurred when governments tried to provide greater economic opportunities for Africans, often at the expense of Asians or Europeans. The most dramatic event which could be counted as a negative factor of this kind was probably the decision in 1972 by President Amin of Uganda to expel almost all the Asians in Uganda who were not registered as Uganda citizens. This gave rise to a forced migration of some 30,000 people from Uganda in a period of a few weeks, many of them emigrating to Britain (see Fig. 17.3). Many Kenyan Asians have also migrated to Britain but over a much longer period of time. Several hundred non-citizen Kenyan Asians have been given notice to leave each year since 1967 by the Kenya government and many families have also left in anticipation of being in this situation at some future date or because of other difficulties. Approximately half the Asian population of Kenya in 1963 had left the country after ten years of independence, the choice of Britain as a destination being partly related to perceived opportunities in Britain. Another strong factor was the simple fact that there are fewer legal obstacles preventing entry to Britain than is the case for many other countries so far as these particular migrants are concerned, since most of them have British passports.

Modern migration

Before the period of colonial rule in East Africa some regional economic differences already existed as a result of the varied physical nature of the area and the cultural differences between the groups who had migrated into it. During colonial times, however, much more distinct regional disparities developed, largely as a result of the varied impact of commercial economic influences on different areas. Contrasts between rural areas occupied by Africans and those settled by Europeans were particularly marked but the gradual growth of towns gave rise to an even greater contrast, that between rural and urban areas. As inequalities of eco-

17.3 Closed Asian stores in Central Kampala. One of the most immediate consequences of the departure of Asians from Uganda was the closure of numerous stores in all the main commercial centres, including over half the shops in Kampala the capital. Some, but by no means all, of these shops have since been re-opened under African ownership.

nomic opportunities developed between different areas so migration between such areas tended to grow, with Africans moving in search of paid employment in commercial farming areas or towns.

Detailed analysis of inter-regional migrations in Kenya based on the 1962 census and other contemporary source materials (see Ominde, 1968) showed something of the nature of such movements. More recent information from later censuses and other sources in each of the East African countries has helped to clarify this. During the colonial period, migration from one rural area to another was dominated by the movement of Africans to work as labourers on the European farms and plantations in areas like the Kenya Highlands or the Asian sugar plantations near Lake Victoria in Uganda. Although the ownership of such farms has often changed since independence was achieved, the pattern of migrations has tended to continue.

Not all migration from one rural area to another was directed towards land held by non-Africans even in the colonial period, however, for as some African groups adopted commercial farming practices so in-migration from other areas developed, as in the migration from many parts of Uganda to the cotton and coffee farms of the Ganda. (For a study of recent migration in Uganda see Masser & Gould, 1975.) In more recent times, however, migration from rural to urban areas has tended to be increasingly significant, to the extent that all three East African governments have shown some concern at the rates of urban growth, much of which has resulted from in-migration.

In the early 1970s Kenya's urban population was increasing at more than 7 % per annum and already most of the population living in Kenya's largest cities were migrants, born outside these cities. Patterns of migration are difficult to define in detail because of the limited data available but there is some evidence to suggest that distance-decay operates, with the majority of migrants moving relatively short distances to their destination. The situation is complex, however, and is dependent on many factors in addition to the distance between origin and destination and the cost of moving between them. There is, for example, fairly clear evidence that different tribal groups react differently to migration opportunities. The Maasai, despite their long history of migratory–circulatory movements, have shown little tendency to migrate to urban areas whereas their neighbours, the Kikuyu, have moved to the towns in large numbers. Such differential migration would appear to be strongly related to what Mabogunje called the rural control subsystem (see p. 89) which, in addition to exercising strong influences against movement outside the tribal group, in the case of the Maasai, also affects an individual's perception of what is attractive in life and in what terms success in life can be measured. The fact that, as one recent survey showed, urban migrants obtained an average income 182% larger than their rural income during the first three months after migration may be of little significance to a Maasai cattle-herder even if he is aware of this.

Migration is selective not only in terms of ethnic groups, however, but also in other ways. A study of the eleven largest towns of Kenya in the early 1970s found that 62% of the in-migrants were male and that 80% of the male migrants were aged less than 30 at the time of migration. A survey of the urban labour force in Tanzania about the same time (*Annual Manpower Report, Tanzania*, 1971) also emphasised that migrations were selective by age and sex, but produced rather different results from the Kenyan study mentioned. It again emphasised the youthful nature of the in-migrants but suggested that there had been a dramatic change in the sex composition of the migration stream, which was heavily male-dominated in the mid-1960s but showed in 1971 a slight majority of women migrants. This increase in the proportion of women migrants is common in other LDCs and reflects the fact that men are increasingly bringing their families to town, often marrying young women from their 'home' area shortly after the time of their own migration. This is a sign of the increasing

stability of the urban labour force, for traditionally many migrants to urban areas have returned to their rural homes after a few years and left their family at home throughout their period of urban residence.

Another type of female migrant of increasing importance in Tanzania – and other parts of East Africa – is the unmarried woman in search of employment in the urban areas. Many such migrants are better educated than the majority of married female migrants and indicate another aspect of differential migration, selectivity on the basis of education. In fact, migration of both men and women in Tanzania appears to be selective of people with some formal education, reflecting the pattern of better employment opportunities for the educated in urban rather than rural areas. It is also the consequence of the increased expectations which tend to result from education and which can rarely be satisfied in rural areas.

Table 17.1 indicates what people interviewed in a 1971 Tanzanian survey considered to be their main reason for moving to town. This emphasises the importance of employment opportunities and family links as motives for migration though it possibly fails to bring out some of the negative factors in the home area which may have influenced the decision to migrate. Investigations in both Uganda and Kenya have tended to stress the importance of land-shortage and lack of opportunities in the 'home' area as push factors.

The 1971 Tanzanian survey also contained information concerning the geographical origins of urban migrants. Of the seven towns studied, all but one (Arusha) received the largest group of in-migrants from the regions for which they were the main economic centre, while the next-largest group came from adjacent regions and the smallest proportion of the total from more distant regions. Thus, in very general terms, this pattern suggests the operation of distance-decay in migration. It was apparent that those who travelled furthest tended to be better educated than short-distance migrants, a pattern of differential migration which often occurs in other parts of the world.

About 60% of all migrants had moved directly from their place of birth (usually in a rural area) to the town in which they were resident at the time of the survey. Where stepwise mi-

Table 17.1 *Main reasons given by Tanzanian urban migrants for moving to town (all statistics are percentages unless otherwise indicated)*

Town	Main reasons for migration									Total number interviewed
	Government transfer	Transfer in other employment	For education	To do job already arranged	To seek employment	Accompanied parents	With husband	On visit	Others	
Dar es Salaam	3	2	5	3	25	19	25	11	7	2,796
Tanga	4	2	6	4	25	19	25	9	7	550
Arusha	5	5	4	8	28	17	23	8	3	284
Mwanza	1	4	4	5	24	22	25	11	5	521
Tabora	4	6	4	3	19	21	26	12	3	178
Dodoma	8	3	3	6	20	21	26	12	4	170
Mbeya	7	4	8	4	14	14	26	12	13	152
Total	3	3	5	4	25	18	25	11	6	4,651

Based on *Annual Manpower Report, Tanzania*, 1971, p. 98.
Rounding of totals means that some percentages do not total 100 for individual towns.

gration was apparent, migrants had normally made few such steps and had tended to stay for fairly long periods at any stopping place. The most mobile of the population, in the sense of those who had moved most often to new residences, like those who travelled furthest, tended to be among the better educated of the migrant population.

The increasing amount of migration in East Africa, especially that from rural to urban areas, is seen as a major problem by the various individual governments. All three have undertaken rural development schemes of some kind largely in an attempt to stem the flow of people from the countryside to towns which, at their present stage of development, are incapable of coping effectively with the influx. The amount of migration and its selective nature have several major consequences in this situation.

First, there are often insufficient employment opportunities in the urban areas to meet the needs of the in-migrants. This results in unemployment, with its attendant dissatisfaction, or under-employment where more people are employed to carry out a task than is necessary and consequently all tend to receive inadequate payment for the achievement of decent living standards. Ultimately this situation may drive some people to become beggars – a common

feature of the largest cities – or to become criminals. A whole range of problems may result from the shortage of employment opportunities but the situation is made worse by the failure of urban authorities, largely through their sheer lack of wealth, to provide adequate housing (see Fig. 17.4), health, education and other facilities for the increasing urban population. One result has been the growth of 'shanty towns' such as that in the Mathare valley in Nairobi, where thousands of people live in houses made from any materials they can acquire and where basic needs of light, heat, water, sewerage and other facilities are provided inadequately or not at all. Only recently have town planners begun to accept that shanty towns are an almost unavoidable element of city life in LDCs and therefore that better results may be achieved by providing help to improve them rather than by attempting to destroy them.

The selective nature of migration to the urban areas creates other problems. The male–female imbalance in most towns (see the population pyramids for some Tanzanian towns, Fig. 17.5) and the lack of normal family relationships can create obvious social difficulties. One side effect of this has been the development of prostitution and venereal disease as major problems in the larger towns. The considerable

17.4 A street in Nairobi. This view is typical of many of the poorer parts of African cities, with its badly maintained buildings, varied construction materials and muddy, uneven road surface. It is far from representing the worst conditions in urban Africa, however, and might be regarded as a desirable area by many migrants to the city or the poorer inhabitants of Nairobi's shanty settlements.

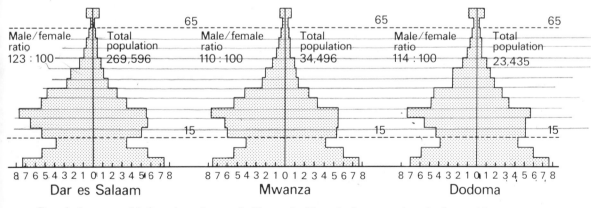

17.5 Population pyramids for selected towns in Tanzania. Note the large numbers in the working age groups and the male/female imbalance. In the 25–29 age group, the proportion of males to females in Dar es Salaam is 137:100, in Mwanza 139:100 and in Dodoma 131:100. (Totals of population aged more than 75 years are not given in separate five-year age groups.) (Source: Census of Tanzania, 1967.)

numbers of educated people who fail to find employment or to achieve living standards in keeping with their education or expectation can also be a source of political problems, though these have so far been of rather less significance in East Africa than in some areas of Latin America and Asia. Obviously if there is a continuation of the trend for increased female migration noted in the Tanzanian survey mentioned earlier and the development of more stable family relationships in urban areas then many of these problems may be lessened.

In the rural areas from which many migrants have moved, both economy and society have been considerably affected by the loss of the younger, better educated men to the towns. Out-migration of this kind has obviously affected agriculture even in areas where women are responsible for much of the agricultural work. Possibly even more important though has been the tendency in many groups for the complex web of relationships and activities which formed the basis of traditional life to break down. Moreover, returning migrants often refuse to accept many traditional ideas, having learnt new values during their time in the urban areas. Tensions have therefore developed in many groups and migration has often encour-aged change in the rural areas of origin as well as in the urban destinations. Governments in all three East African states are now concerned with rural development schemes, as has already been mentioned, but this concern is most marked in Tanzania. Here a virtual rural revolution is in progress through the development of 'ujamaa' villages based largely on self-help principles, which are an attempt to raise rural living standards and so avoid the development of too great a differential between rural and urban areas.

Rural–urban migration has not resulted only in problems, however. It has, for example, alleviated pressures on land in some areas (e.g. Kikuyuland in the Kenya Highlands), and planned migration is now a part of government policy in Tanzania in an attempt to relieve over-population in some rural areas and encourage development in others. The mixing of different tribal groups which has resulted from migration is also seen by some people as an important feature of the political development of East Africa and migration is clearly one of the elements of the 'modernisation' process which LDCs like those in East Africa are at present undergoing and which have affected many other countries already.

18

Case Study 10
Rural migration in
the *sertão* of
North-east Brazil

The sertão, *the interior plateau region of North-east Brazil, provides an interesting example of the effects of land allocation and land tenure, heightened by climatic unpredictability, on migratory movements. These push factors have given rise to important intra- and inter-regional migration flows which in years of particularly severe drought have assumed gigantic proportions.*

North-east Brazil consists of nine states (Fig. 18.1), covers an area of 15.5 million square kilometres and in 1970 had a population of 28.1 million (about 30% of the total Brazilian population). Within this vast region, two broad sub-regions may be identified in terms of natural conditions and economy. Along the coast and stretching inland, in places for up to 250 kilometres, is the heavily populated *zona da mata* (forest zone). This area was originally covered by tropical forest but has been settled by agriculturists since the sixteenth century and now constitutes an important sugar-producing region containing a number of very large cities. Behind this coastal strip the amount and reliability of rainfall decreases. The *zona de mata* gives way first to a transitional zone and then to an undulating interior plateau covered, in its natural state, by spiny scrub and cactus woodland called *caatingas*. This sub-region is the *sertão* (backlands). The most distinctive feature of the *sertão* is its unpredictable climate, which has given rise to a number of different types of internal and inter-state migrations.

The *sertão* experiences two seasons: the rainy winter season and the dry summer season. Under normal conditions the rainy season extends from January to July and the dry season from August to December, but the beginning and end of these two seasons vary alarmingly, with, for example, the rainy season beginning as early as December or as late as March. Not only is the onset and length of the rainy season variable, but the amount of rainfall is also irregular. The annual average rainfall is approximately 690 mm, but it may be as low as 190 mm or as high as 1,000 mm. Although 690 mm may seem to be a perfectly adequate rainfall, it must be remembered that the whole of North-east Brazil lies within 18° of the Equator and that the average daily temperatures of between 24 °C and 32 °C cause high losses through evaporation and reduce rainfall effectiveness.

At the end of the eighteenth century the *sertão* was a region of cattle ranches supplying beef to the relatively densely settled coastlands. Its population was still small, but grew rapidly throughout the nineteenth century as the agricultural frontier advanced into the semi-arid interior. By 1900 the population of the North-east was 6 million, of whom 3 million lived in the *sertão*. During this period cotton was established as the interior region's most impor-

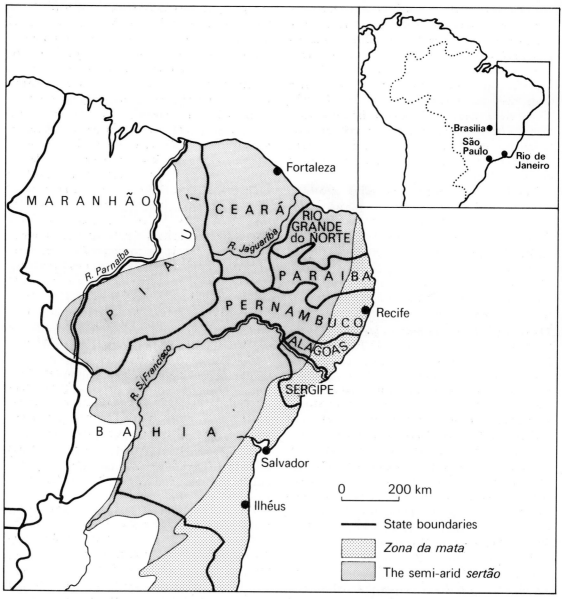

18.1 North-east Brazil: some general features.

tant cash crop and the types of land tenure and land use which are typical of the *sertão* today became established.

On the more moist soil of the valleys, particularly on the margins of the *sertão*, are found peasant smallholdings (*minifúndia*); in the semi-arid plateaux large plantations (*latifúndia*), combining cattle ranching and subsistence agriculture are more common. The large land-holdings are usually worked by share-croppers (*moradores*) of mixed Indian and European descent (*mestizos*) whose land is allocated to them by a manager who also supervises the collection of the share of the cash crop due to the landlord. (For a clear and readable account of share-cropping in the *sertão* see Johnson, 1971.) The share-croppers usually provide their own seed and implements (generally no more than hoes, billhooks and axes). In addition to paying the landlord a share of the cash crop, usually cotton, the *moradores* often have to spend some time tending the landlord's crops, which may include sugar cane, bananas, oranges and feed-grasses for the cattle. Besides receiving a proportion of each share-cropper's cash crop harvest, and selling the produce from his own plots, the landlord usually has a herd of cattle. These are looked after by a *vaqueiro* (cowhand) who not only supervises cattle grazing but also trains horses, makes saddles and protective clothing from leather, and oversees milking and cheese-making.

The land in the *latifúndia* varies greatly in quality. The best lands, which are overwhelmingly given over to basic food crops and fruits, lie in the river valleys where seasonal flooding replenishes the topsoil with alluvium, while the least desirable lands lie on the higher hillsides. Share-croppers usually farm one large hillside plot (called a *roçado*), which is cleared by cutting the thin forest growth and then burning the brush as it lies on the ground. Fertility declines after two or three years and the land is then left fallow for from five to eight years before new clearings are made. (This means that the subsistence food crops must be planted in a new clearing, but cotton will continue to be produced in the old clearing for eight to twenty years.) In addition to hillside clearings, industrious and long-established share-croppers may be allocated choice lowland plots. The most important crops grown by the share-croppers are maize, manioc, potatoes, rice, beans, squashes and cotton. Livestock generally consists of pigs, goats and poultry and, less commonly, cattle, sheep, horses and donkeys.

The migratory patterns of the region are related to land tenure, land allocation and climatic unpredictability, and may be divided into four types: movements within a particular *latifúndio*, movements between *latifúndia*, coastal and city-ward migrations, and migrations to other parts of Brazil.

On most *latifúndia* in the *sertão* there is no scarcity of land but there is a shortage of choice plots, and this has given rise to much movement of home sites within the large landholdings. As people leave to take up plots elsewhere, houses and plots become vacant and share-croppers occupying inferior houses and farming the least desirable hillsides move to choicer sites. (Johnson (1971) records that in a nine-month period

in 1966/7 in one *latifúndio* in the state of Ceará, five families moved away, five families moved in and six families moved from one house to another within the plantation.) The desire for choice sites is also the reason for many movements between large landholdings. Another reason for movement between *latifúndia* is marriage. When he marries, a son may live for a short period in his father's house until another one becomes available, until a new house is built or until he has made arrangements to take up land on a neighbouring plantation. Whether inter-plantation migrations take place because of the shortage of good land or because of marriage, investigations suggest that such migrations are usually short-distance, either to adjacent *latifúndia* or to *latifúndia* within the same *municipio* (the smallest administrative unit in Brazil). Thus it is possible to isolate important push and pull factors and to see the effects of distance-decay in this type of migration. Investigations have also shown that much of this movement is true migration and not a type of circulation in that only a minority of share-croppers return to a former plantation. One type of circulation does arise from the fact that some share-croppers also own and work *minifúndia* and family labour may be divided between the two. The protective patronage of a landlord in times of drought, as well as the fact that many smallholdings are too small to support a family, lead to this dual type of existence.

For most share-croppers intra- and inter-plantation movements may be considered the norm but in years of exceptional aridity out-migration from the *sertão* to the coast and from the North-east altogether become important. For many *sertanejos* (the name given to the inhabitants of the *sertão*) these movements are temporary, but for younger persons particularly, they may result in permanent migration. Thirty-seven droughts have been recorded in the *sertão* since the first Portuguese colonisation of the region: four in the seventeenth century, eleven in the eighteenth century, thirteen in the nineteenth century and nine in the twentieth century. The most recent droughts occurred in 1958 and 1970. When a drought occurs, hunger and starvation (cases of cannibalism were reported during the 1877 drought) lead first to coast-ward and city-ward migrations. At such times the coastal towns and cities become grossly overpopulated. In 1877, for instance, Fortaleza's population grew in a matter of weeks from 25,000 to 114,000 and Aracati's from 5,000 to 60,000. Arrival at the coastal cities, however, has seldom meant the end of suffering. In December 1878 alone, over 14,000 people died of smallpox in Fortaleza and it has been estimated that between 1877 and 1879 one half of the state of Ceará's population of 1 million died. The droughts of the nineteenth century grew in significance because of the increasingly large number of *sertanejos* involved. The reaction of state and national governments since that time has been to encourage migration from the *sertão* while at the same time attempting to mitigate the problems of the region.

During the 1877–9 drought, the governments of the states of Pará and Amazonas, as well as of Ceará, which was the worst hit of the *sertão* states, paid the passages of many migrants willing to settle in the newly developing rubber-producing states of the Amazon lowlands. Estimates suggest that about 55,000 *sertanejos* sailed to the Amazon states during 1878. Sponsored and free migrations to these states continued until the decline of wild rubber collecting just before World War 1, and began again at a lower volume during World War 2 because of the rubber shortages. In the inter-war period many migrants went west to the relatively undeveloped state of Maranhão and farmed the land using the slash and burn method of clearance, while others joined the growing flow of migrants southwards, particularly to the cities of São Paulo and Rio de Janeiro. This southward movement has become the predominant one since World War 2, although not all the migrants have moved to the largest cities. There have been efforts to re-direct migrants from the North-east to the newly developed lands on the agricultural frontier in the states of São Paulo and Paraná. More recently (since 1956) substantial numbers of *sertanejos* have made their way to the new federal capital of Brasília.

In the *sertão* itself efforts have been made to minimise the effects of drought and to raise living standards in two ways. First, there have been attempts by the Brazilian Institute of Agrarian Reform, as part of a national programme, to eliminate unproductive *latifúndia* and to consolidate the estimated 900,000 mini-*fúndia* in the North-east into a smaller number of viable family farms. Progress, however, has been slow. A much more ambitious scheme is the SUDENE (Superintendency for the Development of the North-east), created in 1959 following the severe drought of the previous year. This federal scheme was designed not only to initiate new regional development schemes but also to co-ordinate the work of existing development agencies. Among the broad aims of SUDENE are: to improve the infra-structure of the region, to increase the production and promote the wider use of electricity, to improve the health situation by carrying out water supply and sewerage projects, to improve education, to improve methods of cultivation and to extend irrigation, to colonise the thinly populated parts of the state of Maranhão, and to expand industrial employment. As with land reform, the influence of the SUDENE in the rural areas of the *sertão* is still slight, due in part to the size and isolation of the area and in part to the conservatism and apathy of many of the large landholders. Of more direct influence over a long period has been the government agency specifically concerned with water conservation and counteracting the effects of drought. This agency was established in 1901, and although re-named in 1919 and 1945 its activities have remained virtually the same. It is now known as the Departamento Nacional de Obras contra as Secas (the National Department of Anti-Drought Works) and by the end of the 1950s it had been responsible for the sinking of approximately 6,800 wells and the building of 243 dams.

In spite of the work of these government agencies, economic and social changes in the *sertão* are likely to be modest in the foreseeable future and the pattern of intra- and inter-plantation migration seems certain to continue to dominate local rural movements. Although it is possible to over-emphasise the role of droughts in migration in the North-east (it is suggested by some scholars that most *sertanejos* leave the North-east under normal climatic conditions: see, for example, Fischlowitz, 1969), it seems unlikely that the massive migrations resulting from the ecological push of periodic drought will be diminished to any great extent in the immediate future.

19

Case Study 11
Labour migration into
Western Europe

Western Europe (here defined as France, the German Federal Republic (GFR), Benelux and Switzerland) has been the scene of large-scale economically motivated migrations in the period since World War 2. Italy and the countries of North Africa were the major senders of migrant labour in the immediate post-war years but in the 1960s and 1970s they have been joined by Spain, Portugal, Yugoslavia, Greece and Turkey. This international movement of labour has given rise to social and economic problems in both the sending and receiving countries. Future policies of individual countries are unclear but much closer control of movements is likely to emerge in the future.

Throughout this study the terms migrant and immigrant are used to describe all persons residing and working outside the country of their birth. An increasing amount of this movement is true migration as defined in Chapter 11, but much of it must still be regarded as long-term circulation.

Since the second half of the 1950s there has been a massive increase in the number of foreign workers in the highly industrialised countries of North-west Europe. It has been estimated that in 1975 there were 10 million foreign workers in the EEC (European Economic Community) countries and 15 million in the whole of industrialised Europe. According to a UN estimate, if present trends are continued there will be 22 million foreign workers in Europe by 1980. In

the early 1970s France and the GFR were most dependent upon foreign labour, followed by Switzerland, Belgium and the Netherlands (Table 19.1).

The post-war labour movements in Western Europe began almost immediately after World War 2, while the economies of the warring nations lay in ruins or were in need of large-scale modernisation. Switzerland, its industries untouched by war, took advantage of the situation and boosted its economy to supply goods and services to surrounding countries. In order to do this, Switzerland entered into labour-migration agreements with its neighbours. As post-war economic expansion gathered pace throughout the whole of Europe, particularly in the middle and late 1950s, other countries, especially France and Belgium, also entered into agreements to import labour. During this early period of post-war economic recovery Italy and North Africa were the major sources of immigrant labour. During the late 1940s and the 1950s the bulk of the GFR's labour needs were met by the massive influx (mainly between 1946 and 1959) of over 12 million refugees and expellees from the east. (These included the German nationals (*Reichsdeutsche*) who at the end of World War 2 were living in those parts of the pre-war German state which were claimed by Poland and the USSR, and the so-called *Volksdeutsche* who lived as minorities in the

Table 19.1. *Foreign workers in Western Europe, 1972*

Country	Total number (thousands)	As a percentage of the total labour force
Belgium	200	7
France	2,200	9
Luxembourg	33	30
Netherlands	80	2
Switzerland	600	30
West Germany	2,300	9

Source: Various official sources.

countries of Eastern Europe. Both of these groups fled or were expelled at the end of the war. In addition there were large numbers of refugees from the Soviet zone (later to become the German Democratic Republic) in East Germany.) The Federal Republic did, however, enter into agreements to recruit labour in Italy in 1955 and in Spain in 1960, and after the building of the Berlin Wall in 1961 the number of foreign labour recruitment agreements rose sharply.

The decline in the number of refugees entering the GFR from the east in the early 1960s coincided with the early stages of that country's so-called 'economic miracle' and it resulted in the re-direction of potential Italian migrants from France and Switzerland to the GFR. The continued demand for labour in Belgium, France and the Netherlands since 1960, together with the emergence of the GFR as a major recruiter from that date, caused rapid changes in the numbers, origins and destinations of foreign workers. Italians and North Africans continued to be recruited on a large scale but they were joined by large numbers of Spaniards, Portuguese, Yugoslavs, Turks and Greeks. The importing countries displayed preferences for workers from particular countries and recruited accordingly. The migrant workers themselves showed certain preferences and together these two forces have created clear (legal and illegal) migration streams. A brief analysis of the numbers and origins of foreign workers in France and the GFR clearly illustrates these tendencies.

In France, by 1973 (Table 19.2) Algerians

formed the biggest immigrant group and it is against these workers that there is most prejudice, not only because of their colour but also because they are less passive than other groups. The members of this group, who are predominantly male, come to France for a limited period and, if they are married, usually leave their wives and families behind. The next most important group is the Portuguese, whose numbers have grown rapidly in recent years and who seemed likely to become the largest group following the decision of the French government in 1972 to reduce the annual influx of Algerians from 35,000 to 25,000. One interesting feature of the Portuguese immigration is that a small number of them have settled in declining rural areas and taken over abandoned farms. The number of Spaniards in France, although large, is slowly dwindling and that of the Italians, once the largest group, is falling more rapidly as employment opportunities increase at home and in other West European countries. Among the smaller groups are sizeable numbers of Moroccans and Tunisians, a reflection, as in the case of the Algerians, of France's former North African colonial ties.

The number of foreign workers or *gastarbeiter* (literally 'guest workers') in the GFR in 1970, and changes during the 1960s in the dominant countries of origin, are illustrated in Table 19.3. The table shows not only the massive increase, more than 300%, in the yearly levels of immigration between 1960 and 1970, but also the way in which the main centres of recruitment have moved from Spain and

Table 19.2. *Foreign-born workers living in France, 1973*

Algerian	798,690
Italian	573,817
Moroccan	218,146
Polish	108,264
Portuguese	742,894
Spanish	608,759
Tunisian	119,546
Turkish	24,531
Yugoslav	75,828
EEC (except Italy)	716,247

Source: Various official sources.

Italy to the eastern Mediterranean. This most recent source of supply is not likely to decrease in the forseeable future. It is estimated that in Turkey alone there is a waiting list of about 1 million applicants for jobs abroad.

In the early phases of foreign labour recruitment the immigrants were offered and took the lowest-paid, most menial and most unattractive jobs, especially in agriculture, mining, the building trade and in the service sector. Since the early 1960s, however, there has been an increasing movement into jobs in all branches of the economy, particularly in manufacturing. By the early 1970s 50% of the assembly-line workers in the car industry in the GFR were immigrants, and in France the proportion was only slightly lower at nearly 40%. Although large numbers of immigrants have moved out of the dirtiest jobs in their adopted homelands, they have often moved into repetitive and boring ones which have been increasingly shunned by the indigenous population. Thus the immigrants have provided a constant supply of relatively docile and cheap labour at the unskilled and semi-skilled levels.

As the numbers of foreign workers rose massively during the 1960s and as the area of recruitment widened, the economic and social consequences of the situation for both the receiving and the sending countries became more evident and were taken seriously at the highest

Table 19.3. *Immigration of registered* Gastarbeiter *into West Germany in 1960 and 1970, and the total number of* Gastarbeiter *in West Germany in 1970*

Country of origin	Number of registered *Gastarbeiter* entering W. Germany in:		Total number of *Gastarbeiter* in 1970
	1960	1970	
Greece	23,364	64,026	242,184
Italy	26,745	48,836	381,840
Portugal	—	20,119	44,796
Spain	141,263	168,300	171,671
Turkey	—	123,626	352,898
Yugoslavia	4,400	202,360	423,228

Source: Various official sources.

government level. One of the most serious problems to emerge is the high degree of segregation of large numbers of the immigrant population, at best in special workers' barracks or hostels (Fig. 19.1) and at worst in overcrowded conditions in the inner parts of cities, or, as in France, in peripheral shanty towns (*bidonvilles*) made of such materials as wood, corrugated iron, flattened oil cans, cardboard, tarpaulin and rope. It was estimated in 1966 that between 75,000 and 100,000 North Africans, Portuguese and Spaniards were living in *bidonvilles* in France. The overcrowding and degradation are not helped by the fact that large numbers of immigrants have entered their host countries illegally with the sole purpose of living as cheaply as possible while they earn money to send or take home.

Another increasingly urgent problem is the status of the immigrant worker within the society of his host country. When labour movement began it was viewed as a short-term answer to labour shortages in certain sectors of the economy. Agreements with sending countries allowed the recruitment by government agencies and by private industry on a contract basis. Many of these were one-year renewable contracts and resulted, in the main, in the migration of men mostly under the age of 45. Gradually this pattern has changed, in spite of a high turnover (estimated to be around 50% per annum) of immigrants. Increasingly, workers bring or send for (legally and illegally) their wives and children, and there is a rapidly growing population of French, German, Swiss, Dutch and Belgian-born children of immigrant parents. In the GFR, for instance, by the early 1970s more than half the foreign workers had their families with them and the average foreign family was three times as big as the average West German family. As families have become re-united and as the possibility of the reduction of the foreign labour force through reduced quotas or by repatriation has become stronger, the demand for naturalisation has increased rapidly. If the children of the new West Europeans expect and demand equal opportunities, especially during periods of economic recession, then serious social problems could ensue.

The consequences of labour migration for the sending countries are no less problematic. Such movement has relieved them of surplus labour

19.1 Italian workers resident in Switzerland in the canteen of a workers' hostel. Foreign worker accommodation policies vary throughout Western Europe. Advocates of specially built worker accommodation or tied housing stress the advantages of housing provision immediately on arrival in the host country, daily contact with large numbers of fellow countrymen and nearness to the place of work.

and reduced local unemployment. It has also resulted in the influx of much income in the form of migrants' remittances to dependants (Table 19.4). In Spain, for instance, money sent home by migrant workers is the second largest source of foreign income after tourism. However, much of the money has been used to purchase cars, houses, domestic appliances and small businesses rather than in developing local, regional and national economies. In addition, the loss of many of the most able-bodied

Table 19.4. *Money sent home to countries of migrant workers (worldwide) for selected countries, 1972*

	Millions of US dollars	As a % of total imports
Algeria	308	15.0
Greece	571	24.0
Italy	722	13.7
Morocco	126	16.0
Portugal	818	37.0
Spain	599	8.9
Tunisia	53	12.0
Turkey	740	47.0

Source: *Time,* 3 December 1973.

men and women of each generation is causing increased concern in the exporting countries.

The future is unclear. The exporting countries welcome the foreign currency and the reduction of unemployment; the importing countries find themselves increasingly dependent on foreign labour but are very sensitive to the growing social problems in their midst. The GFR stopped the recruitment of foreign labour in November 1973 and France followed suit in 1974. In view of the current labour shortages these are likely to be short-term measures. After a plebiscite in 1974 Switzerland decided not to impose a ban. One solution which has been widely advocated is the controlled rotation of immigrants. Under this scheme a worker would work abroad for a short period without his dependants and at the end of his contract would return home to be replaced by another worker from the same country. In the eyes of its promoters, this system has the double advantage of providing the much-needed labour for continued economic growth without raising the social and economic problems which attend a more lax approach to labour migration. Whatever policies emerge in the 1980s one thing is certain; their success will have to be based on a closer co-operation between sending and receiving countries and upon a greater awareness of their economic interdependence.

Part Five

Exercises

1 (a) Construct a graph to show the following information relating to Japan:

Year	Total pop. (millions)	Crude birth rate (per 1,000)	Crude death rate (per 1,000)	Year	Total pop. (millions)	Crude birth rate (per 1,000)	Crude death rate (per 1,000)
1921	56.7	35.1	22.7	1948	80.0	33.5	11.9
1922	57.4	34.3	22.4	1949	81.8	33.0	11.6
1923	58.1	35.2	22.9	1950	83.2	28.1	10.9
1924	58.9	33.9	21.3	1951	84.5	25.3	9.9
1925	59.7	34.9	20.3	1952	85.8	23.4	8.9
1926	60.7	34.6	19.1	1953	87.0	21.5	8.9
1927	61.7	33.4	19.7	1954	88.2	20.0	8.2
1928	62.6	34.1	19.8	1955	89.3	19.4	7.8
1929	63.5	32.7	19.9	1956	90.2	18.4	8.0
1930	64.5	32.4	18.2	1957	90.9	17.2	8.3
1931	65.5	32.1	19.0	1958	91.8	18.0	7.4
1932	66.4	32.9	17.7	1959	92.6	17.5	7.4
1933	67.4	31.5	17.7	1960	93.4	17.2	7.6
1934	68.3	29.9	18.1	1961	94.2	16.9	7.4
1935	69.3	31.6	16.8	1962	95.2	17.0	7.5
1936	70.1	30.0	17.5	1963	96.2	17.3	7.0
1937	70.6	30.9	17.1	1964	97.2	17.7	6.9
1938	71.0	27.2	17.7	1965	98.3	18.6	7.1
1939	71.9	26.6	17.8	1966	99.1	13.7	6.8
1940	72.2	29.4	16.5	1967	100.2	19.4	6.8
1941	72.9	31.8	16.0	1968	101.3	18.6	6.8
1942	73.9	30.9	16.1	1969	102.5	18.5	6.8
1943	74.4	30.9	16.7	1970	103.7	18.8	6.9
1944	73.8	n.a.	n.a.	1971	105.0	19.2	6.6
1945	72.1	n.a.	n.a.	1972	107.5	19.3	6.5
1946	75.8	n.a.	n.a.	1973	109.1	19.4	6.6
1947	78.1	34.3	14.6	1974	110.6	18.6	6.5

Source: *Japan Statistical Yearbook*, 1976.
n.a., not available.

(b) Comment on the features indicated on your graph in relation to the demographic transition model (Fig. 2.2, p. 6).
(c) On the basis of your more general reading suggest reasons for the changes in birth and death rates in Japan since 1920.

2 (a) Construct an age–sex pyramid for Chile using the statistics provided below.

Age distribution of population, 1970

Age group	Males		Females	
	a	b	c	d
0–4	563,720	(6.5)	546,700	(6.3)
5–9	616,100	(7.1)	619,740	(7.1)
10–14	556,660	(6.4)	553,780	(6.3)
15–19	442,640	(5.1)	457,960	(5.2)
20–24	356,960	(4.1)	387,000	(4.4)
25–29	294,300	(3.4)	319,720	(3.7)
30–34	241,740	(2.8)	266,180	(3.0)
35–39	246,640	(2.8)	267,380	(3.1)
40–44	218,640	(2.5)	230,160	(2.6)
45–49	168,040	(1.9)	180,840	(2.1)
50–54	144,800	(1.7)	159,780	(1.8)
55–59	124,820	(1.4)	138,340	(1.6)
60–64	103,580	(1.2)	113,240	(1.3)
65–69	75,000	(0.9)	91,080	(1.0)
70–74	51,840	(0.6)	62,120	(0.7)
75–79	29,300	(0.3)	36,620	(0.4)
80–84	15,880	(0.2)	23,400	(0.3)
85 +	10,420	(0.1)	18,200	(0.2)
Not known	60,420		59,400	
Total	4,321,500		4,531,640	

Source: *UN Demographic Yearbook 1975.*
Figures in columns a and c indicate totals of males and females respectively by age groups.
Figures in columns b and d express each sex–age group as a percentage of the total population (less those whose age is not known).

    (b) Describe the main features of the pyramid and suggest what they imply concerning birth and death rates in Chile.

3 (*a*) Construct age–sex pyramids for countries A, B and C using the data provided in the table below. (All values given are percentages of the total population.)

Age group	Country A		Country B		Country C	
	Males	Females	Males	Females	Males	Females
0–4	8.7	8.5	4.6	4.4	4.7	4.5
5–9	7.4	7.2	4.7	4.5	4.9	4.8
10–14	6.4	6.2	4.5	4.3	4.8	4.7
15–19	5.4	5.3	4.3	4.1	4.3	4.4
20–24	4.4	4.3	4.6	4.4	3.6	4.0
25–29	3.7	3.6	3.9	3.5	2.9	3.3
30–34	3.0	3.0	3.3	3.0	2.7	3.1
35–39	2.5	2.5	3.0	2.9	2.9	3.4
40–44	2.1	2.1	2.9	2.9	3.0	3.3
45–49	1.8	1.8	2.8	2.9	2.8	3.2
50–54	1.4	1.5	2.5	2.6	2.5	2.8
55–59	1.1	1.2	2.3	2.5	2.3	2.7
60–64	0.9	0.9	2.0	2.3	2.2	2.6
65–69	0.6	0.7	1.7	2.0	1.7	2.3
70–74	0.4	0.5	1.2	1.6	1.1	1.7
75–79	0.2	0.3	0.8	1.1	0.7	1.0
80+	0.2	0.2	0.8	1.0	0.4	1.0

Based on information in *UN Demographic Yearbook 1975*.

(*b*) The three age–sex pyramids you have constructed relate to the Netherlands (in 1971), Portugal (1972) and Peru (1973), though not necessarily in that order.
   Suggest, with reasons, which pyramid relates to which country. (Comments about migrant workers from Portugal in Case Study 11 may help you to answer this question.)

4 Examine the information provided below concerning the proportion of the total population aged less than 15 years in selected regions and then:
(*a*) Explain how variations in crude birth and death rates have operated to bring about the situation indicated, and
(*b*) Suggest what future problems are likely to result from this situation and outline some of the efforts being made to resolve them in particular areas or countries.

Region	Estimated pop. aged less than 15 years in mid-1970s (%)	Region	Estimated pop. aged less than 15 years in mid-1970s (%)
Africa	44	North America	27
South-west Asia	44	Central America	46
South and South-east Asia	42	South America	40
East Asia	33	North-west Europe	24
Australasia	30	USSR and Eastern Europe	27

Sources: Various.

5 Describe and explain the patterns of population growth indicated in the table below:

Mid-year population estimates, crude birth and death rates (by major regions)

Region	Mid-year population totals (millions)			Crude birth rate (per 1,000) 1965–73 average	Crude death rate (per 1,000) 1965–73 average
	1950	1960	1970		
Africa	217	270	344	47	21
North America	166	199	228	18	9
Latin America	162	213	283	39	10
Asia (excl. USSR)	1,355	1,645	2,056	38	16
Europe (excl. USSR)	392	425	462	17	10
USSR	180	214	243	18	8
Oceania*	12.6	15.8	19.4	25	10

Source: *UN Demographic Yearbook 1973.*
* Includes Australia, New Zealand, Melanesia and Polynesia.

6 Select a predominantly rural area in the United Kingdom which contains approximately twelve parishes and for which you have available a 1:50,000 Ordnance Survey map sheet. From the 1971 census returns for these parishes (available from most large libraries) record the total population and area of the selected parishes. Then:
  (*a*) Using, as appropriate, the census data and information provided on the OS map sheet, construct dot distribution and density maps of the population of your selected area.
  (*b*) Comment on the difficulties involved in the construction of the maps.
  (*c*) Discuss the relative advantages and disadvantages of the two types of map, paying particular attention to ways in which the maps might be misleading to someone using them.

7 Summarise the information provided in Fig. 3.1(*b*) concerning the possible future population structure of Great Britain and briefly suggest some of the socio-economic implications for Great Britain if *either* the high variant *or* the continuing low variant should prove to be an accurate projection.

8 Study the map (opposite) of population density by sub-regions for Great Britain and then:
  (*a*) Describe the main features of the pattern shown, and
  (*b*) Select one area with a density of over 1,000 per square kilometre and one with a density of under 75 per square kilometre and explain why the areas selected have such high and low densities respectively.

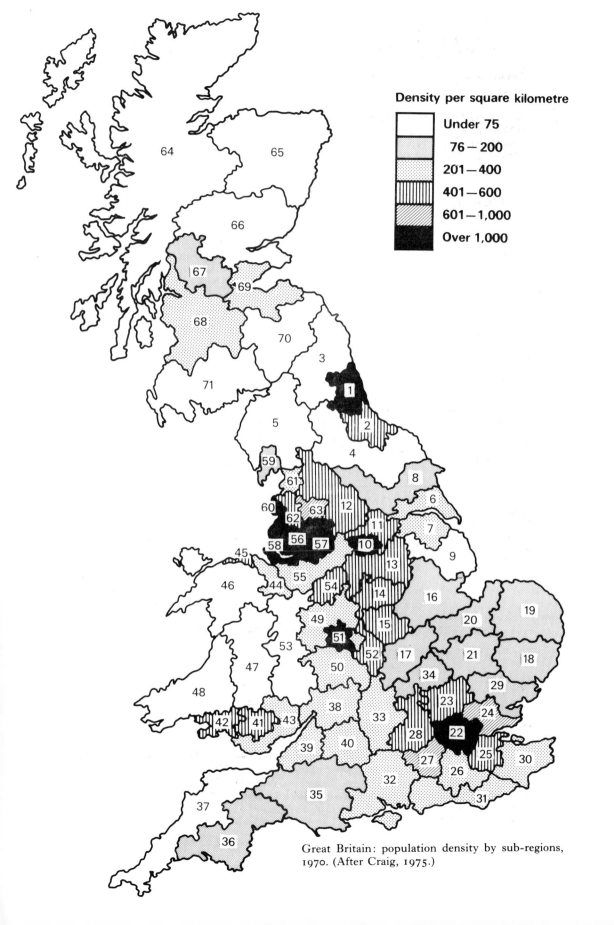

Under 75

76 — 200

201 — 400

401 — 600

601 — 1,000

Over 1,000

Great Britain: population density by sub-regions, 1970. (After Craig, 1975.)

9 (a) Study Fig. 3.2, which shows the distribution of population in East Africa, and then describe the pattern of population distribution in either Kenya or Tanzania.
   (b) On the basis of your further reading, suggest reasons for regional variations in the distribution described.
   (c) Explain how regional development has been influenced by regional variations in population distribution in the country selected for study.

10 (a) Select at random twenty countries from those for which information is provided in Fig. 3.6 and use the Spearman rank correlation coefficient technique to obtain a measure of the degree of correlation between GNP per capita and the percentage of the population living in urban areas.
   (The coefficient is derived from the formula

$$R = 1 - \frac{6\Sigma d^2}{n^3 - n}$$

where R is the Spearman rank correlation coefficient, Σd^2 is the sum of the squares of the difference in rank of the variables, and n is the number of samples taken.)
   (b) In the light of your calculation in part (a) and the evidence shown on the scattergraph (Fig. 3.6), comment on the relationship between GNP per capita and the percentage of the population living in urban areas.
   (c) Discuss the nature and significance of increasing urbanisation in LDCs.

11 Make a critical assessment of the division of *either* Africa *or* Latin America into population/resource regions as depicted in Fig. 4.6.

12 Consider the concept of overpopulation by reference to the present situation in India. (Case Study 5 may serve as a helpful starting point.)

13 (a) Examine the information provided concerning world food production in selected regions. Describe the regional differences highlighted by this information and suggest why such differences exist.

Indices of food production in selected regions (1961–5 average = 100)

Regions	Total food production						Food production per head					
	1969	1970	1971	1972	1973	1974*	1969	1970	1971	1972	1973	1974*
Western Europe	115	117	121	119	125	130	109	110	114	111	116	120
North America	115	113	124	122	129	124	107	104	113	110	111	110
Eastern Europe and USSR	125	130	132	133	148	146	117	121	122	122	135	132
Latin America	120	124	125	127	128	135	101	102	100	98	97	99
Africa	117	121	124	124	121	127	102	102	101	99	93	96
South and South-east Asia	118	124	125	121	132	128	102	104	102	97	103	97

Based on data in *The State of Food and Agriculture 1975* (FAO, 1976).
* Estimated.

   (b) Outline the major problems faced by one selected LDC in its attempts to increase food production per head and explain how such problems have been (or might be) overcome.

14 Study the statistics provided in Tables A to C relating to migration to Australia in 1972 and:
   (a) Construct:
       (i) A map to show the countries of origin of the migrants. Devise a method of showing variations in the volume of migration from the countries concerned.
       (ii) A population pyramid to show the age, sex and marital status of the migrants.
       (iii) A graph to show the occupations of both the male and female migrants.
   (b) Use your map, diagram and graph to form the basis of a short essay, entitled 'The selective nature of migration to Australia in 1972'.

Table A. *Nationality of migrants to Australia, 1972 arrivals*

Nationality	Assisted	Other	Total	Nationality	Assisted	Other	Total
British				American (US)	2,189	2,710	4,899
Country of citizen-				Austrian	186	108	294
ship:				Dutch	860	406	1,266
Australia	418	2,051	2,469	French	1,235	220	1,455
Canada	108	1,843	1,951	German	1,256	507	1,763
Bangladesh, India,	2	3,666	3,668	Greek	2,234	1,989	4,223
Pakistan,*				Italian	2,938	1,611	4,549
Sri Lanka				Lebanese	24	2,443	2,467
Ireland*	1,405	452	1,857	Portuguese	816	436	1,252
Malta	937	578	1,515	Spanish	911	270	1,181
New Zealand	33	3,390	3,423	Swiss	483	199	682
South Africa*	226	866	1,092	Turkish	875	755	1,630
United Kingdom	36,193	13,360	49,553	Yugoslav	5,149	2,109	7,258
and colonies				Other, including	3,980	5,349	9,329
Other countries	59	1,858	1,917	stateless			
Citizenship not	1,193	1,582	2,775				
stated							
Total, British	40,574	29,646	70,220	*Total, non-British*	23,136	19,112	42,248
				Grand total	63,710	48,758	112,468

* Included with 'British nationality' for the purpose of this table.

Table B. *Occupations of migrants to Australia, 1972 arrivals*

Occupation group	Males	Females
Professional, technical and related workers	5,763	3,595
Administrative, executive and managerial workers	2,170	318
Clerical workers	1,863	4,940
Sales workers	1,520	704
Farmers, fishermen, hunters, timber getters and related workers	737	25
Miners, quarrymen and related workers	117	—
Workers in transport and communication	1,954	335
Craftsmen and production-process workers	14,601	1,683
Labourers	4,238	—
Service (protective and other), sport and recreation workers	1,502	3,253
Occupation inadequately described or not stated	2,391	553
Persons not in work force:		
Children and students	19,298	17,720
Others	1,669	21,519
Total	57,823	54,645

Table C. *Sex, age and marital status of migrants to Australia, 1972*

Males				Females				Total number of persons			
Age last birthday on arrival	Never married	Married	Widowed or divorced	Age last birthday on arrival	Never married	Married	Widowed or divorced	Age last birthday on arrival	Never married	Married	Widowed or divorced
0–4	7,274	—	—	0–4	6,736	—	—	0–4	14,010	—	—
5–14	9,843	—	—	5–14	9,278	—	—	5–14	19,121	—	—
15–24	10,875	3,349	44	15–24	7,328	6,988	78	15–24	18,203	10,337	122
25–44	5,052	15,178	524	25–44	2,583	14,166	546	25–44	7,635	29,344	1,070
45–64	302	3,746	266	45–64	286	3,511	1,317	45–64	588	7,257	1,583
65+	49	990	331	65+	89	672	1,067	65+	138	1,662	1,398
Total	33,395	23,263	1,165	*Total*	26,300	25,337	3,008	*Total*	59,695	48,600	4,173

Source of data in Tables A, B and C: *Official Year Book of Australia, No. 59, 1973.*

15 Examine the statistics of population and migration for Jamaica provided in Tables A to D below, and then attempt the following exercises:

(*a*) Use the information provided to comment on:
  (i) the main features of population growth in Jamaica since 1970, and
  (ii) the patterns of migration from Jamaica to North America and the United Kingdom.
(*b*) Suggest to what extent the information provided indicates the selective nature of migration from Jamaica.
(*c*) Explain what consequences this selective migration is likely to have in Jamaica.
(*d*) On the basis of your more general reading, investigate the causes of migration from Jamaica.

Table A. *General demographic statistics*

Year	Population at 31 Dec.	Mean pop.	Birth rate (per 1,000)	Death rate (per 1,000)	Rate of natural increase (per 1,000)	Infant mortality rate (per 1,000 live births)
1970	1,890,700	1,869,100	34.4	7.7	26.8	32.2
1971	1,911,400	1,901,100	34.9	7.4	27.5	27.1
1972	1,953,500	1,932,400	34.3	7.2	27.0	30.9
1973	1,982,700	1,968,400	31.4	7.2	24.2	26.2

Table B. *Main streams of Jamaican migration*

Countries	1970	1971	1972	1973
United States	15,033	14,571	13,427	9,963
Canada	4,659	3,903	3,092	7,000*
United Kingdom	2,372	1,759	1,620	1,485
Total	22,064	20,233	18,139	18,448

* Estimated.

During the period for which information is provided the majority of migrants to the United Kingdom were children, who are dependants of earlier migrants. The total of migrants to Canada in 1973 was influenced by a Canadian government decision to allow earlier illegal immigrants to apply for permanent residence, but there was also a marked general increase in migrants. Migration to Canada is based on a points system which favours skilled migrants.

Table C. *Age distribution of Jamaica migrants to the United States, 1973*

Age group	Male	Female	Total	%
0–4	189	219	408	4.0
5–9	708	657	1,365	14.0
10–19	1,616	1,750	3,363	33.5
20–29	995	991	1,986	20.0
30–39	756	541	1,297	13.0
40–49	412	364	776	8.0
50–59	207	282	498	5.0
60–69	74	138	212	2.0
70+	14	40	54	0.5
Total	4,971	4,992	9,963	100

Table D. *Jamaican migration to the United States by occupation*

	1971	1972	1973
Professional, technical and related workers	1,078	810	562
Farmers and farm managers	50	6	—
Managers, officials and proprietors	183	194	158
Clerical and kindred workers	783	797	595
Sales workers	121	105	82
Craftsmen, foremen and kindred workers	1,411	1,150	821
Operatives and kindred workers	1,007	967	674
Private household workers	1,839	1,617	761
Service workers except private household	501	436	355
Farm labourers and foremen	145	91	73
Labourers except farm and mine	136	138	124
Housewives, children, others with no occupation or occupation not reported	7,317	7,116	5,758
Total	14,571	13,427	9,963

Source of data for Tables A, B, C and D: various official Jamaican sources.

16 Consider the geographical background to the following trends revealed by the 1970 US census:

'The U.S. population is almost 205 millions. This is an increase of 25 millions over the 1960 figure. California has taken over New York's position as the most populous state. Florida, Arizona, Colorado, Nevada, Washington and Oregon experienced substantial net gains by migration between 1960 and 1970. States showing net losses by migration during the same period included Alabama, Louisiana, Arkansas, South Carolina, Kentucky, West Virginia, Pennsylvania, North and South Dakota, Nebraska, Kansas, Iowa, Montana and Wyoming.'

17 Study carefully the Tables A to C (pp. 154–5), which give details of foreign workers in Switzerland, and the map (p. 156) showing the cantons of Switzerland.
 (*a*) Comment on the changes in the relative importance of the main countries of origin of foreign workers between 1955 and 1974 as shown in Table A.
 (*b*) With the aid of simple distribution maps, comment on the distribution within Switzerland of the main national groups of foreign workers in 1974 as shown in Table B. To what extent do the distributions reflect the significance of distance-decay and intervening opportunities?
 (*c*) Note the distinction in Tables B and C between foreign workers on yearly contracts, seasonal foreign workers and foreign workers who cross into Switzerland each working day. Comment on the differences in these categories (i) between the different national groups of foreign workers and (ii) between men and women.
 (*d*) Comment on the occupational differences between the three categories of foreign workers as shown in Table C.
 (*e*) Use the information gathered in (*a*)–(*d*) together with information from other sources to write an essay on 'Foreign workers in Switzerland'.

Table A. *Foreign workers in Switzerland** 1955–74 by country of origin*

Year	German Fed. Rep.	France	Italy	Austria	Spain	Others
1955	59,208	8,140	162,343	35,441	6,017	
1959	71,426	8,841	242,806	30,382	11,323	
1960	72,365	11,932	303,090	31,604	6,408	10,007
1961	73,466	16,163	392,060	30,152	21,801	14,670
1962	77,678	18,790	454,402	29,001	44,226	20,609
1963	78,389	21,166	472,052	27,879	63,653	26,874
1964	78,550	24,012	474,340	27,715	82,320	33,964
1965	67,668	23,775	448,547	24,184	79,419	32,735
1966	58,378	25,624	432,776	21,245	77,247	33,278
1967	59,089	29,521	425,236	20,155	75,945	38,136
1968	60,404	33,980	409,344	20,246	80,861	43,220
1969	57,199	36,842	398,929	19,865	95,696	50,698
1970	52,975	41,486	371,814	19,920	112,636	60,654
1971	50,229	50,176	340,213	18,903	132,024	68,935
1972	48,516	54,416	310,877	17,948	136,292	80,936
1973	42,995	57,880	273,536	16,374	134,766	95,301
1974	40,573	58,368	227,895	15,121	112,703	96,686

* Living in Switzerland in August of each year in question.

Table B. *Foreign workers in Switzerland in August 1974 by nationality, by canton and by category*

Canton	German	French	Italian	Austrian	Spanish	Others
Zurich	8,516	373	37,032	2,569	17,396	22,639
Bern	1,793	3,446	18,004	710	14,737	7,644
Luzern	761	44	6,226	345	4,711	4,270
Uri	88	4	1,289	66	468	926
Schwyz	226	19	3,033	165	905	1,421
Unterwalden	197	8	1,129	78	944	974
Glarus	102	2	2,100	53	541	553
Zug	312	8	2,052	137	862	1,409
Fribourg	184	371	2,696	50	3,282	1,226
Solothurn	558	513	6,938	173	2,466	3,140
Basel: city	9,274	12,735	6,481	529	5,352	4,420
Basel: country	2,393	3,114	6,875	200	3,398	2,837
Schaffhausen	3,707	27	1,698	106	868	1,931
Appenzell	171	7	1,280	214	937	1,135
St Gallen	1,381	76	10,179	6,662	5,193	6,282
Graubünden	910	140	11,779	698	3,262	4,774
Aargau	5,368	283	15,017	718	4,969	7,882
Thurgau	1,826	28	6,073	889	2,619	3,629
Ticino	625	134	51,153	178	2,455	2,326
Vaud	654	5,020	13,256	179	16,199	6,282
Valais	307	1,169	10,257	137	4,958	2,466
Neuchâtel	143	4,230	4,806	32	3,198	1,904
Geneva	1,077	26,617	8,542	233	12,983	6,616
Switzerland	40,573	58,368	227,895	15,121	112,702	96,686
Category of worker:						
Yearly contract	19,046	8,792	126,814	7,546	58,263	68,114
Seasonal worker	1,436	1,280	65,303	1,465	54,338	28,140
Cross border daily	20,091	48,296	35,778	6,110	102	432

Table C. *Foreign workers in Switzerland in August 1974, by category, sex and occupation*

Occupation	Yearly contract workers		Seasonal workers		Workers who cross into Switzerland each day		All categories of foreign workers		
	Men	Women	Men	Women	Men	Women	Men	Women	Total
Agriculture, livestock, horticulture	3,894	705	6,560	659	515	51	10,969	1,415	12,384
Forestry and fishing	404	7	681	11	32	—	1,117	18	1,135
Mining	481	10	942	7	203	4	1,626	21	1,647
Food, confectionery, tobacco	5,852	4,678	950	1,151	2,684	1,449	9,486	7,278	16,764
Textiles	6,168	8,481	15	71	1,348	1,333	7,531	9.885	17.416
Clothing and shoe-making	2,894	10,801	13	100	1,041	6,528	3,948	17,429	21,377
Wood and cork	5,608	725	1,064	69	2,821	313	9,493	1,107	10,600
Paper-making	1,838	1,539	4	16	536	400	2,378	1,955	4,333
Graphics	2,614	1,671	19	33	1,187	304	3,820	2,008	5,828
Tanning and leather	269	427	1	3	112	121	382	551	933
Rubber	1,841	1,089	28	7	553	209	2,422	1,305	3,727
Chemicals	3,981	1,681	67	9	4,334	2,097	8,382	3,787	12,169
Stone-working	4,557	584	2,164	19	1,330	139	8,051	742	8,793
Metal and machine industries	49,806	14,201	1,837	61	23,339	3,608	74,982	17,870	92,852
Watch and clock making	2,542	4,596	2	6	2,381	2,901	4,925	7,503	12,428
Other manufacturing industries	1,021	814	18	19	883	285	1,922	1,118	3,040
Building and construction	29,518	773	105,202	611	12,899	134	147,619	1,518	149,137
Trade and banking	13,304	8,805	1,149	299	6,856	13,245	21,309	22,349	43,658
Transport	4,836	695	631	82	2,547	712	8,014	1,489	9,503
Tourism	12,681	12,742	12,751	11,720	1,478	1,430	26,910	25,892	52,802
Health and welfare services	7,491	20,725	72	1,498	434	1,062	7,997	23,285	31,282
Teaching and science	3,603	3,448	27	97	355	166	3,985	3,711	7,696
Domestic	435	5,215	15	186	39	2,308	489	7,709	8,198
Others	9,340	9,185	469	547	2,919	1,184	12,728	10,916	23,644
Total	174,978	113,597	134,681	17,281	70,826	39,983	380,485	170,861	551,346

Source of Tables A, B and C: *Swiss Statistical Yearbook, 1975.*

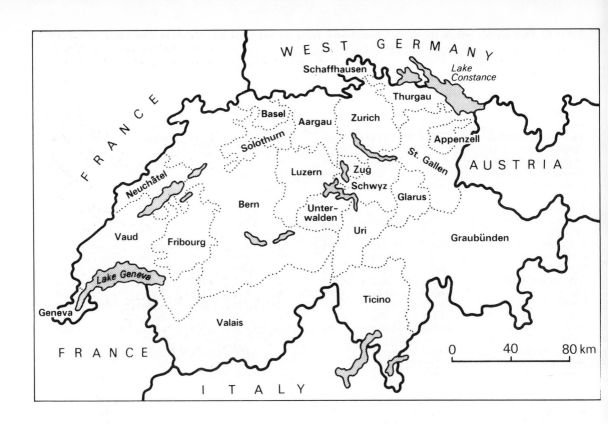

18 (*a*) The accompanying outline is a suggested typology of migrations in the conterminous United States between 1960 and 1970. Complete the typology by entering the appropriate details (see Case Study 8).

	Long-distance	Medium-distance	Short-distance
Rural—urban			
Urban—urban Suburban—suburban			
Urban—suburban	////////	////////	
Rural—rural			
Urban—rural	////////	////////	

(*b*) Suggest a classification, in the form of a typology, of the migratory patterns in England and Wales between 1951 and 1971 (see Case Study 7).

19 Study carefully the map below of the conterminous United States, which shows the percentage of families below the low income level ($3,743) in 1969. The low income level, below which families are officially classified as poor, is established (and periodically revised) by the President's Council of Economic Advisers.

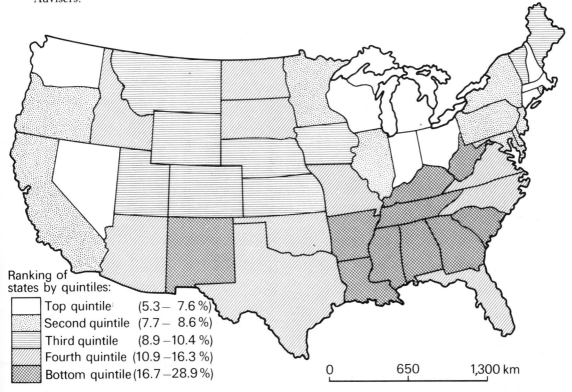

Ranking of states by quintiles:

Top quintile	(5.3 – 7.6 %)
Second quintile	(7.7 – 8.6 %)
Third quintile	(8.9 – 10.4 %)
Fourth quintile	(10.9 – 16.3 %)
Bottom quintile	(16.7 – 28.9 %)

USA: percentage of families below low income level, 1969. (Source: US Bureau of the Census.)

For the purposes of this exercise all the states in the Union (including Alaska and Hawaii, which are not shown on the map) have been ranked according to the percentage of families below the low income level and then divided into five groups, each consisting of ten states. Each group is one-fifth of the whole and is called a quintile. The top quintile consists of the ten states with the lowest percentage of families below low income level, the second quintile consists of the next ten states in the ranking and so on to the bottom quintile which includes the ten states with the largest percentage of families below the low income level.

(a) Describe the pattern revealed by the map.

(b) Choose *two* states, one from either of the top two quintiles and *one* from the bottom quintile and attempt to explain the differences in the levels of poverty between the two states in terms of relative location, resource base, social factors and economic structure.

(Case Study 8 should be re-read before attempting the exercise.)

20 Comment on the social and economic background of the UK population trends revealed in the table below.

Distribution of the population of the UK (as a percentage of the UK population) 1911–71

	Census			Mid-year estimates						1971 (millions)
	1911	1921	1931	1951	1961	1966	1969	1970	1971	
Standard regions of England:										
North	6.7	6.9	6.6	6.2	6.1	6.1	6.0	6.0	5.9	3.3
Yorkshire and Humberside	9.3	9.3	9.4	9.0	8.8	8.7	8.7	8.6	8.7	4.8
North-west	13.8	13.6	13.4	12.8	12.4	12.3	12.2	12.2	12.1	6.7
East Midlands	5.3	5.3	5.5	5.8	5.9	6.0	6.0	6.0	6.1	3.4
West Midlands	7.8	8.0	8.1	8.8	9.0	9.1	9.3	9.3	9.2	5.1
East Anglia	2.8	2.8	2.7	2.8	2.8	2.9	3.0	3.0	3.0	1.7
South-east	27.8	27.9	29.4	30.2	31.0	31.1	31.1	31.1	31.1	17.3
South-west	6.4	6.2	6.1	6.5	6.5	6.7	6.7	6.8	6.8	3.8
Wales	5.8	6.0	5.6	5.1	5.0	4.9	4.9	4.9	4.9	2.7
Scotland	11.3	11.1	10.5	10.1	9.8	9.5	9.4	9.4	9.4	5.2
Northern Ireland	3.0	2.9	2.7	2.7	2.7	2.7	2.7	2.7	2.8	1.5
Total de facto population (*millions*)	42.1	44.0	46.0	50.3	52.8	54.7	55.5	55.7	55.6	55.6

Source of data: *Social Trends No. 3* (HMSO, 1972).

21 Study the map below showing inter-regional migration in Great Britain between 1961 and 1966 and:

(a) Comment on the overall pattern of regional loss and gain;

(b) Comment on the significance of age-selectivity in inter-regional migration.

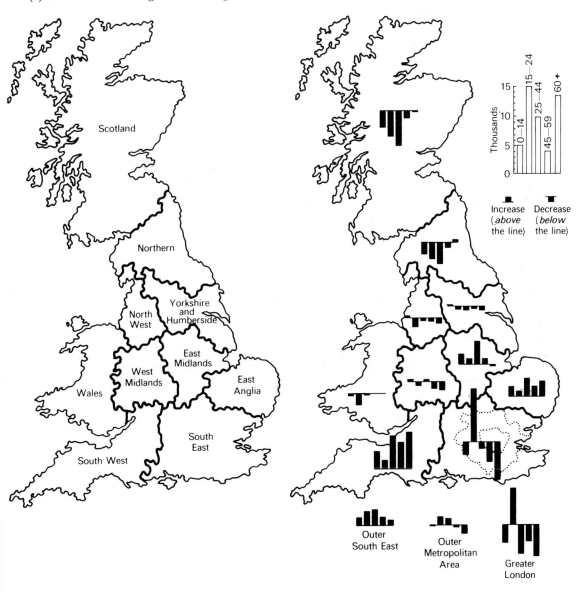

Great Britain: Inter-regional migration, net balance by age groups, 1961–6. (Source: *Social Trends No. 5*. HMSO, 1972.)

22 Comment on the geographical background to the regional variations in the journey to work patterns indicated in the following table.

Great Britain: journey time to work of head of household by region of residence, 1971 (%)

	Journey time to work (minutes)						Work at home	No usual place of work	Median journey time (minutes)
	1–12	13–22	23–37	38–52	53–75	76+			
North	32	30	17	6	3	—	5	8	16
Yorkshire and Humberside	29	26	18	6	5	—	7	8	18
North-west	30	28	20	9	4	1	2	7	18
East Midlands	28	34	18	6	3	1	3	8	17
West Midlands	31	30	20	6	3	1	4	6	17
East Anglia	42	26	8	2	2	1	9	9	12
Greater London	18	19	21	15	14	2	2	8	28
Outer Metropolitan area	26	22	14	8	14	6	3	6	21
Other South-east	34	23	20	5	2	3	4	9	16
South-west	38	27	13	3	2	1	6	11	14
Wales	32	22	16	7	7	2	7	8	17
Scotland	37	25	16	5	5	1	4	6	16
Great Britain	30	26	18	7	6	2	4	8	18

Source: *Social Trends No. 3* (HMSO, 1972).

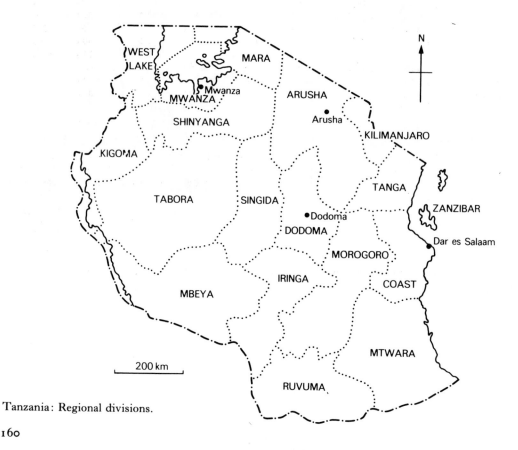

Tanzania: Regional divisions.

23 (a) Map the information provided in the accompanying table, using the map of Tanzanian regional divisions opposite as a base.

(b) Describe briefly the patterns of migration illustrated by your map.

(c) Use information provided in the table in Case Study 9 (p. 134) and in any other sources you have available as the basis for an essay entitled 'Urban migration in Tanzania'.

Population of four towns in Tanzania by place of birth

Place of birth*	Arusha Pop. total	% of all migrants	Dar es Salaam Pop. total	% of all migrants	Dodoma Pop. total	% of all migrants	Mwanza Pop. total	% of all migrants
Same location	9,623	—	87,565	—	6,322	—	14,092	—
Arusha	4,066	18.2	1,322	0.7	274	1.6	187	0.9
Coast	86	0.4	64,202	35.3	128	0.7	116	0.6
Dar es Salaam	429	1.9	—	—	638	3.7	683	3.4
Dodoma	2,123	9.5	3,686	2.0	6,058	35.4	292	1.4
Iringa	225	1.0	3,497	1.9	770	4.5	250	1.2
Kigoma	64	0.3	2,183	1.2	334	2.0	1,267	6.2
Kilimanjaro	7,013	31.4	6.774	3.7	632	3.7	638	3.1
Mara	174	0.8	1,711	0.9	175	1.0	2,374	11.6
Mbeya	333	1.5	4,976	2.7	818	4.8	555	2.7
Morogoro	275	1.2	21,393	11.8	1,091	6.4	406	2.0
Mtwara	120	0.5	14,062	7.7	322	1.9	170	0.8
Mwanza	271	1.2	2,671	1.5	373	2.2	1,094	5.4
Ruvuma	167	0.7	5,687	3.1	438	2.6	285	1.4
Shinyanga	77	0.3	1,153	0.6	139	0.8	894	4.4
Singida	1,085	4.9	1,268	0.7	1,101	6.4	358	1.8
Tabora	294	1.3	6,033	3.3	1,239	7.2	2,794	13.7
Tanga	1,592	7.1	8,959	4.9	818	4.8	492	2.4
West Lake	189	0.8	3,774	2.1	258	1.5	2,715	13.4
Zanzibar	177	0.8	5,548	3.1	102	0.6	227	1.1
Other Africa	2,271	10.2	11,874	6.5	812	4.8	3,133	15.4
Outside Africa	1,322	5.9	10.939	6.0	572	3.3	1,402	6.9
Not known	34	—	343	—	24	—	66	—
Total pop.	32,010		269,620		23,438		34,490	

Based on *1967 Population Census, Tanzania, Vol. 2, Statistics for Urban Areas.*

* Place of birth refers to the region and *not* the town of the same name. The town of Dar es Salaam counts as a region for census purposes. 'Other Africa' refers to people born in African countries other than Tanzania, 'Outside Africa' to those born outside Africa.

Bibliography

General sources

Beaujeu-Garnier, J. (1966). *Population Geography*. London.

Cox, P. R. (1976). *Demography*, 5th edn. Cambridge.

Demko, G. J. *et al.* (eds.) (1970). *Population Geography : a Reader*. New York.

Haggett, P. (1975). *Geography : A Modern Synthesis*, 2nd edn, chapters 6, 7, 8 and 13. New York.

Petersen, W. (1975). *Population*, 3rd edn. New York.

Stanford, Q. H. (ed.) (1972). *The World's Population*. Toronto.

Scientific American (1974). *The Human Population*. San Francisco.

Young, L. B. (ed.) (1968). *Population in Perspective*. New York.

Zelinsky, W. (1970). *A Prologue to Population Geography*. London.

Much useful material is included in two series of articles which have appeared in the *Geographical Magazine*:

1. A series on the Third World, published between March 1973 and April 1974, on themes which include population growth, rural–urban migration, and various aspects of population/resource relationships.
2. A series entitled 'Inquiry into People', published between February 1974 and February 1975. This series includes population studies in the following countries: England, Wales, Scotland, Northern Ireland, USSR, France, Romania, Peru, Jamaica, China, Egypt, Gambia, Nigeria, USA, Japan, India, Thailand.

A wide range of statistical sources related to themes introduced in this book is available in most large libraries. Of particular value are statistical reports produced by various government ministries and similar agencies, national yearbooks and international publications such as the *United Nations Statistical Yearbook, United Nations Demographic Yearbook* and the annual reports of the Food and Agricultural Organisation of the United Nations, *The State of Food and Agriculture*.

Part One

Benjamin, B. (1968). *Demographic Analysis*. London.

Benjamin, B., Cox, P. R. and Peel, J. (eds.) (1973). *Resources and Population*. London.

Berry, B. J. L. (1973). *The Human Consequences of Urbanisation*. London.

Boserup, E. (1965). *The Conditions of Agricultural Growth*. London.

Caldwell, J. C. and Okonjo, C. (eds.) (1968). *The Population of Tropical Africa*. London.

Chorley, R. J. and Haggett, P. (eds.) (1967). *Socio-economic Models in Geography*. London.

Clark, C. (1967). *Population Growth and Land Use*. London.

Clarke, J. I. (1972). *Population Geography*, 2nd edn. Oxford.

Clarke, J. I. (1971). *Population Geography and the Developing Countries*. Oxford.

Coates, B. E., Johnston, R. J. and Knox, P. L. (1977). *Geography and Inequality*. Oxford.

Dwyer, D. J. (1975). *People and Housing in Third World Cities*. London.

FAO (1975). *The State of Food and Agriculture*. Rome.

Fielding, G. J. (1974). *Geography as Social Science*. New York.

Frankel, F. R. (1971). *India's Green Revolution.* Princeton.

Gilbert, A. (1974). *Latin American Development.* London.

Glass, D. V. (ed.) (1953). *Introduction to Malthus.* London.

Hall, P. (1974). *Urban and Regional Planning.* London.

Hauser, P. M. and Duncan, O. D. *The Study of Population.* Chicago.

Hodder, B. W. (1973). *Economic Development in the Tropics.* London.

Howe, G. M. (1970). *A National Atlas of Disease Mortality in the United Kingdom.* London.

Howe, G. M. (1972). *Man, Environment and Disease in Britain.* Newton Abbot.

Jones, E. (ed.) (1975). *Readings in Social Geography.* Oxford.

Jones, E. and Eyles, J. (1977). *An Introduction to Social Geography.* Oxford.

Jones, R. (ed.) (1975). *Essays on World Urbanization.* London.

Kagambirwe, E. R. (1972). *Causes and Consequences of Land Shortage in Kigezi.* Kampala.

Kosinski, L. (1970). *The Population of Europe.* London.

McKeown, T. (1976). *The Modern Rise of Population.* London.

Meadows, D. H. *et al.* (1972). *The Limits to Growth.* London.

Mitchell, P. K. (1972). West Africa counts its people. *Geographical Magazine,* **44,** 318–21.

Morgan, W. T. W. (1973). *East Africa.* London.

Mountjoy, A. B. (1971). *Developing the Underdeveloped Countries.* London.

Myrdal, G. (1963). *Economic Theory and Underdeveloped Regions.* London.

Office of Population Censuses and Surveys (1975). *Variant Population Projections 1974–2011.* London.

Open University (1975). *Population,* Course D291, Unit 3. Milton Keynes.

Park, C. W. (1965). *The Population Explosion.* London.

Parry, H. B. (1974). *Population and its Problems.* Oxford.

Sauvy, A. (1974). *General Theory of Population.* London.

Schumacher, E. F. (1973). *Small is Beautiful.* London.

Taylor, G. R. (1972). The concept of optimum population. In Q. H. Stanford (ed.), *The World's Population.* Toronto.

Trewartha, G. T. (1969). *A Geography of Population: World Patterns.* New York.

Wrigley, E. A. (1969). *Population and History.* London.

Wrigley, E. A. (1967). Demographic models in geography. In R. J. Chorley and P. Haggett (eds.), *Socio-economic Models in Geography.* London.

Part Two

Berger, R. (1971). Reality on the Chinese communes. *Geographical Magazine,* **43,** 326–32.

Blaikie, P. M. (1975). *Family Planning in India: Diffusion and Policy.* London.

Buchanan, I. (1972). *Singapore in South-east Asia.* London.

Buchanan, K. (1970). *The Transformation of the Chinese Earth.* London.

Burnley, I. H. (1974). *Urbanization in Australia: the post-war experience.* London.

Chu Li and Tien Chieh-yun (1974). *Inside a People's Commune.* Peking.

Craig, J. (1975). *Population Density and Concentration in Great Britain 1931, 1951, 1961.* London.

Drake, M. (ed.) (1969). *Population in Industrialization.* London.

Dwyer, D. J. (ed.) (1974). *China Now.* London.

Fisher, C. A. (1975). Singapore: a booming city state. *Geographical Magazine,* **48,** 104–10.

Frankel, F. R. (1971). *India's Green Revolution.* Princeton.

Harriss, B. (1971). The Green Revolution in Ludhiana district, India. *Geography,* **56,** 243–6.

Jacoby, E. (1972). Effects of the Green Revolution in South and South-east Asia. *Modern Asian Studies,* **6,** 63–9.

Johnson, B. L. C. (1972). Recent developments in rice-breeding and some implications for Tropical Asia. *Geography,* **57,** 307–20.

Haslemere Group (1973). *The Death of the Green Revolution.* London.

Saw, Swee-Hock (1972). *Singapore: Population in Transition.* Philadelphia.

Spengler, J. J. (1975). *Population and America's Future.* San Francisco.

Wade, N. (1974). Green Revolution: a just technology, often unjust in use. *Science,* **186,** 1093–6.

Wade, N. (1974). Green Revolution: problems of adapting a Western technology. *Science,* **186,** 1186–92.

Part Three

Banton, M. (1972). *Racial Minorities.* London.

Blacksell, M. (1974). Reformed England and Wales. *Geographical Magazine,* **46,** 235–40.

Clout, H. D. (1972). *Rural Geography: an Introductory Survey.* Oxford.

Gottmann, J. (1961). *Megalopolis.* New York.

HMSO (1969). *Local Government Reform* (Redcliffe–Maud Report: short version). Cmnd. 4039.

Jansen, C. J. (ed.) (1970). *Readings in the Sociology of Migration.* Oxford.

Jones, H. R. (1973). Modern emigration from Malta. *Transactions, Institute of British Geographers,* **60,** 101–19.

Keenan, J. (1972). An era ends for Tuareg nomads. *Geographical Magazine,* **44,** 465–71.

Keown, P. A. (1971). The career cycle and the stepwise migration process. *New Zealand Geographer*, **27**, 175–84.

Kosinski, L. A. and Prothero, R. M. (eds.) (1975). *People on the Move : Studies in Internal Migration*. London.

Lawton, R. (1968). The journey to work in Britain: some trends and problems. *Regional Studies*, **2**, 27–40.

Lee, E. S. (1966). A theory of migration. *Demography*, **3**, 47–57. (Reprinted in Demko *et al.*, 1970.)

Mabogunje, A. K. (1970). Systems approach to a theory of rural–urban migration. *Geographical Analysis*, **2**, 1–18.

Manners, G. *et al.* (1972). *Regional Development in Britain*. London.

Musgrove, F. (1963). *The Migratory Elite*. London.

Peach, G. C. K. (1975). Immigrants in the inner city. *Geographical Journal*, **141**, 372–9.

Petersen, W. (1958). A general typology of migration. (Reprinted in Jansen, 1970.)

Ravenstein, E. G. (1885). The laws of migration. *Journal of the Royal Statistical Society*, **48**, 167–235.

Roseman, C. C. (1971). Migration as a spatial and temporal process. *Annals of the Association of American Geographers*, **61**, 589–98.

Stouffer, S. A. (1960). Intervening opportunities and competing migrants. *Journal of Regional Science*, **2**, 1–26.

Swindell, K. (1974). Sierra Leonean mining migrants, their composition and origins. *Transactions, Institute of British Geographers*, **61**, 47–64.

Zelinsky, W. (1971). The hypothesis of the mobility transition. *Geographical Review*, **61**, 219–49.

Part Four

Brooks, R. H. (1971). Human response to recurrent drought in North-eastern Brazil. *Professional Geographer*, **23**, 40–4.

Champion, A. G. (1973). Population trends in England and Wales. *Town and Country Planning*, **41**, 504–9.

Davis, J. F. (1972). United States population changes 1960–70. *Geography*, **57**, 140–4.

Edwards, K. C. (1964). The new towns of Britain. *Geography*, **49**, 279–85.

Estall, R. (1972). *A Modern Geography of the United States*, chapters 1 and 2. London.

Fischlowitz, E. (1969). Internal migration in Brazil. *International Migration Review*, **3**, 36–46.

HMSO (1969). *The Intermediate Areas* (Report of the Hunt Committee). Cmnd. 3998. London.

Husain, M. S. (1975). The increase and distribution of New Commonwealth immigrants in Greater Nottingham. *East Midland Geographer*, **6**, 105–29.

Johnson, A. W. (1971). *Sharecroppers of the Sertão*. Stanford, California.

Jones, P. N. (1970). Some aspects of the changing distribution of coloured immigrants in Birmingham 1961–66. *Transactions, Institute of British Geographers*, **50**, 199–219.

Kleinpenning, J. M. G. (1971). Objectives and results of development policy in North-east Brazil. *Tijdschrift Voor Economische en Sociale Geografie*, **72**, 271–89.

Krausz, E. (1971). *Ethnic Minorities in Britain*. London.

Lawton, R. (1957). Irish immigration to England and Wales in the mid-nineteenth century. *Irish Geography*, **4**, 35–54.

Lawton, R. (1967). Rural depopulation in nineteenth century England. In R. W. Steel and R. Lawton (eds.), *Liverpool Essays in Geography*. Liverpool.

Lewis, G. M. (1969). The distribution of the Negro in the Conterminous USA. *Geography*, **54**, 410–18.

Masser, I. and Gould, W. T. S. (1975). *Inter-regional Migration in Tropical Africa*. London.

Ominde, S. H. (1968). *Land and Population Movements in Kenya*. London.

Osborne, R. H. (1964). Population. In Watson, J. W. and Sissons, J. B. (eds), *A Systematic Geography of the British Isles*, chapter 16. London.

Peach, G. C. K. (1968). *West Indian Migration to Britain: a Social Geography*. Oxford.

Saville, J. (1957). *Rural Depopulation in England and Wales*. London.

Salt, J. (1973). Job finding in a united Europe. *Geographical Magazine*, **45**, 768–70.

Soja, E. W. (1968). *The Geography of Modernisation in Kenya*. New York.

Southall, A. W. (1961). Population movements in East Africa. In Barbour, K. M. and Prothero, R. M. (eds.), *Essays in African Population*. London.

Turner, M. F. (1961). Population changes in England and Wales 1951–61. *Geography*, **46**, 357–60.

Thomas, W. S. G. (1974). Gastarbeiter in Western Germany. *Geography*, **59**, 348–50.

Time (1973). Will migrants become the victims again? 3 Dec. issue, pp. 12–19.

Willatts, E. C. and Newsom, M. G. C. (1953). The geographical pattern of population changes in England and Wales, 1921–1951. *Geographical Journal*, **119**, 431–54.

Zelinsky, W. (1962). Changes in the geographic patterns of rural population in the USA. *Geographical Review*, **52**, 592–524.

Index

Copyright © 2002 by Max Velthuijs
This paperback edition first published in 2004 by Andersen Press Ltd.
The rights of Max Velthuijs to be identified as the author and illustrator of this work
have been asserted by him in accordance with the Copyright, Designs and Patents Act, 1988.
First published in Great Britain in 2002 by Andersen Press Ltd., 20 Vauxhall Bridge Road, London SW1V 2SA.
Published in Australia by Random House Australia Pty., 20 Alfred Street, Milsons Point, Sydney, NSW 2061.
All rights reserved. Colour separated in Switzerland by Photolitho AG, Offsetreproduktionen,
Gossau, Zürich. Printed and bound in Italy by Grafiche AZ, Verona.

10   9   8   7   6   5   4   3   2   1

British Library Cataloguing in Publication Data available.

ISBN 1 84270 375 7

This book has been printed on acid-free paper

Frog
and the Treasure

Frog
and the Treasure

Max Velthuijs

Andersen Press · London

"Let's hurry up and finish our breakfast, Little Bear,"
said Frog. "Today we are going to dig for treasure!"
"Dig for treasure?" said Little Bear. "What does that mean?"
"Come with me and you'll find out," said Frog.

"We are going to dig a deep hole," he explained.
"We are going to dig and dig, until we find treasure."
"But what if there isn't any treasure?" said Little Bear.
"There is always treasure," said Frog. "I promise."

All at once, Frog stopped and pointed at the ground.
"This is where we'll find treasure," he said. "Right here!"
"How do you know?" said Little Bear.
"I just *know*," said Frog.

Frog started to dig. Little Bear watched, full of admiration.
It looked very hard work.
Soon enough, Frog was tired. "Now it's your turn, Little Bear,"
he said.
Little Bear wasn't sure, but he took the spade . . .

. . . and bravely he began to dig. But the spade was far too big and much too heavy for him.

"This is useless," said Frog after a while. "We'll never find treasure at this rate. Give it back to me."

So Little Bear watched while Frog dug, deeper and deeper –
until he could hardly be seen.
"Frog!" called Little Bear. "Is there any treasure yet?"

"No, not yet . . ." came Frog's voice from far below.
"Careful, Little Bear, here comes a stone . . ."
 But Little Bear couldn't hear. He leant over into the
hole, and . . .

. . . in he fell!

There they sat in the deep, dark hole.

"I'm hungry," said Little Bear. "I want to go home."

"We can't," said Frog, quietly. "This hole is too deep.
We can't climb out. We're trapped."

Little Bear started to cry. "We'll be here forever!" he wept.

"I'll never go fishing with Rat again and Hare will miss
me so!"
Frog was scared, too. He didn't know how to comfort
Little Bear. "Be brave, Little Bear," he said. "Let's shout
for help. Someone is sure to hear." So they called and
called – but nobody came.

Then Frog had another idea. "Let's sing," he said. "Let's sing a sitting-in-the-hole song to cheer ourselves up." The moon rose, the night came. Frog and Little Bear

sang and sang, until they were so tired that they slept,
even though they were far away from their own warm,
little bed . . .

Early next morning, Duck was out for a walk when she came
across a mountain of sand.
"How very curious!" she exclaimed. "This wasn't here
yesterday!"
Then she saw the hole and went to find Pig.

Pig leant over and called down into the hole, "Hello?
Is anybody there?"
"Yes, we are!" shouted Frog and Little Bear together. "It's us.
Frog and Little Bear! We can't get out!"
"I think we should go and fetch Rat," said Pig.

Duck hurried off, shouting at the top of her voice.
"Rat! Rat, come quickly! Frog and Little Bear are trapped
in a hole and they can't get out!"

Rat knew exactly what to do. He fetched a ladder
from the barn and he and Duck hurried to the scene
of the disaster.

Rat lowered the ladder into the hole, which was so deep that soon the ladder disappeared.
"Climb up, Little Bear!" called the animals. "And Frog, you must follow! Don't be scared. We'll help you out!"

Carefully, Little Bear started to climb.
When he was close enough to the top of the hole,
his friends pulled him to safety.
Then it was Frog's turn . . .

Everyone cheered when Frog's head appeared above
the ground. "Hooray!" they shouted, as Rat helped
him out of the hole.
"But what were you doing down there?" asked Hare,
anxiously. "Such a deep hole is extremely dangerous.

We must fill it in at once."
"It was me," said Frog quietly. "I promised Little Bear we
would find treasure but there was none. Now there's just
a big, useless hole and it's all my fault."
Frog was so disappointed.

"Ah, but you did find treasure," said Rat solemnly, kneeling down and picking up the stone lying nearby. "This stone is more than a hundred million years old!"

He polished the stone on his sleeve until it gleamed.
Then he handed it to Frog.
Frog could hardly believe his eyes. He beamed with pleasure.

"Thank you, Rat," he said, proudly. "But I think this is Little Bear's treasure. I shall give it to him – because he was so brave, and because I promised!"

Other Andersen Press Paperback Picture Books by Max Velthuijs

"Frog is a masterpiece of creation and design." *Guardian*

Frog in Love

Frog in Winter

Frog and the Stranger

Frog is Frightened

Frog is a Hero

Frog is Frog

Frog and the Birdsong

Frog and the Wide World

Frog and the Very Special Day

Frog Finds a Friend